MEMORIES OF A RETIRED COP

By Robert Meyerholz

AUTHOR'S INTRODUCTION

I joined the New Haven Police Department in New Haven, Connecticut on January 9, 1961. My 17 year career as a Police officer enabled me to be part of people's everyday lives. I have seen the best and the worst of humanity. I am sharing with you these true-life stories of what it's like to be a cop. Some are sad. Some are funny. Some are shocking. I have delivered a baby and saved a man's life. It's all part of the job of being a Police Officer. Please enjoy this novel that was written from my heart.

BEFORE I BECAME A POLICE OFFICER

In the spring of 1960, I was still working at Nelke Motors as their Parts Manager. Nelke Motors was located at 226 Whalley Avenue – the once successful Studebaker, Packard & Mercedes-Benz dealer. Business was bad. The once luxurious Packard was now no longer building cars. Studebaker was only building the Lark model. Mercedes-Benz sales were skyrocketing. At $65.00 per week salary and no future raises coming, I had a wife and 2 beautiful children. I had to do better for my family. I always wanted to be a Police Officer. I wrote to the Connecticut State Police and also the New Haven Police Department, inquiring about qualifications. Within a short time I received answers from both agencies. One qualification was that you had to be able to swim. I never learned how to swim. I wanted to be a Policeman so that weekend I went down to the West Haven beach across from the old Chick's Drive in. Alone, I taught myself how to dog paddle and then the backstroke and finally I was swimming. I then joined the YMCA. I got into shape preparing for the agility test for either department. I became a strong swimmer. New Haven notified me first and they set a date for me to take all the tests to qualify. Pushups, sit ups, everything was a breeze. Almost 2000 people applied for 18 positions to become Probationary Policeman. The first night at the Payne Whitney Gym, more than 1000 were disqualified. During the written test, another 500 were disqualified. Finally, I was notified that the Board of Police Commissioners at the department's Training Academy would interview me. The most important question was "Why do you want to be a Police Officer?" My answer was "I want to make a difference in people's lives." Another question was "Would you treat everyone equally, regardless to the color of their skin and nationality?" "Absolutely," was my answer. Finally, on my 24th birthday, November 16, 1960, I was notified that I passed the test and was put on a 2 year waiting list. Only 18 candidates would be selected from a list of approximately 400 eligible candidates. Originally more than 1000 applicants applied for the job. On December 29, 1960. I received a letter from Chief Francis V. McManus to report to Sergeant Biagio DiLieto at the Police Academy on January 9, 1961 for assignment to duty as a Probationary Patrolman. My dream came true. •

Sometime in 1966, I was dispatched to a bomb scare at Almar's Diner, located on Middletown Avenue. It was about 1:30 PM and I arrived just behind a fire truck. There was a Greyhound bus parked outside and maybe 40-50 people walking around by the front door. Someone had called Fire and Police Communications to report that a bomb was going off at 2:00 PM and to clear all the people from the Restaurant. The Firefighters and I entered the restaurant to look for anything suspicious – a box or package that didn't belong there. After about an hour of searching, all clear was announced and everyone was allowed back into the restaurant, including employees. All calls to communications are recorded. I drove to the Records Division on 200 Orange Street. I listened to the actual bomb threat telephone call and I was shocked to hear the voice. It was one of Almar's Waitress's named Helen. "Why?" I asked myself? Helen was a good waitress and a nice person. Helen was from the south and she had a distinct accent. The female caller said, "Y'all better clear out this damn Restaurant because she's gonna blow at 2 O'clock." I called Almar's from Communications and played the tape for the Manager. He listened and said, "Helen, right?" "Right, don't say anything to her until I get back there because she will be under arrest for a felony." I took Helen in the office with the Manager. I said, "Helen. Are you willing to talk to me without calling a Lawyer?" She said, "Yes." "I have evidence that you made the bomb threat call. Do you have anything to say in your defense?" She said, "Every time these damn cheap Army recruits come here on that damn bus, I bust my butt for them and they never leave me a tip. I'm tired of it." "Okay, Helen, you are under arrest." I read her, her rights and took her out of there in handcuffs. These young Army recruits are told to bring no money or valuables with them. They are now the property of the United States Army. It is not their fault. The Restaurant bills the Government for the food. No cash is exchanged. Helen could not understand that. A bomb threat is a very serious matter. •

MY FIRST BABY DELIVERY STORY

I graduated from police academy on March 6, 1961. Each day on the 4:00 PM to 12:00 AM shift we rookies would be dropped off on different beats in New Haven. This day an Officer named Burt Gifford dropped me off on Dixwell Avenue and Webster Street. He said, "I'll see you at 11:45 PM on this corner. Ok, kid?" Guess I'm on my own now. As I walked north on Dixwell Avenue, I twirled my nightstick feeling proud of myself. I feared nothing until about 6:30 PM when a man came running out of an apartment building yelling that his daughter was having a baby. I wanted to run the other way but I couldn't. We ran up the 3 flights of stairs into a room where a young black lady was in labor. Everything I learned in police academy was a blank. On television they always ask for hot water and towels. That's what I asked the man for. In the meantime a small head was protruding from mama. I eased the baby out and then the cord was visible. I took a towel and placed it on mama's stomach and placed the baby boy on the towel. Please, the following remark is in no way racial but that baby was pure white/pink. That threw me off but within 10 minutes the baby turned a beautiful olive color. I guess that's normal. In the meantime I had the father call for an ambulance using my name to verify that is was a legit call. I was just about to cut the cord after tying both ends firmly with shoelaces when I heard the ambulance in the distance – what a relief that was. The ambulance took the mother and baby exactly the way I placed him on her stomach. They did not cut the cord as they thought it was better for the hospital personnel to cut it. I absolutely felt like a part of the community as I left that apartment. I walked down Dixwell Avenue with the nightstick twirling in the wind and my head held up high. I couldn't wait until I got home that night to tell my wife that I delivered a baby, a baby boy. •

MY FIRST MOTOR VEHICLE ARREST

In the summer of 1961, fresh out of Police Academy in March, I was assigned a walking beat on Washington Avenue. It was a Saturday and it was during the 4:00 PM to 12:00 midnight shift. My walking patrol area was on Washington Avenue from Congress to the 6 corners and all side streets off of Washington Avenue. Unlike today, Washington Avenue was bustling with restaurants, stores, bakeries, cars, trucks and lots of pedestrians. Washington Avenue was a one-way street from Howard Avenue to Congress Avenue. I was walking in the area of Lafayette and Liberty Streets. Suddenly, I observed a car coming the wrong way on Washington Avenue. With caution, I stepped off the curb and flagged down the driver. In the same professional manner that I was taught in Police Academy, I asked the driver for his license and registration. He asked, "What's wrong?" I said, "You are driving the wrong way on a one way street." His reply, "So are you going to make a fuc*ing federal case out of it?" At the same time, I was looking at his driver's license. Address: Cedar Street. So, he lived 1/2 block away. He knew it was a one-way street. I was going to give him a verbal warning but his nasty attitude earned him a ticket. It was my very first Motor Vehicle Violation. I had issued a few parking tickets but not a moving violation. I then realized that no matter how courteous or professional a Policeman is there will always be nasty, disrespectful people. •

After graduating from Police Academy in March of 1961, I was assigned to the 4:00 PM to 12:00 midnight shift. Each day a squad car would drop us off alone at 4:15 PM and pick us up at 11:45 PM. The second week, I was dropped off on Dixwell Avenue and Webster Street. That beat went from Henry Street to Broadway. I had my 38 Colt police special revolver, my nightstick, my blackjack, badge and, of course, my ticket book. The Captain reminded me to walk through the projects a few times so the folks would see that we were out there protecting them. My first walk through went well, I said hello to a few people and they were friendly. The second walk through was not so good. The black teenagers from a distance called me every white cracker and MF name in the book. They didn't tell us about this in class. They told us that the blue uniform commanded respect. Really? Not today, it's not working like they said it would. Why chase the kids? I wouldn't hit a kid. I got on the police red phone on the corner of Dixwell Avenue and Webster Street and called Headquarters and spoke to the Captain. I told him about the kids. "Can you get close enough to kick them in the ass Bob?" "No Captain. These kids are fast." He sent a car over to assist me. Two black Officers, Burt Gifford and Chick Coles pulled up. How could I tell them? Will they understand? Will two seasoned black police officers understand that some black kids called a rookie white police officer a racial slur? They pulled up to the curb on Dixwell and Webster. "What's wrong kid?" they asked. "Nothing guys." "Come on kid. Something happened right kid? It's OK. Did these kids call you a white cracker or a honky?" "Both," I said. "Heck kid, they call us worse than that." "They do?" "Yeah. Chase them little bastards like you are going to hit them with your nightstick and they will leave you alone." I couldn't find the kids so I didn't need to chase them. The rest of the night went well. The kids didn't bother me and I didn't bother them. I have many more stories about Dixwell Avenue to tell. •

MY FIRST TRAFFIC ASSIGNMENT

On Monday March 6, 1961, after graduating from Police Academy, I was transferred to Precinct No. 1 (Headquarters) for assignment to duty in Squad B at 3:45 P.M. It was my very first day as a Patrolman for the City of New Haven, Connecticut. Wearing a crisp new uniform with a shiny new badge number 267, I was ready to save the world. As I read the assignments on the bulletin board, there it was. Officer Robert Meyerholz: Beat 18 (Downtown). Next to my name was an asterisk: *(Traffic duty- Church & Chapel-1600 to 1800 hours). I asked my Sergeant, "Sir, what does that mean." His answer, "It means at 4:00 PM you turn the traffic signal light out at Church & Chapel and get your butt out in the middle of the intersection and direct traffic with both hands and wearing your white gloves that were issued to you. You will remain in the intersection until approximately 5:45 PM when the traffic flow eases up. You will also be responsible for pedestrians crossing at that intersection." This I was not prepared for. Major traffic jams on my first day. Roll Call was dismissed at approximately 3:55 PM. There was only one way to walk to Church & Chapel. That was to walk west on Court Street and turn south on Church Street. Within seconds, it seemed, I arrived at Church & Chapel. I took my assigned traffic control key on my keychain and opened the traffic control box. ON–OFF–FLASH. Guess it was off that I wanted. I got in the middle of the intersection. I started a steady flow of traffic on Chapel Street using arms, hands, etc. Then I stopped the traffic completely and signaled for the pedestrians to cross. Then I started Church Street, which was one-way north, moving north. Within maybe 45 minutes, I got the hang of it. A friend driving by beeped his horn at me and waved. I waved back. BAD IDEA. Screech. Several cars came to an abrupt stop. I never realized the power and authority a Policeman had with his hands wearing those white gloves. I made it. By 6:00 PM, I turned the traffic light back on and felt pretty darn proud of myself. The rest of the night, I walked the beat and talked to many, many people. Seemed that all the young ladies loved the uniform and seemed friendly. Of course I was age 24 and in excellent shape with a full head of hair. I also had a gold wedding ring on my finger that kept me out of trouble. •

MY FIRST PARKING ENFORCEMENT ASSIGNMENT

As I said earlier, after graduating from Police Academy, I was assigned to the squad B (4:00 to 12:00 midnight) shift. Every other day they would schedule us so we would get to learn the different parts of the city. Mainly, where the trouble spots were and where the most crime was. One day in the summer, I was assigned a walking beat on State Street from Grove Street to Water Street. There, I was responsible for parking violations, especially from 4:00 to 6:00 PM. As I walked past Lincoln Furniture then located on the east side of State Street just south of Grand Avenue, there were 2 signs in front of the store. *COMMERCIAL VEHICLES ONLY BETWEEN SIGNS.* That meant delivery trucks or smaller vehicles with combination license plates. There were three cars parked between these signs. I got out my ticket book and put parking tickets on all three vehicles. Suddenly, a small bald headed man came running out of the store. "What are you doing?" he exclaimed. "My job mister," I answered politely. "This is my store!" the man yelled. "So? These vehicles are in violation mister," I answered while still being polite. "You must be a rookie." Yelling at the top of his lungs he said, "I know the Chief. I will have you removed from this beat by tomorrow." I thought about his threatening words and gave him an answer. "Mister, could you please do that for me? I hate this beat. Would you talk to the Chief and get me off this beat? I would appreciate that." He turned beat red in the face and stormed back in the store and never came back out. I learned that when the public threatened me, to used reverse physiology. Turn a negative into a positive. The next day, only one truck was parked between those 2 signs. No bald man came running out of the store. I was never called into the Chief's office, for doing my job. Being a Police Officer was a lifelong dream come true. •

THE SPOUSES OF POLICE OFFICERS NEED TO BE RECOGNIZED

The spouses of Police Officers, both male and female, need to be recognized. My beautiful wife Mary of 60 years kept a secret all the years that I devoted my life to Police work. On the day I retired, December 10, 1978, when we got home from the ceremonies, she said, "Finally. Thank God I don't need to worry about you anymore." "What do you mean honey?" "Every time you walked out that door in your uniform and I kissed you, I thought that it would be the last kiss and the last time I saw you." "Since when did you feel that way honey?" "Since the first day you wore your uniform." All these years I never knew about her thoughts. I would have resigned years ago. Mary said, "I know. I know you loved your job more than anything." But, I loved Mary more than anything. I would not be writing this post had I known how Mary felt. Mary is a strong and devoted woman and any success I achieved, I owe it to my Mary; my sweetheart and my best friend. •

A FUNNY STORY-DUMB AND DUMBER

It's time for a funny story. One Saturday in the summer of 1968, I was off duty and looking for parts for my own car at Tarducci's Used Auto Parts on Middletown Avenue. They had an honor system where you would take your own tools and remove the parts you need for your car, then stop at the office and pay for them. One of the guys came out in the yard and said, "John Tarducci needs to see you in the office". I entered through the side door and John said, "Bob, I got 2 guys out in the yard and I have been watching them. They passed the office three times with used parts in their hands and haven't stopped once to pay for any of them." I was dressed in old clothes and had greasy hands and I sure didn't look like a cop. Just then the 2 men walked out again, past the gate with used parts and put them in their trunk. I had plenty of back up in the office so I approached and said, "Hey guys, what's up?" Their trunk was full of used parts. "Man," they said, "we been coming here for years man and these guys are stupid. We never pay for nothing." These two idiots are bragging to me about how much they have been stealing from Tarducci's. I said, "Damn. What did you get today?" "2 batteries, a starter motor, an AM-FM radio, a 4 barrel carburetor." "Wow, all that for nothing?" "Yep. They sure are stupid here man." By now, John Tarducci Sr. and the boys were just behind the fence, waiting for my signal. I took out my badge and yelled, "John, let's go. These men have some stuff that they forgot to pay for." I don't know what the final figure was, but, one man went to the bank and the other stayed in my custody until his friend came back and paid for every single part in that trunk. Then they were both told to never come back to Tarducci's. I did a complete police report with the names and addresses of both men plus the license plate number of the vehicle. I concluded that no arrest due to restitution made and no further police action necessary. John said, "Bob, you the man." I forgot what I needed for my own car and went home. •

YOUNG SPEEDER WITH CORVETTE

In the summer of 1964 I was patrolling the 12:00 to 8:00 AM shift in Westville. At about 1:00 AM, I was waiting for a red light on Ramsdell and Fountain Street. I hear a motor of a fast moving vehicle traveling west on Fountain Street. The car passed that intersection at a very high rate of speed heading up Fountain Street toward Woodbridge. The operator turned off his headlights so I couldn't see the license plate. I turned right and proceeded to pursue the vehicle. It appeared to be a Corvette. I put on my red lights and crossed the Woodbridge line. The vehicle was out of site. As I approached the intersection of Ansonia Rd and Rimmon Road, I could see black skid marks and a little smoke in the road that turned right into Rimmon Road. I also smelled burning tires. I decided to turn my red lights off knowing I was no match for a Corvette but maybe I could outsmart the driver. I proceeded several miles until I observed taillights in the distance. Just past Beecher Road, I caught up to a red Corvette. I hit my red lights and siren at the same time. The Corvette pulled over. I notified my dispatcher of my location and the license plate number of the Corvette and requested that Woodbridge PD meet me there. A young operator got out of the car laughing and said, "Ha ha. I'm out of New Haven and you can't touch me." As the Woodbridge car pulled up, I said, "Ha ha oh yes I can. Speedy information allows a Policeman in hot pursuit to cross city/town lines to make an arrest." He didn't know that. I was unable to clock his speed but I charged him with reckless driving and operating a motor vehicle without headlights. Three weeks later he went to court and pled guilty. He paid a substantial fine. •

I was off duty one Saturday afternoon driving my own personal vehicle in the summer of 1970. I crossed the Q Bridge and noticed 2 vehicles parked against the guardrail going into Church Street South, exit 4 or 5 men were standing by the vehicles. Thinking it was an accident; I passed the 2 cars and pulled over with my flashers on to assist. I was risking my own safety, but I knew that Policeman are required to assist with any emergencies like accidents 24 hours a day. I displayed my badge and asked if I could assist. "Nope," one said. "We're just talking." I said "Gentleman, this is a dangerous place to stop, please get in your cars and leave." Same guy said, "We ain't moving, man. That badge means nothing so stick it up your a**." Cars getting off at the Church Street exit were whizzing by at a high rate of speed so for my own safety, I left the scene but got to a police call box on Frontage and York Street and first called the State Police and then called Headquarters. I had a good description of the vehicles and Massachusetts license plates. The State Police arrived at the scene a few minutes later, but reported that both vehicles were gone. I put out a broadcast with the description of both vehicles. I got a call at 10:00 PM from the West Haven PD that one vehicle was parked in front of the Penny Arcade at Savin Rock. I drove to West Haven and met with West Haven Police. The man sitting in the driver's seat was the one with the big mouth. The other men were not wanted. The West Haven Policeman put him in the back seat of his car. I tried to talk to him and maybe resolve it without an arrest, but he said, "Don't talk to me, just lock my ass up and take me to jail man." That's what we did. He got his wish. Monday morning in court I was there. The Judge told him that, this Officer was doing his job for your own safety. The man said, "F**k these cops man." That got him 30 days in the Whalley Avenue County Jail. •

VW CHASING DOG

Back in 1966, sometime in the spring, I was working an extra assignment job on Congress Avenue and West Streets – it was either the SNET or UI Company. They had a manhole cover open and there were men working underground. I was directing traffic around the site. There was a big mongrel dog sitting on the sidewalk, just watching us, an old and friendly dog. All of a sudden, he took off barking and chasing a car traveling west on Congress Avenue. He came back and sat in the same spot. 5 minutes later, he was off chasing another car traveling east on Congress Avenue. Suddenly, I realized something. This dog was only chasing Volkswagen beetles. What? Am I on Candid Camera? Impossible. Dogs don't know one car from the other. Do they? I called the 2 guys working down in the hole. They came up the ladder. "Hey guys, I want you guys to look at something." Just then her comes a VW beetle going west. The dog goes running after the beetle, barking and biting at the tires. They said, "It's the VW motor noise he doesn't like." OK, sounds right. Just then, here comes a VW van, going the same way. He sits on the sidewalk and ignores the van with the same VW engine in the back. The guys looked at me and went back down the ladder. Here comes another VW beetle and off goes the dog chasing it for a half block. All I could come up with was this roaming dog, at one time was hit by a VW beetle and he hates VW beetles. I called the Animal Shelter to pick him up before he got run over. They arrived but the dog took off and disappeared. Smart dog. •

A POLICE OFFICERS DECISION

Any decision a Police Officer makes can affect a person's life forever. Common sense must always prevail when a person's life and livelihood are in the Officer's hands. The last week of February 1973, at about 1:30 AM, I was dispatched to Orchard Street, between Davenport and Sylvan Avenue. My radio car, number 21, was also designated as a major accident investigation car. My responsibilities were enormous when investigating serious accidents. A car struck a man in his early 60's as he walked between two parked cars and into the street. I called for an ambulance and administered first aid to help stop the bleeding. The man had severe head injuries. Finally, the ambulance arrived and took the man to Yale New Haven Hospital. A young woman was driving the car that struck him as he attempted to cross the street. A short time later, I was notified that the man had died. He was from New York and had no family here. I comforted the driver of the car who was very distraught. After checking her license, registration and insurance, there were no obvious signs that she had been drinking or impaired in any way. I asked her if I could call a relative or a friend to take her home. I even offered to call her a taxi. She said she was fine, heartbroken that a man had died, but fine. I reassured her that from what I saw, the man probably caused his own death. I advised her to go home and that I would be in contact with her. I immediately started my investigation as to the cause of the accident. With my camera, pen and pad in my hand, along with my measuring devise, I measured the width of the street. I took a diagram of every street light on the block. Recorded the serial numbers on each utility pole. Recorded the lumen (brightness) that each light produced. The most important street light directly over the accident scene was out. A check with the UI Company disclosed that it had been out for a few days and was scheduled to be replaced. The man had dark complexion and was dressed in dark clothing. A toxicology report disclosed that the man's blood alcohol content was double the amount of a person that was deemed intoxicated. I sent my completed fatal accident report to the County Coroner's Office. My role was not to judge who caused the accident, the pedestrian or the driver of the car, but to do a complete accident investigation report so the Coroner will have that information to assist him in making a fair and impartial decision. After a hearing in the Coroner's Office months later, It was determined that the man caused his own death by stepping in front of a moving vehicle,

MEMORIES OF A RETIRED COP

between 2 parked cars at night while he was intoxicated. The driver of the vehicle was heart broken, but she did not cause the man's death. The female driver of the car was sent a formal letter, exonerating her completely of any wrong doing in this unfortunate fatal motor vehicle vs. pedestrian accident. Justice must always prevail. The female driver of the vehicle wrote a nice letter to Chief Biagio DiLieto a few days after the accident occurred. The Chief sent her a letter back. I've attached both letters in the Supplements section at the end of the book for reference. •

One of my favorite places to work extra duty was The Oxford Ale House, located on Whitney Avenue near Audubon Street. Bobby Lucibello, the owner of the club, was a really great guy. Sometime during the mid 70's, on a Saturday night, Eight To The Bar came to perform there. Myself and another Policeman were on duty that night and we took turns rotating from the front door to the interior of the club. Ned, one of the bouncers, was working the front door. Admission was only a $5.00 cover charge. At about 10:00 PM, Ned signaled for me to come to the front door. Ned stated that a very tall black gentleman pushed past him without paying the $5.00. Ned found him at the bar and the man stated he wanted to make sure his friends were there before paying the $5.00. Things are not done that way but we made allowances. One half hour later, the man had not returned to pay the $5.00 admission charge. He was still standing at the bar drinking. That's when I got involved. I found the man and escorted him outside to the sidewalk. I said, "Mister, either pay the $5.00 like everyone else or leave." "Who the f**k are you man?" I said, "Mister leave now." That's when he took a swing at me. Missed by a mile. He was taller and younger and he had a few drinks but I was sober and more experienced. We were actually wrestling on the trunk of a parked car and I finally got the cuffs on him. I called for the paddy wagon. As I was putting him in the wagon, a gentleman identifying himself as a Yale law student stated that he witnessed the incident on the sidewalk and that I used excessive force toward the black man. "Did you see the man swing at me?" "No. I did not. I saw you putting handcuffs on him behind his back." "Yes, because he was under arrest." "You didn't need to put handcuffs on him." "Yes, I did. That's standard Police procedure." He wanted my name and badge number. I wrote it all down for him. He then blocked the front door and refused to move. Finally, I placed him under arrest for interfering with a Police Officer and put him in the same paddy wagon. Ned asked, "Is it a full moon tonight Bob?" I looked up. Yes it was. •

HUSBAND WHO BEATS HIS WIFE (CALLED A COWARD)

I have a story, not sure of the exact date, but sometime in the summer of 1966, in the mid afternoon I was patrolling in Westville. My partner, Officer Al Morrone, was off duty so a new rookie Policeman was driving Al's patrol car. We answered a call of a domestic on Rock View Circle. A woman called to say her husband was beating her. She called from a bedroom telephone so he wouldn't know she was calling the Police. I rushed to Rock View Circle and arrived before the rookie. I approached the apartment and knocked on the door. A large black guy answered the door. He said, "Did you call this pig on me?" to his wife who was somewhere in the apartment. I said, "Mister, don't call me a pig." I asked him to open the door so I could enter and make sure the lady was all right. He tried to slam the door in my face and at the same time calling me a pig again. Once that door locks, the lady could be in real danger so that wasn't going to happen. I put my foot in the door jam and this time he called me Mr. Pig and fought me to slam that door in my face. That's it. The fight was on. Where is my backup?! I yanked him through the wooden screen door and we ended up on the grass area wrestling. I got on top of him and had him under control. As I was putting the handcuffs on him, the wife jumped on my back and started punching me on my head, neck and back. This is the same woman that called the police and reported that her husband was beating her. I threw her off of me and thank God, a neighbor called the police station to say that a policeman was in trouble. I couldn't get to my radio. The paddy wagon pulled up with my backup behind him. I arrested them both, charging her with an assault on a Policeman and him for breach of peace. The rookie said, "I got lost. Couldn't find Rock View Circle." I was peeved, really peeved. This was his area and I was the backup car. "Why didn't you ask the dispatcher where Rock View Circle was?" "I was too embarrassed," he said. Domestic calls are dangerous to Police Officers that respond. Officers should never be alone at a domestic dispute. I told the rookie that we all start off new to police work and sometime we can't find an address so pick up the radio mike and ask the dispatcher for help. •

The following story is one of my absolute favorites. This is what New Haven in the 60's was all about: one night in the late 1960's, I was on patrol in the Newhallville area. It was a little after 1:00 AM. I was waiting at a red traffic light heading north on Dixwell Avenue and Bassett Street. One car was in front of me. The light changed to green and the car did not move. I beeped the horn. Nothing. It turned red again. Then, it turned green again. Beep-beep. Nothing. I got out of my police car after calling in the license plate for my protection. The driver's window was open. The driver was snoring and he was sound asleep. The car was in DRIVE and his foot was on the brake pedal. I carefully reached in and put the car in park and removed the keys. I woke the driver up. He looked around and didn't know what happened. "Mister," I said, "have you been drinking tonight?" "Damn straight Officer. I just came from the Elks Club on Webster Street and can't find my house. I'm driving and driving and can find my house." I put him in my police car and parked his car in the Zeoli's Texaco Station on the corner and locked the doors. "Mister, what's your name?" "Ozzie Gooding." "Where do you live Ozzie?" "238 Shelton Avenue, second floor. I just want to go home, please." "Okay Ozzie. You were straight with me so I'll take you home." I drove to 238 Shelton Avenue and parked in front and opened the rear car door for Ozzie. We walked up on the porch. Ozzie couldn't find the right door key so I rang the bell. The hall light came on and down the stairs came Mrs. Gooding. She opened the door and looked at us both. "Ozzie? Why are the police with you?" I helped Ozzie up the stairs and he turned around and whispered, "Officer don't go. Please don't leave me alone with her, please man." I explained the situation to Mr.'s Gooding and told her there will be no arrest. Ozzie was honest and cooperative with me and he was getting a break tonight. I gave her the car keys and told her to please move the car from Zeoli's Gas Station before 8:00 AM. I told her that I left a note on the windshield saying that the car would be moved in the morning. She thanked me and said to Ozzie, "You and me are going to talk in the morning about this drinking business." I left. •

Now, about two weeks after meeting Ozzie Gooding, who was the most honest and cooperative person I ever met, I was on duty alone at a Bar & Grille on the corner of Winchester and Division Street. It was called Coes (Cofrancesco). It was a Saturday night. It was like a night club and very popular, but it was also a rough place with many fights. My assignment was to stay on the sidewalk unless there was trouble inside. This night, all hell broke loose. A fight at the bar between 5-6 guys broke out. The Bartender was calling the station for backup for me. I walked in and tried to break it up. It was impossible alone. Next thing I realized there was a man to my left, swinging at the guys fighting so I assumed that it was an off duty Policeman or Detective. Nope. After my back up arrived, we made several arrests, putting them in the paddy wagon. I turned around to thank this man. It was Ozzie Gooding. Ozzie said, you took me home a few weeks ago. right? Yes, I did. But, I asked him, "How did you remember me?" "By your glasses and the way you walk, man. You got that walk man." Yes Ozzie. It was me. Then Ozzie said, "I ain't comin back here no more because the brothers are going to be pissed off at me tomorrow." I felt bad but Ozzie helped me because he wanted to. He didn't have to get involved but he wanted to. Ozzie died years ago well into his 80's and he still lived at 238 Shelton Avenue. It was in the New Haven Register. A Google search shows that 238 Shelton Avenue is now a lot, no longer is a 2 family house located there. May God bless Ozzie Gooding. •

DAMAGE TO CONSTRUCTION EQUIPMENT

On June 13, 1966, I was assigned to work an extra traffic assignment on Weybosset Street at the intersection of Cross Street. I would be working for C.W. Blakeslee. I arrived at 7:45 AM for the 8:00 AM traffic assignment. Upon arrival I was met by the construction foreman, Berney Kuhn. The traffic assignment was to repave Weybosset Street from Cross Street to Westminster Street. Berney informed us that we would not be working today. Over the weekend, vandals severely damaged the Blakeslee equipment. Berney showed me the damage: the road grader has a slashed tire, the fuel tank was full of sand, the ignition wires were ripped out and the battery was smashed. The road grader had been parked in an empty lot over the weekend near the intersection. I offered to stay on duty and try to determine who did this damage. Berney informed me that he could not authorize paying me because all the workers were being sent home without pay. The assignment could not be completed without the road grader. I told Berney that I would work for nothing just to solve this senseless crime. Thousands of dollars of damage was done to the road grader. Also a bulldozer was damaged. Berney said, "If you want to stay Bob, that's fine. I just can't pay you." I picked up a legal pad and pencils and started by looking for evidence in the soft dirt around the construction equipment. I found 7 sets of sneaker prints surrounding the road grader. I carefully made diagrams of the prints and made exact measurements of each sneaker print with a tape measure. Then I waited patiently until school got out at 3:00 PM. I believe it was the last week before summer vacation. One at a time, as the kids walked by looking at the road grader, I checked their sneakers. Each sneaker has a unique print, from circles to diamonds to other designs. Within a short time, I caught five of the vandals who admitted to the damage. They implicated two others. I now had the names and addresses of 7 vandals. I drove to Station Two where I reported for regular duty at 4:00 PM, I was now on my regular eight-hour shift. After leaving Station Two, I started my investigation. I filled in my Sergeant as to what I was doing. One at a time, I paid a visit to the parents of the seven vandals. All the parents had homeowners insurance and the thousands of dollars' worth of damage done to Blakeslee's road grader and bulldozer was covered. Bernard Kuhn sent a beautiful letter to Chief McManus. I attached this very old letter plus Chief McManus's reply to Blakeslee Company. •

14-YEAR-OLD MURDER SUSPECT

In 1968, there was a 14-year-old boy being held at the Juvenile Detention Center on Orange Street for shooting and killing his 14 year old friend with a 12 gauge shot gun. The friend was visiting him and they were clowning around like kids often do. The phone rang and it was the girlfriend of the boy in Detention. His friend wanted to talk to the girlfriend and he said, "No, and if you keep bugging me, I'll go get my father's shot gun and blow your f**king head off." The boy continued to bug him. Not realizing he was serious, He handed the phone to the other boy and went to the closet and got his fathers loaded 12 gauge shot gun and cold bloodedly shot the other boy, killing him instantly. Then he took the phone and coldly told his girlfriend that he blew his friend's f**king head off. Well at about 8:00 PM, I was sent to the Detention Center because one of the attendants called out sick on the 8:00 to 4:00 AM shift. My assignment was to closely watch this child murderer until the midnight shift arrived. I locked my weapon in the office and was directed to his room. He was playing solitaire. I wasn't worried about a physical attack from this kid, because I was 6'1" and 240 lbs. and he was maybe 5'4" and 120 lbs. but he had just killed his best friend in cold blood for nothing. To pass the time, we played cards. He looked at me with those cold eyes and said, "Where's your gun, cop?" I said, "In a safe place, why?" "Because if you had it, I would take it away from you and put a bullet in your f**king head." This 14-year-old boy was the coldest person I have ever met. I called the office and ordered this boy handcuffed behind his back, for my own safety as well as his. From 9:00 PM until 12:00 midnight, that was the longest three hours of my life. At midnight, I told my relief not to turn their back on this boy, not even for a second. We handcuffed him to his bed. I lost track of the case and never knew what happened to him. He was probable released from juvenile detention when he turned twenty-one. •

ARREST OF JIM MORRISON OF THE DOORS

On December 9, 1967, I was working extra duty at the old New Haven Arena. There were approximately 30-35 Officers on duty for the concert. All Officers had to report at 7:00 PM, two hours before the concert to check all offices, rest rooms, dressing rooms etc. for any unauthorized non-paying persons. The old arena building had wooden doors and windows that were easily forced open to allow people to sneak in – that's why it was important for us the check the building before each event. Jim Morrison and an unidentified female were hiding in a shower stall. An Officer checking those areas discovered them and told them to leave. The young lady ran out of the building but Mr. Morrison decided to give the Officer a hard time. Telling the Officer to mind his own business. There was reported shoving and Morrison got maced and arrested. As he was being escorted out of the building, his manager intervened and agreed to have Mr. Morrison surrender after the concert. Lieutenant James Kelly was in charge and gave his approval with a warning to Mr. Morrison to cool off and act properly. I was stationed on the floor in front of the center of the stage. The concert went on as planned. Toward the end, Mr. Morrison started to tell the story about his dealings with the New Haven Police. The audience, mostly young people started to stamp their feet on the old wooden floor, making a thunderous noise. Lt. Kelly jumped up on stage and warned Mr. Morrison to knock it off. 10 minutes later, Morrison was again agitating the crowd and Lt. Kelly went behind the stage and ordered the overhead lights on. He also had Morrison's mike cut off. At that point Lt. Kelly told Morrison that the concert was over and he was under arrest. Officer Wayne Thomas jumped on stage and assisted Lt. Kelly in escorting Morrison to the rear of the stage. I then jumped up on stage and took Lt. Kelly's place, permitting Lt. Kelly to remain on the stage to direct crowd control. Morrison was escorted to a waiting paddy wagon in the parking garage. He was taken to Headquarters at 165 Court Street and booked on several charges. By the time he was fingerprinted and processed, it was after midnight so his booking picture was dated December 10, 1967. There is a short YouTube video of the actual arrest. Looking at the video, I am shown after jumping on the stage to assist Officer Leary in escorting Jim Morrison to the waiting paddy wagon parked in the garage behind the stage. •

OVERSIZED SANDWICH IN N.H.P.D CAFETERIA VENDING MACHINE

I was working the midnight shift one cold night in February 1976; it was a Saturday night. We had pot roast for dinner a week before so Mary had left over pot roast. She packed two large pot roast sandwiches on large rye bread for me to take to work. We had a Cafeteria in the New Police Station so I could enjoy my sandwiches rather than go to the Highway Diner for my lunch period and deal with the Saturday night drunks that came in after the bars closed. About 3:00 AM, I parked my police car, #60, in front of the police station and went inside and sat in the cafeteria with my pot roast sandwiches. Now, I need to point out that we had vending machines in the cafeteria with tiny sandwiches on white bread with one or two pieces of meat and one slice of cheese for maybe 75 cents. I got a cold soda from one of the machines and sat down. I opened one pot roast sandwich, which Mary cut in half. Just then as I took the first bite, two of my fellow Police officers walked in. "Damn Bob. Where did you get that sandwich?" I could not resist. I told them from the vending machine. They walked around to the vending machine and looked in every window. No large pot roast sandwiches could be seen. "Yo Bob? Show us where you got that sandwich man." I got up and walked around to the vending machines and carefully selected an empty window. "Right there guys," I said, pointing to the empty window. "Guess I got the last two sandwiches." They looked so disappointed so I offered my second sandwich to them. As they were enjoying this delicious pot roast sandwich made from love by Mary, I told them the truth. "Damn Bob, we knew you were bull jiving man but we weren't sure. Don't matter Bob, this sandwich is delicious." Just having some clean harmless fun between three brother Police Officers. •

In the summer of 1972, among other responsibilities as a New Haven Policeman, I drove the three-wheel Harley Davidson motorcycles. One evening on the 4:00 to 12:00 shift, I was stationed in the Grand Avenue area. I decided to park on the corner of Lloyd Street and Grand Avenue. I was sitting there checking out traffic and pedestrian activity. I attracted the attention of 3 or 4 neighborhood boys who came over. Checking out my bike. One wise guy kid commented that, "He ain't no cop. He's the Good Humor man," and laughed. The other boys did not laugh, they were more respectful toward me. I had an idea. I started the Harley and left the area and drove over to the Good Humor Corporation on the corner of James Street and River Street. I drove right in the garage. The night manager, Al Torello, was on duty. I said hello to Al and asked for a favor. I told Al the story about the kids. He took a box of 24 toasted almond bars and even set a block of dry ice in the rear compartment. He placed the ice cream on the dry ice. I thanked him and drove back to Lloyd and Grand and parked in the same spot. It took a while but finally, the same boys returned. The wise guy said, "Yo, it's the Good Humor man," and laughed. I got off the bike and opened the rear compartment and said, "Boys, I only have toasted almond left, OK?" Mr. Wise guy said, "See, I told you guys he wasn't a real cop, man." At 12:00 PM I signed off at Station 2 and went home, never telling the other Officers what I did. I knew what would happen the next night. Well, next day at 4:00 PM, I was assigned to Lighthouse Park with my 3-wheeler. Another, mean looking cop was assigned to Grand Avenue with his 3-wheeler. The eight-hour shift went by. Checking in at midnight, we compared our nights. The mean Officer said, "Guess what? These little bas**ards came over to me on Grand Avenue and asked for ice cream. They said the other cop gave them ice cream last night. Where do these kids get such stupid ideas anyway?" "No respect," I said. •

ONE WAY STREET VIOLATION

Back in the days when I patrolled Westville in 1962, one of my stops to chat with my little friends was Cooper Place. I loved talking to my little friends. They always had stories to tell me like, "mommy goes real fast sometimes" or "my daddy says stop signs are stupid." "Oh, really?" I would answer. Cooper Place was a one-way circular street. Pulling in from Fountain Street, drivers would turn right and follow the circle until in exited back on Fountain Street. One day, the kids told me about a man that lived there that drove the wrong way every day because his apartment was closer to Fountain Street. Because the kids were used to looking in one direction only as they crossed the street, I viewed this violation as serious. The man owned a new car dealership on Amity Road. According to the children, every day just after 5:00 PM this man would enter Cooper Place and instead of following the traffic pattern, he drove straight, against traffic the wrong way to his apartment parking lot just two driveways down on the right. It was quicker than driving all the way around the circle. The next day, I sat parked waiting for him. Not only did he drive his luxury car the wrong way but at a high rate of speed. I stopped him and called in his dealer plate number for my protection. I was prepared to give him a stern verbal warning but he opened his mouth. "Did the little brats squeal on me?" he asked. My little friends were not little brats so he said the wrong thing to me. He got his ticket that he rightfully deserved. In the distance I could see my little friends jumping up and down watching Officer Bob give a ticket to a bad guy. He never did that again. •

A RACIST LANDLADY

Being a New Haven Police Officer, I saw more prejudice than the average person would ever see. Are we all treated the same? NO. Does skin color matter? YES. Does where we come from matter? YES. As I mentioned before, I worked in the Hispanic Community in Fair Haven. I was off duty one Saturday morning in 1966, visiting some friends on James Street: a young Puerto Rican family with two beautiful children. They were looking for an apartment in New Haven but had problems reading the advertisements and talking on the telephone. Their English wasn't too good so I offered to help them. I glanced through the New Haven Register, apartments and found one on Ann Street. First floor and the rent was reasonable. I called the number. A lady answered. I specifically said I was calling for a friend. She said the apartment was still available and would I like to see it this morning. I asked my friends and they said yes. We drove to Ann Street right off of Congress Avenue. Waited for 10 minutes for the landlady. She pulled up. We got out of our car. We all walked toward the apartment. The landlady got behind me and grabbed my arm. "Is this for you or for them?" "It's for my friends, why?" "It's $300.00 a month cash," she said. I asked my friends if they had cash (dinero)? Si. Tenemos dinero. I told the landlady that I was a Policeman and they were my friends and that hey were nice family people. She had no choice but to give my friends the rent. She was angry but she kept quiet. The next week I got a truck from a friend and I helped them move from James Street to Ann Street. We had all the heavy appliances on the truck so I backed up on the sidewalk to the front porch just to unload the appliances. Movers do that all the time. Within two minutes, two police cars pulled up and said they had a complaint of a truck on the sidewalk. They confided in me and said the complaint was from the landlord of the house. I had to park the truck across the street and we had to carry the heavy appliances. I had to remain professional at all times and obey all laws. The very first night, two Policemen knocking on their door at 3:00 AM awakened my friends. They had a complaint of a fight in the apartment. Two nights later, the same thing happened. Finally, my friends had to move because of the harassment and false complaints to the Police Department. The landlady did not want 'them' in her house. She made it impossible for them to stay there. This is the ugly side of bigotry. •

FEMALE VICTIM FROM MEXICO

In the summer of 1966, at about 10:00 PM, I was dispatched to a two family home on Liberty Street. It was a time when I was working closely in the Hispanic Community, learning the culture and language. The call was a report of an attempted rape of an 18-year-old Mexican girl. I was nowhere close to speaking Spanish fluently, so with the assistance of an interpreter, I put the following story together. The girl's name was Blanca and she was from Acuna, Mexico. Blance was living with a middle aged Mexican couple that owned a nearby business. An agreement was made that Blanca would be their domestic helper, to cook and clean for them as they worked during the day, for room and board plus $25.00 a week spending money. The couple also paid for her plane ticket to come to America and after one year, Blanca would be free and on her own. Four months had passed, but tonight the man decided to attack Blanca as his wife was away for a few days. She ran to a neighbor's house and they called the police. That's when I got involved. Blanca was not injured, but she was frightened and alone. All of her personal belongings, including her clothes were still in that house. She only had the clothes she was wearing. I went next door and knocked on the door. The man opened the door and I told him that Blanca was not coming back, ever but she needed her clothes and other personal items. He said, "Un momento," and closed the door. Ten minutes later he opened the door and handed me a large pile of ladies clothes and closed the door. I then realized he cut all of Blanca's clothes into pieces. My sergeant was on scene and he said, "It is now a civil matter Bob so don't get involved." However, later that night I arrested this bastard for attempted rape. Blanca had nothing, just the clothes on her back. I found a safe place for her to stay and the next morning, I took her to Alexander's in Milford where we had a store credit card and let her put $100.00 on my credit card so she would at least have clean clothes to wear. She really stretched that $100.00 – shorts, tops, underwear and a pair of sandals. I was looking at one of my own daughters shopping and having fun. Although homeless, Blanca felt that someone cared and that someone was me. When I told this whole story to Mary, she was not happy. Absolutely not jealous, but she said, "You stuck your neck out for a young girl and God knows how it could of ended." She gave me the old familiar lecture of, "Bob, you can't change the whole world," but if anything happened to Blanca, I would never forgive myself.

Blanca's safety was now in my hands. I could not let her down. Blanca met a boy her age and the last time I saw them they were very happy.

(Conclusion) Since that traumatic night on Liberty Street for Blanca, I found her a safe home with my friends Phyllis Berrios and her Cuban husband, Wilfredo. Phyllis was the daughter of Pepe and Anna Berrios, who operated a fine Spanish Restaurant on State Street just north of Elm Street. It was called La Mina De Oro (The Gold Mine). Phyllis and her husband also ran a dry cleaning business on Grand Avenue near James Street. Blanca took care of their home while they worked. Blanca was now safe and happy. Blanca met a handsome 21-year-old man named Lee from Puerto Rico. They found an apartment in New Haven and moved in together. Blanca was no longer a frightened and vulnerable woman, living in a strange city, thousands of miles away from home. Blanca now had friends and a relatively normal life. About 6 months later, Lee became home sick for Puerto Rico so Lee and Blanca moved to Puerto Rico. On their last day here, I paid them a visit to say adios y buenas suerta (Good bye and good luck.) Blanca bought me a record (disco) as a reminder of our mutual friendship and trust. It was called "Yo Te Amo." It was by a popular singer at that time named Yaco Monte. The song can be heard on Youtube these days. The kindness you show to a person today could mean a lifetime of friendship. •

MEN ELECTROCUTED RETRIEVING TV ANTENNA

In the spring of 1962, I was still a rookie walking the beat on Grand Avenue. The Officer on radio car patrol picked me up to give my feet and legs some relief from walking the beat. At about 2:00 PM, we got an emergency call to respond to a vacant house on William Street that was being torn down for Redevelopment. Upon arrival, the New Haven Fire Department was already on scene. 2 men had received permission to remove a television antenna complete with a 20-foot aluminum pole that was strapped to the chimney on the roof of the vacant house. They parked their pickup truck in the back yard. As they carefully let the antenna drop to the ground, they swung the pole around to place it in the back of the truck. Part of the pole came in contact with the Rail Road high-tension wires. They were both electrocuted instantly. The Foreman who was in charge of demolishing several houses on William Street admitted that he gave them permission to remove the antenna and pole from the house. He told them to be careful of high-tension wires under the Olive Street railroad bridge. It was my first experience of seeing death first hand. It was very traumatic for me. Shortly after this tragic accident, the demolition crew stopped letting people take items from homes that were scheduled for demolition. Many television roof antennas in the past were removed without any problems. That privilege was now a thing of the past. •

NEW BURGER KING OPENS

Burger King opened a new Restaurant on the corner of Whalley and E. Ramsdell Street in 1970-71. The first week, management had big problems with the neighborhood kids coming in after school and weekends and harassing the patrons and staff. I was dispatched to investigate the complaints. I suggested hiring an off duty Policeman. Wound up that I was familiar with the neighborhood so I was hired part time for Friday and Saturday nights and other Policeman for during the week. That Friday I arrived at about 7:00 PM and parked my personal vehicle on the side of the building. I walked in the front door and the kids were throwing pickles and catsup at each other. I immediately took a stand and said, let's go outside kids. I took maybe seven or eight teenagers outside and read the riot act. I told them my name and why I was now on duty there. I said, "You guys are more than welcome to patronize the new Burger King, but this nonsense is stopping now, today." If looks could kill, I would be dead. They walked slowly to the rear of the building and toward the projects on E. Ramsdell Street. Looking at my car, one said, "Nice car man, wouldn't look good with busted windows." I stopped the group and said, "If one of my windows is broken on my personal car tonight, I will go to your house and break all your windows." One kid answered and said, "You don't know where I live man." "Yes I do," I responded. "You live in the projects and I know your mom." "You do?" "Yes and I'm going to talk to her about your behavior when I see her," I said. "What's your name?" He said, "Jimmie." I shook his hand and said, "I'm Bob. You look like the leader of this gang." "I am," he said. "How did you know that?" "Because you look the toughest," I said. I went inside and got four FREE Whopper tickets from the manager and handed them to Jimmie. I said, "Bring in your mom for a whopper." He handed me back two tickets and said, "I only need two. One for me and one for my mom." That really impressed me. I got to meet Jimmie's mom two weeks later, but remember how I told Jimmie I knew his mom... well, after meeting her and sitting in the booth with them, I said, "I thought I knew you." Anyway, after my first day on the job at Burger King, we never had a problem with the kids again. I showed them that the nonsense was over but I also showed them respect and gave them a choice. I bet he turned out to be a productive and successful man. •

MAN EXPOSES HIMSELF TO CHILDREN

In early 1964, maybe March or April, I arrested a man for exposing himself to children. I remember it was a Friday afternoon. I was working the 3:00 PM to 11:00 PM shift. My first stop was usually Cooper Place to say hello to my little friends. As usual the kids were waiting at the curb to greet me, but today was different. As I pulled to the curb, the kids were all trying to talk to me at the same time. "Bob, Bob, guess what? Guess what??" "One at a time kids. What happened?" They told me about a car parked on the corner of Cooper Place and Fountain Street as they walked home from school shortly after 3:00 PM. The man with curly black hair called them over to his car. While sitting in the driver's seat he exposed himself to the children. They then all ran home. "Did you tell your parents kids?" I asked. "No, because we wanted to tell you first, Bob." "Kids. What did the car look like?" One little girl said, "Just like my daddy's car, only it was white." "Where is daddy's car now?" "It's in the back parking lot." I got out of my police car and followed the children to the back lot. Daddy's car was a 1959 Chrysler, only his car was blue. I immediately put out a general broadcast to all police departments to be on the lookout for a 1959 Chrysler, color white, operated by a white male with black curly hair. I then informed all the parents of the incident. The rest of the night and all the next day (Saturday) I searched for that car. No luck. Sunday I left Station 2 on Sherman Parkway at 3:00 PM and headed for the area of Cooper Place. As I was proceeding west on Fountain Street passing Colby Court, I observed a white car parked on the corner of Fountain and Cooper Place. As I got closer, the car started moving and turned right into Fountain Street. I made a U-turn and gave chase. I stopped the vehicle just west of Colby Court. It was a white Chrysler, white male with curly black hair driving. I radioed in my position to the police dispatcher with the registration plate number of the car and approached the car. I had to assume the role of a Police Officer and not an angry parent. I simply said, "Why did you expose yourself Friday afternoon to those small children?" "I'm sorry," he answered. "I can't help myself." It took all my willpower not to punch this guy in the face. I cuffed him and took him to the Detective Division after towing his car. Later that night, I learned that last week in Hamden, This same guy tried to force a little kid into his car. Thank God my little friends knew enough to run and then tell someone. •

After about one year walking the beat downtown, Dixwell Avenue, Fair Haven, Congress Avenue, etc. I finally was transferred to Station 2 on Sherman Parkway. Station 2 had very little walking beats and mostly patrol car beats. My transfer came on March 26, 1962. I was immediately assigned a patrol car. Now, I felt like a Patrolman. To be able to perform police work to its full potential. Yes, now I had the ability to chase bad guys. I was going to save the world. Or at least, save New Haven. On the night of October 6, 1962, I had just left Station 2 at 11:00 PM. As I cruised down Dixwell Avenue in a northbound direction toward Hamden, I pulled into Manzi's Atlantic Service Station that was closed for the night. I thought I saw someone climbing through a rear window of the service station. I parked the police car and checked the window. It was broken so I called for backup and climbed through the broken window, being careful not to cut myself. Once inside I pulled out my Colt service revolver and turned on my flashlight. Upon checking the office, there were drawers open, indicating that someone was in there. I was now on high alert. Very carefully I searched the garage area and found a man, hiding under a workbench. Very often burglars work together in pairs, so I had to be extra careful that someone was not behind me with a weapon. I ordered the man out from under the workbench at gunpoint and searched him before I handcuffed him. My back up then arrived and I opened the front door to let him in. The 24-year-old burglar had a $10.00 transistor radio in his pocket. Nothing else was taken. I went to court with him and told the Judge that he was cooperative and only stole a cheap radio. They let him go on probation. He was not a hardened criminal. •

One afternoon in October 1963, at about 5:00 PM, I was dispatched to the Amity Shopping Center in regard to a serious motor vehicle accident involving personal injuries. My radio car, #21, was designated as a major accident investigation car. Upon arrival, a man driving a Fiat with his 13-year-old son with him had just left the Amity Bowling Lanes. As they crossed the Amity Shopping Center, another vehicle struck their vehicle broadside on the right passenger side causing extensive damage to both vehicles. The man was lying on the ground with numerous facial injuries next to his driver's door that was open. His 13-year-old son was sitting in the driver's seat. I called for an ambulance. While waiting for the ambulance, the Fiat driver stated that the impact knocked him out of his car and also knocked his 13-year-old son from the right front passenger seat and into the driver's seat. The driver of the second car was not injured. However, that driver stated that the 13-year-old boy was driving. Just then, my Sergeant arrived at the accident scene. After hearing conflicting stories, my Sergeant ordered me to arrest the driver of the Fiat for permitting a minor to operate a motor vehicle and arrest the boy for operating a motor vehicle without a license. The Fiat driver was a well-known Westville dentist whom I never met before. His description of the accident made sense to me so I asked my Sergeant to give me a couple of hours to possibly find a witness to this accident. He said, "You have until the end of your shift, 11:00 PM Bob and then go to the Hospital and issue summons to the driver and the boy." "Thank you Serge," I said. I went door to door at the Amity Shopping Center looking for a witness to this accident. No luck. Finally, I noticed two men on the sidewalk who worked at the Finest Super Market smoking a cigarette. "Hey guys, did you by chance see this accident?" "Yeah," they said. Earlier, they were both out on the sidewalk taking a smoke break and they stated that this car, going at a high rate of speed, crashed into the right side of the Fiat and knocked the driver right out of the car and knocked a young boy over to the driver's seat. Are you gentleman willing to give me a written statement and are you also willing to go to court if necessary and testify as to what you saw? "Yes," they both answered. "Yeah man, the other cat (guy) was wrong," was their answer. Thank you God. I called my Sergeant to meet me at the Amity Shopping Center. I introduced him to the two witnesses and got written statements and arrested the other driver for reckless driving. Had I arrested the doctor, a great injustice would have occurred to him and his son. His insurance company would have denied his claim, thinking he broke the law by allowing a minor to operate his vehicle and they both would have had a police record that they did not deserve. I knew in my heart that the doctor was telling the truth. I just needed to buy some time; I just needed to find a witness. You can't learn this stuff in Police Academy. You must follow your instincts and always put your heart into your job. A Policeman's decision can affect a person's life, forever. Good or bad. •

UNDERCOVER POLICE OFFICER

During the 1960's, Chapel and Howe Street area was a hot spot for activity; prostitution, female impersonators, perverts, loitering, etc. One night after dark I was on patrol in the area. I noticed the same Chevy with a white male operator with long hair, beard and mustache wearing a pull over poncho over his clothes. After seeing the same car three times in an hour, I decided to do a spot check. His taillights were out, which gave me a reason to pull him over. I pulled him over on Dwight Street near Chapel Street and asked him for his license and registration, but he could not produce them. He said, "Let me go." Y"es, after you show me your license and registration." "I don't have them. You are making a big mistake Officer. Let me go." Finally, I decided to call the paddy wagon and sent him downtown for questioning. He was acting very suspiciously. No driver's License or Registration and driving a car? Very suspicious. Soon afterwards, I got a call from the Captain of Detectives. "Bob," he said, "you arrested an undercover Detective." "What?" "Yeah, the hippy with the poncho is undercover." How would I know who he was? The Captain said, "You did a beautiful job because the bad guys that he was following, observed you arrest him and put him in the paddy wagon. Now when he gets out of jail, they will trust him." They will think that he is a bad guy like them. "So Bob," the Captain said, "if you see the poncho guy, leave him alone." "Okay. Yes sir Captain, leave the poncho guy alone, got it." •

HEART WARMING STORY ABOUT A DAD AND HIS 14 YEAR OLD DAUGHTER

I have a heartwarming story about a dad and his 14-year-old daughter. In honor of my beloved daughter Terry Ann Meyerholz who at age 44 on April 1, 2000 passed away. Terry, our first child, was born October 31, 1955.

One Saturday evening, in the fall of 1969, I was scheduled to work a teenage dance at the Jewish Community Center on Chapel Street. Just before leaving the house, Terry asked, "Dad can I go with you, please?" I called Stan Sprechman and asked him if I could bring my 14-year-old daughter with me. Terry is mature and I knew she wouldn't interfere with my Police responsibilities. "Of course you can bring your daughter with you," Stan said. Terry got dressed quickly and we left our East Haven home for the Jewish Community Center. We arrived at about 7:00 PM for the scheduled 8:00 PM dance. I got Terry situated at a table near the front door where I would be stationed most of the night. I got her a soda and kissed her forehead. Everything went very smooth. I caught a few kids smoking in the men's room, but nothing major. The dance broke just after 11:00 PM. It took almost an hour to make sure the kids all had rides home and were all safely out of the building. My car was parked around the corner on Park Street. As Terry and I walked to the car, she said, "Daddy, I'm cold." It did get chilly. Now, remember that I am still in full police uniform. I put my left arm around her shoulder and hugged her close to me, to warm her up. As we walked west on Chapel Street, a couple was walking in the opposite direction. As they passed us, the lady said, "That's disgusting, that Policeman with that young girl, just disgusting." We stopped. I said, "Ma'am, excuse me. I am Officer Robert Meyerholz, badge 267. This is my 14-year-old daughter Terry Ann. We are coming from a teen dance at The Jewish Community Center." She apologized and her husband said something like, "Next time mind your own business dear." We got in our car and drove off towards home. Until the car heater started working, I kept my right arm around Terry. Isn't that what dad's do? •

POLICEMAN SAVED MANS LIFE

I have a heartwarming story that almost ended my short police career. On February 17, 1964, at approximately 5:00 AM, I was dispatched to 89 Brooklawn Circle in regard to a sick person. Upon arrival, a lady dressed in night cloths, was frantically waving to be from her front lawn. I parked my police car and spoke to her. She was hysterical and trying to tell me her husband was in bed fighting for breath. I quickly followed her into the bedroom. Mr. Greenhouse was grabbing his chest. Knowing that the two or three ambulance companies in the New Haven area were miles away, I picked up Mr. Greenhouse and carried him to my police car. I put him in the front passenger seat and put Mrs. Greenhouse in back just behind him with instructions to hold his shoulders tight. There were no seat belts then. I radioed St. Raphael's Hospital that I was en route with a 55-year-old male who was now unresponsive. I arrived in less than 5 minutes to a crew with a gurney outside. They wheeled in Mr. Greenhouse and I escorted Mrs. Greenhouse to the waiting room. I sat with her for about one hour at times holding her hand. At my age of 28, I could see my mom and dad. Finally a Doctor came out. "Mrs. Greenhouse?" he asked. "Yes," she responded. "I have your husband stable but still in very serious condition." "Officer?" he asked me. "Yes Doctor." "Did you bring this man here in your police car?" "Yes, I did Doctor." "He only had minutes to live so you saved his life. Good job Officer." One week later I got a call from Chief McManus's office. "The Chief wants to see you tomorrow morning at 9:00 AM. Be in full uniform." I arrived the next morning in full uniform. I was called in. The Chief showed me a letter from Mrs. Greenhouse. "Read this letter Officer Meyerholz." After reading it the Chief said, "You are a hero to Mrs. Greenhouse. However, if Mr. Greenhouse had died in your police car or if he arrived DOA at the Emergency Room, you would be in serious trouble. Maybe lose your job. Did you realize that?" "Yes sir, I did." "Before you leave my office I have one question, Officer Meyerholz. If this same thing happened tomorrow morning at 5:00 AM, what would you do different?" "Nothing Sir." He half smiled and said, "Get out of my office." Mr. Greenhouse lived for another 20 something years. Policeman sometime have to make split second decisions. It's all part of a job you love. •

POLICEMAN'S LOVE FOR CHILDREN

I have a related story from the one I just told about my love for children. Well, in 1964, I got in a lot of trouble giving Westville neighborhood children a ride around the block in my shiny black 1963 Chevy Biscayne police car with the gum ball red light/siren on top. I would always talk face to face with the mothers of my little friends and ask permission to give them a quick ride around the block. One day, a well-meaning mother called City Hall to inquire about insurance in case the Policeman on the beat got into an accident with her child in the police car. Boy, did this stir up a hornets nest and the call went directly to Chief McManus. I was working the 3:00 to 11:00 PM shift. The next morning I got a call from Station 2 on Sherman Parkway to report at 4:00 PM for a walking beat assignment on Newhall Street. I knew something was wrong. I reported to station 2 with my best walking shoes and a positive attitude because any problems that occurred were of my own doing. I was dropped off on Newhall and Bassett. I proceeded to walk south on Newhall Street checking for any parking or motor vehicle violations like I would do driving a police car. Within two hours, I had four or five kids following me. They were all trying to hold my two hands. I met the parents of four children and asked permission to take them to Camp's (Campie's) Pizza Restaurant on Winchester Avenue for my scheduled lunch period. We had fun, eating pizza and telling police stories. They were amazed that I don't lock up bad kids and I don't shoot people. Only one negative thing happened while walking back to Newhall Street on Ivy Street – an elderly black gentleman sitting on a porch yelled at the kids and warned them not to trust the white cop. "He's getting information from you kids to lock up your mama's." The kids yelled back in my defense that I was their friend and I was protecting them. Sadly, one week later, I was back in Westville driving my car, #21, with a stern warning from Chief McManus to keep those kids out of your police car. I said goodbye to my little Newhallville friends that Sunday afternoon. •

PLAIN CLOTHES LOOKING FOR PROSTITUTES

I have another Chapel and Howe area story: In the summer of 1961, I was fresh out of Police Academy working the 4:00 to 12:00 midnight shift. At about 9:00 PM, I got a message from the Vice Squad to go to Headquarters and change into my civilian clothes for a plain-clothes assignment. Wow, six months on the job and I'm a Detective? I was all excited and felt honored to be chosen. An unmarked car took me to a location off of Chapel Street near Orchard Street, behind a medical building or Doctor's office. I met with the Sergeant. My instructions were to drive this yellow Datsun (Nissan) four door car around the perimeter of Dwight, George, Park and Edgewood Avenue and pretend I was looking for prostitutes. I was the John looking for prostitutes. I was to pull to the curb and if they got in to the car, let them say what they are going to do for me. I could not suggest anything, otherwise, it's entrapment. I had marked money and a tape recorder. My first pick up was on the corner of Chapel and Park. A pretty lady, I think it was a lady, anyways, jumped in and offered me a (BJ) for $10.00. I gave her a marked $10.00 bill and then drove to a secret location and when we drove in this back yard and she saw the paddy wagon and other Officers, she called me every name in the book and tried to scratch my eyes out. After the 4th pick up I said, "Sergeant. This is not for me. Sorry." He released me from that assignment and I put on my uniform and went back to my beat. My heart was in serving the public in uniform. When I got home that night, I told my wife about my plain clothes assignment. Like any curious wife would ask, she said, "Those girls didn't do anything to you, or for you, did they?" "Heck no honey. No way." •

I have another doctor story. In the fall of 1964, The New Haven PD received a complaint from the local school bus companies that drivers were not stopping for stopped school buses who were displaying their emergency red lights. The areas were Ray Road, Curtis Drive, Knollwood Drive, etc. I took out an unmarked police car and met up with one of the bus drivers. To be fair, I did a complete inspection of the emergency *STOP ON RED* signal lights. Front and rear. All emergency lights were working properly. It was about 1:00 PM, the bus had kindergarten kids returning home. I followed the bus east on Ray Road and then turned into Knollwood Drive. We proceeded past Mumford Road dropping off little kids as we proceeded toward Laurel Road. The bus stopped to let off two young children. All emergency lights were on and displayed. As the children crossed in front of the bus, a speeding blue Cadillac shot by without even slowing down. I made a U-turn with the unmarked police car and gave chase. I pulled the Cadillac over using my red grille lights and siren. I was in full uniform when I asked for his license and registration. As I checked them, I notice Dr. in front of his first name. I asked him if he was on an emergency and he responded yes. I urged caution and let him go. He sped off. I have a photographic memory and I remembered his name and home address. I decided to drive to his house and the blue Cadillac was in the driveway. For my own protection, I notified the dispatcher that I would be out at this address for a possible motor vehicle arrest. I rang the bell. The doctor came to the door. I was shocked but not surprised. I said, "Doctor, you lied to me. I need your license and registration, now." He produced his license from his wallet and got the registration from his glove compartment. His wife looked out the front door, but said nothing. I sat in my police car and wrote the ticket for passing a standing school bus. As I handed him the ticket, I said, "Doctor, you could have killed a child crossing the street. Then you lied to me." He said, "Don't you dare lecture me. Give me the damn ticket." I was happy to hand him the ticket. I set a court date hoping that he would contest the ticket, but he paid the hefty fine before the case came to court. •

NUN INVOLVED IN TRAFFIC ACCIDENT

I have a Catholic Nun story. On Thursday February 25th, 1971 at about 4:30 PM, I was dispatched to a two-car motor vehicle accident at the intersection of Church and Crown Street. Upon arrival, I observed that damage to both vehicles was moderate. However, one injury was reported to the driver of the other vehicle. Sister Ann Scappini from the Centro San Jose, located at 312 Congress Avenue, was operating one vehicle and an elderly woman was operating the other vehicle. Her teenage niece was a passenger. The elderly woman was taken to St. Raphael's Hospital in an ambulance with unknown injuries. Sister Scappini was very upset, stating that she was never in a motor vehicle accident. I calmed her down and reassured her that everything would work out. Because of the personal injury, a state motor vehicle accident report had to be filed. Not knowing how to do this, I offered to come to Centro San Jose to assist Sister Scappini in filing the report. I also offered my assistance to the other driver, whom I visited at St. Raphael's Hospital. The next afternoon, I went to the Centro San Jose church and sat down with the Sister. Together, we filled out the state motor vehicle report. Within three or four weeks later, I was surprised to get a memo from Chief Biagio DiLieto stating that the Sister wrote a letter commending me. This is what Policemen do every day, nothing unusual. This is just what we are trained to do. This 43-year-old letter remains in my scrapbook and is highly cherished by me. •

I have another school bus story. It was in 1968, the week before school recessed for the summer. Kathreen Brennen School ordered four school buses from Chieppo Bus Co. to take the seventh and eighth grades to Riverside Park in Agawam, Massachusetts. Being off duty, I enjoyed taking kids to amusement parks. Again, the kids had no idea that I was an off duty Policeman. The pick up time was about 8:00 AM. We loaded the four buses up and proceeded over the Newhallville hill to I-91 to Riverside Park. The kids were noise but well behaved. My bus had two adult chaperones with me. We arrived at the park at about 10:30-11:00 AM. I told the kids to be back no later than 5:00 PM because that's when we were going home. I had a great time going on some rides with the kids, but not the roller coasters. I'll fight five men,but refuse to go on a roller coaster. By 4:45 PM, most of us were back sitting on the bus. I happened to look in the rear view mirror to see some of the kids throwing their garbage out the windows. I got off the bus and on both sides of the bus on the ground were pop corn, pop corn boxes, french fries, paper cups, wrappers, pieces of hot dogs, etc. I said, "Hey guys? dDes everyone want to go home?" "Yeah, we're tired man." "My bus doesn't move until all that mess outside is cleaned up." I turned the motor off and sat back. There is a certain way to talk to young people, firm but respectful. They understood what they had to do for our bus to move. Within twenty minutes, we were on our way back to New Haven. Everything was cleaned up. "Thank you guys," I yelled. I was the second bus in the procession of four buses. Somewhere in Meriden, the bus in front of us got a tire blowout on the left rear. Bang. A grey cloud of air. You could see big pieces of rubber tire fly off the bus. The bus pulled over to the shoulder and I pulled in behind him to put on my emergency flashers. I told the kids to stay on the bus before I got out. Both left rear tires blew out. We called the bus company. The other two buses pulled behind me. We took the kids from the first bus and put them evenly on the other three buses. It was tight but we managed. The kids talked about the BIG BANG blowout all the way home. It was a fantastic day. •

FEMALE SHOPLIFTER AND FROZEN HAM

Around 1968, one afternoon I was dispatched to Pegnataro's Super Market located on Whalley and Boulevard in regard to a female shoplifter. Upon arrival, I parked in the rear lot near the side doors. I entered through these doors and was met by store security. They led me to the manager's office where an average looking woman in her mid 40's was being held. She was accused of concealing several cartons of cigarettes in her clothing as she left the store. I think it was seven cartons of cigarettes. She had prior convictions for shoplifting so she did not quality for PTA (promise to appear). I called for the prisoner conveyance (paddy wagon). When the paddy wagon arrived by the side doors, I escorted the lady who was handcuffed, to the paddy wagon. Her bond would be set by the desk Sergeant when we arrived at Headquarters. She had a funny walk with her knees together like she had to pee. I said, "Are you okay?" "Yes, "she said. Just as we got to the side doors, I heard a PLOP. The lady was concealing a 5 lb. frozen ham between her legs. I thought she had a baby, right there and then. It really startled me until I could see that it was a ham. I brought her back to the office and added another separate charge of shoplifting. "Lady," I said, "why didn't you tell me about the ham? I would have made it all one count of shoplifting." She was wearing panty hose but wouldn't a 5 lb. frozen ham feel cold? I thought I saw it all. I know, thee question you're asking yourself is, "What happened to the ham?" Right in the dumpster. I made sure it wasn't put back in the frozen meat section. We did shop there and I love ham. •

SHODDY AUTO REPAIR WORK

Sometime in the fall of 1966, at about 8:45 PM, I was dispatched to Whalley Avenue just east of the Merritt Parkway. A female motorist was stranded in the middle of the street after her right front wheel fell off her car. She was not injured, but she was very upset. Good thing she was going very slowly. She had just left a well-known automotive center on Dixwell Avenue in Hamden after purchasing four new tires for her car. After leaving there, she got on the Wilbur Cross Parkway and headed home towards Milford. As she entered the Parkway, she accelerated to the speed limit. Hoever, as she did this, her car began to shake violently. She slowed down, terrified and alone and after going through the West Rock tunnel, she got off on Whalley Avenue. She headed toward Whalley and Amity hoping there was a telephone in that area. There was a telephone at the gas station at Whalley and Amity there, but she never made it. The right front wheel fell off of her car and the front end hit the pavement stopping the car instantly. I positioned my police car behind her car with my roof lights illuminated so no one would run into the back of her car. I checked the other three wheels and most of the lug nuts were missing or loose. The other three wheels were ready to come off. I called for a flatbed tow truck, then I called the home and auto store where she got the new tires. Sears and Roebuck, as it were called then. I used the telephone at the Big Top Shop because there were no cell phones in those days. It was just before 9:00 PM. I spoke to the Service Manager and identified myself. I told him what happened and gave him the lady's name. I told him to get down to Whalley Avenue immediately because the lady that bought tires there could have been killed because they obviously did not tighten the lug nuts at all. He reluctantly said he would be right there. He showed up one hour later after the lady's car was towed. He arranged for a loaner car the next day for her and promised to take care of whatever damage was done to her car. Trying to make an excuse that the mechanics are very tired by that late hour because they work an eight to ten hour day. I said, "Lucky it wasn't my wife; I would sue your company." I knew exactly what happened. The mechanic removed all four wheels and installed the new tires on the rims. Then, he mounted the wheels and installed all the lug nuts/bolts finger tight and then forgot to tighten them with his air gun. To me, this should have never happened to anyone. This was gross negligence. The lady could have lost her life. The lady's husband picked her up at Station 2 on Sherman Parkway where I took her. He was so angry. Good thing he did not come to the scene. There would have been big problems between him and the Service Manager. I completely understood how he felt. I gave the couple my name and badge number and told them to call me if Sears didn't make good on the shoddy tire installation. •

6 YEAR OLD STRUCK AND KILLED BY DRUNK DRIVER

I would like to again dedicate my next story to an innocent little 6-year-old boy, who was struck and killed by a drunk driver 52 years ago. This little boy would be my daughter Alice's age today. I've seen the worse in my career.

On January 31, 1963, just after dark, I was dispatched to Temple Keser Israel Synagogue on Sherman Avenue on a report of a pedestrian who was struck by a car. It was a bitter cold snowy night. Upon arrival, I learned that Gerald Tyson, age 6, was struck by a car while he and his dad were crossing Sherman Avenue. The boy and his dad were not at the accident scene. His dad had carried him to St. Raphael Hospital's Emergency Room. I walked to the Emergency Room and spoke to his dad for details. Mr. Tyson said they just left services at the Synagogue and were crossing the street to where his car was parked when this car, traveling north on Sherman Avenue, struck the boy as they were standing in the middle of the street, waiting for a car to pass. The boy was pronounced dead from his injuries. I then interviewed the driver of the car who was waiting at the scene with my partner. Smelling alcohol on his breath, he stated that he had only one beer at an unknown bar. He couldn't remember what bar and he refused a breathalyzer test. The laws were much different then. I could only charge him with Reckless Driving, even though I did not believe the one beer story. The next morning, on my own off duty time, I canvassed every bar on Chapel Street east of Chapel and Sherman Avenue. I had his mug shot photo with me. Finally, I found a bartender that remembered him. He stated to me that yesterday afternoon; he refused to serve this guy because this guy had too much to drink already. I told him about the little boy and he said, "Yes, I will voluntarily give you a written statement and yes, I will testify against him in a court of law. I have children of my own." He said, "I will be glad to testify against him. He walked into my bar drunk and I told him to leave and that he would not be served here." I added a charge of Vehicular Manslaughter through the Prosecutor's Office. The drunk driver served a lengthily prison term. May God bless little Gerry Tyson and so many others killed by drunken drivers. May they rest in peace, knowing that we will never, ever forget them. God bless you Gerry. •

In February 1974, I was on duty on the day shift in Fair Haven. I was driving a 2-month-old Dodge Polara police car. I also had a walking beat Patrolman available on Grand Avenue in case I needed backup. Earlier, we had radio communication. About 1:00 PM, a broadcast came on the police radio that three females were wanted for robbing pedestrians at knifepoint in the area of James and Market Streets. I radioed the beat man, but he didn't answer. I drove on Grand Avenue from James to Ferry, but I couldn't find him. I wanted him to search the neighborhood with me. Four eyes were better than two, as they say. Anyway, I was traveling on Market Street in a west direction. Passing Main Street and looking on both sides of the street for the females, and suddenly, something hit me from the right side. I ended up with my head under the dash and my brief case on my chest. A trailer truck from the New Haven Board and Carton Company located on James Street, ran a stop sign on Main and Market and struck the right passenger side of my 1973 Dodge Polara police car. The front chrome bumper of the trailer truck was two inches from my face after it came crashing through the right front door and fender. I was inches from death. Thank God I did not find the beat Officer because anyone sitting in the right passenger seat would have been crushed. I woke up to my Lieutenant pulling me out of the car, which was brand new in December. The driver of the trailer truck stated that he was blinded by the sun as he drove south on Main Street, never realizing that he was at the end of Main Street as it intersected with Market Street. This back injury caused me periodic pain for four years until I reluctantly retired in 1978. I loved my job and at age 38, I did not want to retire. I continued with the pain, which sometime went away. I would be usually angry when another Officer didn't answer their police radio, but this time, I was so glad that he was not sitting in that right passenger seat. That massive chrome front bumper ripped right through the right front fender and door. My beloved Dodge Polara was totaled. We never found the female street robbers. •

INTOXICATED FEMALE LOSES PANTIES

In January or February of 1962, I was walking the beat on Grand Avenue just after midnight. I had just come on duty. One of my Policeman friends named Bobby O'Brien (RIP) picked me up. It was cold and he let me warm up in his police car. About 12:45, we got a call reporting an intoxicated female that was ejected from a bar on Grand Avenue, corner of Jefferson Street for creating a disturbance after she was shut off. I responded with him. Upon arrival, there was a female trying to get back in the bar and they were holding the door closed. She was cursing up a storm. In those days, public intoxication was a crime and people were arrested for it. Bob was using his experience and charm to encourage the lady to go home but she insisted on having another drink. The lady told Bob what to do with his nightstick so he placed her under arrest and called for the paddy wagon. As we sat in the warm car, the ladies panties fell to the ground around her ankles as she stood on the sidewalk cursing at us. She tried to kick them off and almost fell due to her intoxicated condition. Bob said to me, "Get out and help her before she falls and gets hurt." "Me?" I said. "Yeah you. You're the rookie and I'm trying to teach you something." I got out of that warm car and pulled her panties up, looking around to see if anyone was watching. Just then the paddy wagon pulled up and the wagon driver knew her by name. As she was stepping up into the wagon, her panties fell down again. I looked at Bob and said, "No f**king way." He said, "I'm surprised you did it the first time," and laughed. I guess today you would say I got "punked". Bob and I became best friends. Thank God this didn't get back to the other rookies. Until now. •

OFFICER SAVES FELLOW OFFICERS LIFE AT DOMESTIC DISPUTE

A Police Officer named Rudy Bellacicco saved my life in the summer of 1967. Rudy and I had just come on duty at 8:00 AM. Within the first hour, we both got a call to respond to a girlfriend/boyfriend domestic dispute on the first floor apartment on Elm Street east of Orchard Street. A young woman complained that her boyfriend, who lived in the basement apartment next door, had been harassing her all night, knocking on her door and trying to gain entrance to her apartment. She did not want him arrested, she only warned to stay away from her. Rudy and I went next door and knocked on the basement apartment door. Finally the man opened the door, dressed in boxer shorts only. No shirt and no shoes. Boxers only, claiming that we woke him up. He denied being out of his apartment. We took his name, address, etc. for our report and warned him that if we got another complaint from his girlfriend, he would be subject to arrest. Rudy turned around first in this tiny apartment and started to walk out the door. I turned around and started to follow Rudy when Rudy looked over my shoulder. Suddenly with lightning speed, Rudy's nightstick whizzed past my face. The man had a large black handled knife similar to a large knife used to cut Italian bread tucked in the rear waistband of his under boxer shorts. He had raised the knife over his head and was going to stab me in the back as I walked out of his apartment. Rudy sensed this and acted to save my life. The knife went flying and as a result of Rudy's quick actions, the man's right wrist was broken. The man was taken to St. Raphael's Hospital and treated for a broken wrist before being booked for attempted assault on a Police Officer. To add insult to injury, two weeks later, we were both sued for police brutality for using excessive force. A well-known "cop hater" Attorney took the case. We didn't even arrest this man so why did he want to kill me? What was in his mind? We will never know. This police brutality case was thrown out without ever being heard. The man was found guilty in court, but I never followed the case. More Policemen are killed or severely injured responding to domestic disputes. Wherever you are Rudy Bellacicco, thank you and may God bless you. •

LOVERS IN PARKED CAR

This is a funny story. In 1966, I often patrolled on Congress Avenue and other parts of the Hill. We received a few complaints of lovers or parkers, parking on Ward Street near Sylvan Avenue. That block was very dark. These lovers would leave remnants of their lovemaking on the ground. Sometime beer bottles, McDonald's wrappers and sometime used condoms (gross). One night at about 9:00 PM, Officer Bob O'Brien (RIP) and I parked our police cars ½ block away after spotting a car parked in the dark. We took off our hats and removed our shiny badges and snuck up on the car. A couple of teenagers were in the back seat as we shone our flashlights in the car. They were only kissing, at this point. We scared these kids as they jumped over the front seat and started the motor and sped off. Well, at about 10:00 PM, Bob and I decided to have a cup of coffee at the Toddle House on the corner of Chapel and Dwight. We were sitting there at the counter, sipping our hot coffee when a young man walked in and says, "Hey, I've been looking all over for a cop." "Yes, young man, what can we do for you?" my partner Bob asked. "I was parked with my girl on Ward Street when these two guys came up and shined flashlights in our eyes. I was gonna get out and punch them but my girlfriend stopped me." We had to refrain from laughing but I did spit out some coffee, all over the counter. Bob asked, "What did these guys look like?" "Maybe 6 feet tall and wearing dark shirts and pants. Almost dressed like cops but no hats." Now we really had to fight from not laughing out loud. We promised the young man that we would look out for these two characters. He said, "Thanks. Tell them they are lucky I didn't get out of the car because my girl stopped me." We will, young man. Take care. •

POLICEMANS FAMILY THREATENED

I have a story about the night my wife was threatened. We had just moved to 229 County Street in 1962. I was just off probation, but still assigned to the midnight shift. Each week I would be on a different foot patrol. The week before, I broke up a fight in the Elm City Diner on Chapel and Howe. One of the guys looked familiar and said, "Get your f**king hands off me." No arrest was made. We let both men go their separate ways. The next week, I was walking the beat on Grand Avenue from Olive to East Street when at about 3:00 AM a police car pulled up and said, "Hey Bob, you are wanted home. Someone called your home and threatened your wife and children." We sped to County Street. Mary is a strong woman and she was calm when she stated that the phone rang and woke her up and a man with a pleasant voice said, "Hello, your punk cop husband is walking the beat on Grand Avenue so I'm coming over and raping you and your children. You are on the second floor and you have a light on in your front room in the left window." That was true. A light was on in the living room. Then he hung up. My natural instinct to protect my family kicked in. We just moved in one week ago. We had a brand new telephone number. Not in the book yet. I called information and asked for a supervisor. I identified myself and asked if anyone had called for the number of Robert Meyerholz. "Yes, a man with a very pleasant voice asked for Robert Meyerholz in the City Point area. I told him I had a new listing for Robert Meyerholz on 229 County Street. He said, that's' the one and thanked me. He was very polite." Now it dawned on me. One of the guys fighting in the Elm City Diner was a punk I grew up with. The one that said, get you f**king hands off me. I took the next night off and went to the Elm City Diner. In the hallway was a pay phone and written on the wall was my telephone number. This punk was sitting in a booth with friends. I escorted him to the pay phone and called Mary. I said, "Talk to my wife. Say hello, your punk husband is with me." He did say that. I took the phone. Mary said, "That's him. That's the man that called me." I composed myself really wanting to kick the s**t out of him, but walked out of that Diner. The next morning I tried to get a warrant for his arrest but the Prosecutor said I had a weak case. Not enough evidence. Something scared him and he never came back to the Elm City Diner again. I did see him months later in the Chapel Mall, but he ran out of there like a scared rabbit. •

FEMALE YALE STUDENTS ATTACKED

In the beginning months of 1966, maybe February or March, there was a young man in the Prospect Street area breaking into basement level apartments or dormitories that housed female students at Yale University. At least four reported rapes occurred in a few weeks. That was my general area of patrol on the midnight shift this particular night. With my Sergeants authorization, I took out an unmarked green and white Chevy in an attempt to catch this guy. I started at 12:00 midnight looking for anything suspicious, cars or pedestrians. Finally at about 1:30 AM, I spotted an older Chevy traveling very slowly, traveling north on Prospect near Sachem without headlights. I was driving south. As the car passed me, I observed the driver, who fit the description of the suspect. He took off at a high rate of speed, still traveling without headlights. I made a U-turn and the pursuit was on. My unmarked car had red lights in the grille and a siren. Not much protection for me. I notified the dispatcher that I was in a high-speed pursuit, possibly with the rape suspect driving. Because of the extreme danger of the suspect's car operating without headlights and my unmarked car, I requested no backup, only coverage if I was able to stop him. For twenty minutes we drove up and down the side streets between Prospect and Dixwell Avenue, at times crossing Newhall Street at speeds up to 80-90 MPH. Sometimes, going the wrong way on one-way streets. We were on Thompson Street heading west toward Dixwell Avenue at 80 MPH when I saw Dixwell Avenue approaching, so I jammed on my brakes. The suspect crossed Dixwell at 70-80 MPH, leaving about 75 feet of black skid marks and struck the front porch of a two family house on the west side of Dixwell Avenue. The suspect was able to climb out of the wrecked auto and flee in the back yards. I went to the owner's house on Newhall Street and determined the owner was a bald black male. After he found out what happened, he reported the car stolen. Five months later, the owner came into Station 2 on Sherman Parkway with the driver, his brother in law, and told the truth after his Insurance Company refused to pay the claim on the extensively damaged house. The suspect admitted to at least four burglaries and rapes and I also charged him with a list of motor vehicle violations. I charged the owner of the car with falsely reporting his car stolen. The female Yale students were able to sleep better after the arrest of this rapist. •

POLICEMAN BEFRIENDS LITTLE GIRL

Sylvia Otero was one of my many Hispanic friends when I patrolled Fair Haven in the 60's and 70's. Sylvia was a 9-year-old, skinny little girl with beautiful olive complexion and the sweetest disposition. A few days before Thanksgiving in 1965, I asked Sylvia if her family was having Turkey. "No," she said, but they were having something else. "No turkey for Thanksgiving?" "No," she said. That night I asked my wife Mary if she had bought our Thanksgiving turkey yet. She said that she had not. "Maybe I'll go to Pegnataro's tomorrow and pick up the turkey and trimmings." "Honey? Pick up an extra turkey, cranberry sauce, beans, corn, bread, etc." "Why?" she said. "Because I have a little friend and I want to treat her family to a turkey dinner for Thanksgiving." The next day Mary came home with two turkeys and all the extras. That night, I took my son Bobby Jr,, age 3, daughter Alice, age 7, and daughter Terry, age 9, to Sylvia's house on State Street. We climbed the stairs to the second floor. I knocked on the door. Someone said, "Quien?" (Who is it?) I said, "Bobby El Policia." Sylvia opened the door and invited us in. I introduced my children and Sylvia introduced me to her parents. I said, "Mucho gusto." I handed the bag with the turkey, cranberry sauce, etc. to Sylvia and I said, "This is from my family to your family. A Happy Thanksgiving." It was a beautiful moment. I remember having a cup of my favorite coffee, Cafe Bustelo, and the kids had soda or juice. Two different cultures, two different languages blended into one over a Thanksgiving turkey. We said good night and left for home. Then, I was transferred to a different patrol area and I had not seen Sylvia from 1966 until one night in 1994. After retirement, I was a Security Supervisor at Foxwoods. Sylvia had looked for me for years, but other Policeman never reveal personal information about retired Policeman until one day; Sylvia asked a rookie Policeman if he knew me. No, but I heard that Bob Meyerholz (Bobby) was working at Foxwoods in Security.

To be continued… •

The Sylvia Otero Thanksgiving turkey story continued:

It was sometime in 1994 when I was a Security Supervisor at Foxwoods Resort and Casino in Ledyard, Connecticut. One night around midnight, I got a call from the Foxwoods Telephone Operator. "Bob, were you a New Haven Cop?" "Yes, I was." "Okay, there is a lady on the phone looking for you." I said, "Hello?" The lady said, "Bobby the Policeman?" "Yes, I was a Policeman." She was crying. It was Sylvia. Her first words were, "Bobby, God bless you. I remember you came to my house with your children and gave us a turkey. We all love you." Then I said, "Sylvia, I love you too." We chatted for a few minutes but I was busy at the Casino and had to hang up. Sylvia told me she was living on Blatchley Avenue and had her own children and she gave me her telephone number, but I misplaced it. That's the last time we talked until recently. I got a friend request from Sylvia Evelyn Torres. In my heart, I just knew that this was my friend Sylvia from so long ago. It was. True friends last a lifetime. Mutual respect and love will last for eternity.

To Sylvia: Te quiero mucho. Que Dios te bendigas y tu familia tambien. •

MOTOR VEHICLE ACCIDENT AND RACIAL TENSION

I've often been asked about the Black Panther Party and its relationship to the New Haven Police Department in the late 60's and 70's: During the Black Panther trials in New Haven, (1972-1973) racial tensions were very high. It was a time when Police Officers had to use patience and good judgment, but most of all show respect. A police uniform does not make you better than someone else, but compassion and genuine caring for others earn you respect. One Saturday afternoon, in the summer of 1973, I was dispatched to a very serious three-car accident with personal injuries on Winchester Avenue, just north of Starr Street. The street was completely blocked so I had to park my police car ½ block from the accident scene. As I walked quickly to the scene, I passed a bar on Winchester Avenue with about five or six guys standing on the sidewalk, looking toward the accident scene. One guy said to me, "Hey boy, aren't you afraid to be walking alone in this neighborhood all by yourself?" I had injured people that needed me immediately, pointing out that they were mostly black folks that were injured. I had to ignore him, for now, and proceeded to the accident scene. I called for two ambulances and three tow trucks. Also there was one fire truck at the scene washing down oil and gasoline from the wrecked vehicles. It was a major accident scene with several injuries. Finally, I had everything under control. The injured were being transported to local hospitals and the wrecked cars were towed from the scene. I had 2 other Officers assisting me with traffic. They left the scene. I had to walk back to my police car and had to pass the same bar. I walked up to the man who made the remarks to me and said, "Mister, I want to answer your question about being afraid to walk in this neighborhood. I was born and raised in New Haven. I went to New Haven schools. I buried my mom and dad in New Haven Cemeteries. No, I am not afraid to walk the streets of New Haven." He looked at me and said, "I can dig it man" and turned around and walked into the bar. His friends turned around and looked the other way. "Have a good day men," I said then proceeded to my police car and left the scene. I always showed respect towards everyone. I showed courage and never showed fear. If you are afraid, then turn in your badge and uniform and find another job. •

On a cold winter Saturday night in 1967, I was assigned extra duty at a dance at Albertus Magnus College on Prospect Street. It was called a mixer. I arrived alone at about 7:00 PM. Not expecting any trouble, I was assigned as the only Officer there. The Nun that was in charge of the mixer dance gave me some last minute instructions of what she expected of me. She was concerned about the safety of her girls and I reassured her that I would not let anything happen to any of them. "Even you are safe, Sister," I said. We hit it off well. She took a liking to me right away and I also took a liking to her. It was a short mixer starting at 8:00 PM and ending at 11:30 PM. When the mixer ended at approximately 11:30 PM, I escorted the girls to their dormitories in order to make sure that they were safe with no guys hanging around. I returned to the dance hall and the Nun thanked me and invited me into the kitchen. She said, "While I'm preparing your check Officer; please have a cup of coffee." I poured a cup of coffee and took off my police hat and sat down. I had a high receding hairline and looked older without my hat on. The Nun returned with my check and looked at me and said, "Oh dear, where is that younger Policeman?" Slightly embarrassed, but not wanting the sister to feel bad, I put on my police hat and said, "Sister, you are under arrest." We looked at each other for a few seconds and finally we both burst out laughing. It was one of the funniest and most embarrassing things that ever happened to me while performing my duties as a Police Officer. •

BURGLAR SUSPECT APPREHENDED

In the beginning of 1977, we were plagued with home invasion burglaries in the Westville area. Mostly these burglaries occurred during the night when families were sleeping. One elderly woman that lived alone was beaten, robbed and raped by two male burglars. They left her bound and gagged. She was found the next day by a family member. A horrible experience for anyone to go through. This really bothered me. I said to myself, "I'm going to get these bastards." We decided to use every means available to us to stop these home invasions by using unmarked cars and anything else available to us. On the morning of April 15, 1977, I got a call of a burglar inside of a residence at 81 Marvel Road. I used the silent approach with no red lights or siren. As I approached the residence, the burglar fled in a car. Knowing other Policeman were in the vicinity and backing me up, I radioed a description of the car and the suspect. I was concerned for the safety of the occupants in the house. After making sure they were safe and no other burglars were in the house, I also joined the chase. Officer Heffernan spotted the car on Fountain Street and chased the suspect until he crashed his car. The suspect jumped out of his car and fled in some dark back yards. I joined the search and found him and tackled him and overpowered him. He had the normal burglary tools, large screwdriver, flashlight, etc. in his pockets. The Detective Division and ID Unit also responded. After being questioned by Detective Otha Buffaloe, the suspect admitted to eight other burglaries in the Westville area. The area was once again a safe place to live. This was teamwork at its finest. I was proud to work with Officer Heffernan and Detective Buffaloe. •

While in Police Academy from January to March 1961, we were also training to qualify for the American Red Cross Life Saving Course at the Payne Whitney Gymnasium. Sergeant Biagio DiLieto would make arrangements to get us there. The class had approximately twenty-three recruits, including sixteen New Haven Police Probationary Officers and several more from Yale University Campus Police and surrounding towns. Captain Felix Gilroy was our instructor. He was a wonderful and well-respected Captain. Not until we all jumped in the swimming pool, was it realized that two recruits could not swim. Not one stroke. Without the basic knowledge of swimming, they were told they would not graduate from Police Academy. We were all concerned about their future. Captain Gilroy decided to at least try to teach them how to swim. He asked if the Gym had any flotation devises. Yes, they did. Two red one-gallon gas cans equipped with long shoe lace type strings. One devise fit well around one recruits mid-section but the other, larger recruit, the string was not long enough so the Captain, in a serious tone of voice requested a gas can with a longer string. We all fought the urge to laugh. It was a comical scene. They found some more string and added it to the gas can. Both recruits entered to shallow end of the pool and were ordered to dog paddle to the deep end. To one recruit, he started to paddle toward the side of the pool and Captain Gilroy, pushed him back to the middle with a long pole. In three weeks time, the men not only learned how to swim, but both passed the basic lifesaving course. •

Just before we completed our American Red Cross life Guard course, twi more things happened to us. By now, the Gym personnel were getting tired of us. At least, when we arrived in the morning, we got those looks, OH, these guys again. We were practicing life saving techniques. Throwing the torpedo shaped life preserver toward a potentially drowning victim. One of the recruits wound up the device under arm like throwing a soft ball, attached to 75 feet of marine line and when he went to throw it in the pool, he held on to long so the torpedo went straight up to the ceiling and knocked down two ceiling tiles which came crashing down into the pool. The Gym guy went nuts. He screamed at Captain Gilroy, "Who's going to pay for the damage?" The Captain reassured him that the city of New Haven would pay for any damage. Then came final exams for the lifeguard course. We were paired up during the entire course, but this brawny Detective named Billy who was one of our instructors said, "Okay you guys, line up and one at a time, you are going to save me." Oh no. We actually planned to cheat a little and kick our feet, from the bottom of the pool, to help our partners save us. Billy gave the command to the first recruit and he dove to the bottom of the pool, nine or teen feet deep. One at a time we struggled to save him and we did, diving to the bottom and bringing up his lifeless form. We all made it and received our Life Guard Certificates from The American Red Cross. And we got our certificates without cheating, thanks to Billy. •

On February 1, 1966 I was off duty and driving my own personal vehicle on Eastern Street. A vehicle occupied by three teenagers ran a stop sign on East Grand Avenue and almost collided with my own personal vehicle. They then lost control of the vehicle and all three jumped from the vehicle before it crashed into a snow bank by Eastern Circle. They all fled toward Eastern Circle. I called in for a motor vehicle check. It was determined that the vehicle was stolen four days earlier. These kids had the car stashed somewhere on Eastern Circle and were driving it around for three or four days. I had all three rounded up in one hour. They were Wilbur Cross students and they left their schoolbooks in the stolen vehicle with their names and addresses. I called Wilbur Cross and identified myself. I spoke to the Principles office. All three had been playing hooky for the past several days. When I picked up the first juvenile, he said, "Who squealed on me man?" I said, "Your schoolbooks squealed on you. You left your Wilbur Cross schoolbooks on the back seat of the stolen car. Your two idiot friends did the same thing." Sometime later, I received a letter from Chief McManus that the Board of Police Commissioners voted to award me a Certificate of Commendation for loyalty to duty. Any Police Officer would have done the same thing. I was not a hero. Anyway, I received a certificate of Commendation for which I was very grateful to receive. The owner of the vehicle was very happy to get his car back, with very minor damage from the snow bank accident, and an empty tank of gas. •

DRIVING ON SIDEWALK AL'S LUNCHEONETTE

In 1964, one of the most popular Restaurant's in New Haven was Al's Luncheonette, located on Whalley Avenue on the corner of Winthrop. It was especially popular for the bar crowd on the weekends. A problem developed in January 1964 when customers found a way to drive on the sidewalk and park right in front of Al's so they wouldn't have to walk to the restaurant. The only way to stop the problem was to enforce a motor vehicle law prohibiting motor vehicles from driving on the sidewalk. On the night of February 14th, 1964, Al's hired two off duty Officers, Myself and another Officer named Fred Goetz. At first we tried to warn people not to drive on the sidewalk, but that didn't work. As I stood in front of the main door to the restaurant, one driver jumped the curb and as he approached me, he beeped the horn and asked me to get out of the way. Of course I jumped out of his way. Right! Please see an article from the New Haven Register dated February 17, 1964. As I write this story, I can still remember the delicious pastrami specials on Jewish rye and plenty of half sour pickles and a cold glass of ras-lime soda. Those were the days I remember most about New Haven, Connecticut. •

TV STING

In 1964, New Haven Police had a large sting operation. Something like you now see on the show *COPS*. Hallock's Furniture, on Orange Street, let the Police Department borrow one of their big white furniture delivery trucks. They also gave the police a couple of large empty TV boxes with ADMIRAL or GE printed on them. The plan was for two policemen in delivery men uniforms, armed with dozens of arrest warrants, to go to the criminal's house and park the big white delivery truck in front of the house. One plain-clothed officer would go to the door of the criminal and knock and say, "Mr. Smith," or whatever the name on the warrant said, "you won a FREE television." The other plain-clothed officer would put the empty television carton on the tailgate, making it look authentic and believable. These dumb criminals would open the door and say, "Yeah, I'm Mr. Smith. Give me my free TV." What they would get was a pr. of handcuffs on their wrists and a FREE ride to jail. It only worked for a couple of days until the community got smart about the free televisions that weren't really free at all. I watched a few transactions from a distance as back up, in case they met with resistance. Most just went to jail, scratching their head saying, how could I be that stupid. You just can't make this stuff up. •

LOUIS LUNCH

On January 9, 1962, I completed my one-year probationary period with the New Haven Police Department. I was no longer a Probationary Patrolman; I was now classified as a Patrolman. With the one-year anniversary, I was now entitled to my 2-week vacation. I chose to work extra duty the first week to help catch up with normal household bills that we all have. I was assigned to construction traffic duty on Temple and Center Street, south to George Street, working with the C.W. Blakeslee Company. It was bitter cold that second week of January 1962. There were hundreds of concrete trucks delivering concrete for the new parking garage. A giant crane would lift these large buckets filled with concrete from the trucks to the various floors of the parking garage. Besides directing traffic safely around the trucks and any construction workers on the ground, I had to be alert for anything falling from above. We had to be out of the street by 4:00 PM for the no standing / tow zone violation. Even as a young 25-year-old, the bitter cold along with the standing for eight hours and directing traffic took its toll on me. The weight of that long police overcoat and the weight of my gun belt with all the equipment attached, service revolver, extra bullets, hand cuffs, the claw, flashlight, whistle, keys, added to the discomfort. I would do it all over again tomorrow of I was younger. When we broke for lunch at noon, I headed for Louis Lunch then located on George Street, west of Temple Street for a hamburger and hot coffee. There was actually a vacant seat at the counter so I could sit down and get warm. This was my first time meeting Ken Larson and his wife Lee. •

LASCIVIOUS CARRIAGE

In October 1961, I was still on probation and working the midnight shift downtown. I got a call at home one early evening to report at midnight in street clothes because I was assigned to work with Lieutenant William Pascale Commander of the Vise Squad. This was new and exciting for me. Like being a Detective. We met at Headquarters at midnight and after driving around in an unmarked car, we knocked on the door of a woman's apartment on Elm Street near Garden Street at about 2:00 AM. The lady opened the door and we showed our badges and entered. Her 25-year-old boyfriend was sitting on the couch with his shoes off. Otherwise he was fully dressed. The law assumed that if a gentleman was in a lady's apartment at 2:00 AM, that something was going on. The man was charged with, Lascivious Carriage. One Google definition of Lascivious Carriage is: Conduct which is wanton, lewd or lustful and tending to produce voluptuous emotions. Everyone get that? It's no longer a law but at one time it was enforced. The man went to court three weeks later and paid a $10.00 fine. Lieutenant Pascale was one of the nicest Policemen I ever worked with. He had a reputation for being tough but he was fair. •

OFFICER BOB HERO TO THE WESTVILLE TOTS

In the fall of 1962, after walking the beat for approximately 15 months, I was assigned my first police car. It was a Westville car, designated car 21. My patrol area went from Forest Road from the West Haven city line north to Whalley Avenue. Because it was considered a low crime area, with beautiful homes and a low crime rate, it was a large area. No GPS in those days. I used my Arrow Guild to get around. It was important to me to memorize every street and to get to know as many residents as possible. One street on my beat was called Cooper Place. It was located off of Fountain Street just past Lowin Avenue. My first few times driving through Cooper Place, I noticed a small group of little kids waving at me. They were from age three to maybe nine years old. Each time I did my rounds, the group would get larger. One day I pulled to the curb to say hello. The next time, I showed the kids my equipment in my 1961 black Chevy police car. Siren button, red lights button. I told them my name was Bob. So, they started to call me Officer Bob. One little girl asked me if she could be a police officer when she grew up. "Of course but you need to listen to your parents and be good and always eat all your vegetables so you can become big and strong, like me." One day, I was talking to my little friends and a man approached me with a camera in his hands. He introduced himself as a New Haven Register reporter. He said he wanted to do a story of a policeman that loves kids. I was flattered, but I said that would need to be approved by the Chief of Police. He took several pictures of the children and myself around my Chevy. Months later, the article appeared on the front page of a Sunday edition of the New Haven Register. The title of the article was, "Officer Bob Hero To The Westville Tots." It was approved by then Chief Francis V McManus and Mayor Richard C Lee. I also had a group of kids on Curtis Drive, that would wait every day for me to come around. I absolutely loved all those kids and looked forward to seeing them each day, as I patrolled their neighborhood. Attached in the Supplements section at the end of the novel is the original article that appeared in a June 1963 edition of The New Haven Register. •

FATAL MOTOR VEHICLE ACCIDENT

On August 12, 1963, I was operating radio car #21 in the Westville and Newhallville area. I had been trained in major motor vehicle accident investigation. That meant, in addition to my regular responsibilities, I responded to major motor vehicle accidents involving fatalities and personal injuries. One evening just after midnight, I was dispatched to a two-car accident on Dixwell Avenue and Munson Street. A Winchester worker had stopped to drop off a coworker at his home. The vehicle behind him, a 1958 MGB convertible, struck the rear of his car. The operator of the MGB was pronounced dead at the scene. His forehead had struck the steering wheel and caused what was later determined to be a brain hemorrhage. At this point, the accident scene was now a major accident investigation involving numerous photos, measurements, statements from possible witnesses, even to documenting what gear the MGB was in at the time of the impact. This important information helps the County Coroner to determine who was at fault. I did authorize the man's body to be brought to Yale New Haven Hospital until his family could be notified. Notifications of this nature are always very difficult; to tell a loved one that a family member was killed in a motor vehicle accident. When I arrived at Yale New Haven Hospital, a reporter was there looking for the name of the man that was killed. I refused to give it to him. I told him specifically that I was notifying the Branford Police Department to notify his wife in person of her husband's death. We never call a family on the telephone to tell them a loved one was killed in an accident. It's always done by a Police Officer going to the house. One hour later, a woman arrived at the Yale New Haven Hospital Emergency Room hysterical and said, a reporter called her at home and told her her husband was killed an a motor vehicle accident and he needed the husbands age for the morning paper. This poor accident victim was only age twenty-five and his wife was age twenty-four. I was furious. I went to the New Haven Register the next morning right after I got off duty at 8:00 AM and made a formal complaint against the reporter. I lost some respect for Newspaper Reporters that day. Attached in the Supplements section is a letter Coroner James Corrigan wrote to Chief Francis McManus. •

FUNNY STORY PAT'S LUNCHEONETTE

In the summer of 1961, just fresh out of Police Academy, I learned that to give our families the best quality of life, we would need to work as many extra duty assignments as possible. With a wife and two small kids, I would request extra duty assignments on my two days off. One morning in August, I was assigned to extra traffic duty on Congress and Howard Avenue with another officer named Sal Esposito. Sal was an eight year veteran of the police department. Sal was a husky guy with a large mustache and slightly larger than normal nose. I would later learn a lot from Sal about police work. We both arrived 30 minutes early so we went into Patricia's Luncheonette located on Congress Avenue for coffee. I just met Sal and heard many nice things about him including his humor. We sat at the counter where we were lucky to find two vacant seats. We ordered coffee and something, a hard roll with butter, I think. We chatted about our busy day ahead doing traffic around a large hole in the middle of Congress Avenue. I remember Sal turning around to face me in his swivel seat and tilting his head backward. He said in a very loud voice, "Hey Meyerholz. Does my nose look like a two-car garage with bushes in front of it?" My mouthful of coffee and hard roll went all over the counter. Everyone was laughing. I cleaned off the counter and wiped my mouth and took another sip of coffee. Just then Sal said, "Well, does it?" I again spit my coffee all over the counter. At noontime Sal said, "Well Meyerholz, where are we going for lunch?" "Not me Sal. I'm not eating." Sal – wherever you are, your guidance, wisdom and humor, made me a better Officer. God bless you Sal. Truly, you were one of New Haven's Finest. •

MASONIC TEMPLE SURPRISE VISIT

To know what it's like, to be walking in bitter cold weather and isolation from 12:00 midnight to 8:00 AM the next morning; you would need to be a rookie New Haven Policeman in 1962. It happened to my fellow rookies and I many, many bitter cold nights. This one January night in 1962, I was dropped off on Grand Avenue and Ferry Street. It was about fifteen degrees Fahrenheit. I was dressed in my uniform long winter overcoat with the double row of brass buttons. On my belt, I had my 38 special, one row of extra bullets, handcuffs, the claw, a five-cell flashlight, night stick, one book of parking tickets and one book of moving violation tickets and a black jack in my pockets. I wore gloves and two pairs of socks plus long johns. Eight hours was a long time to be walking and checking every door and window on your beat, never knowing what's in the back yard of the next business. A burglary in progress. A rape in progress. A fire. Always being prepared for the worst. No cell phones, no portable police radios in 1962. Only the issued police whistle. Just you and your training to deal with it, alone and isolated. All that changed one night. An old timer gave me a key to the side door of the Masonic Temple, located on Grand Avenue across from Fab's Dry Cleaning at Atwater Street. He said, "This key was issued by a Masonic Hall Official to be used by the Policeman on the beat. Use it on cold nights to duck in and get warm and rest your legs and back. Keep the office clean. No smoking and no lights. Do not abuse this privilege, okay?" "Yes sir," I said to the old timer who was retiring. As I entered the side door one bitter morning at about 3:00 AM, I made my way in the dark to the front office. Going from bitter cold to a nice warm office, I was in Heaven. I got off my feet and sat down in a chair looking out the front windows. The weight from my gun belt was killing my back so this was relief. The warm air was relief. Instead of just resting and warming up, I had to be curious and wanted to know about the meeting hall for Mason Members in the back. I heard that there was a nice hall in the back for Members to use for meeting and social gatherings. I made my way in the dark, remembering, no lights, and no flashlights. As I walked my eyes adjusted to the dark. I felt a long smooth wooden table, then I felt something cold and clammy. I cupped my flashlight and with a small beam of light I discovered that the wooden table was actually a coffin and a man was in it. I took off like a bat out of hell for the side door. Once outside, I threw that key as far away as I could. The next day, I learned that Mason Members have wakes and funeral services for their member's, right there in the Masonic Temple Meeting Hall. No more keys for me. I would rather freeze my butt off. •

One afternoon in the summer of 1965, I was patrolling in Westville on the 3:00 PM to 11:00 PM shift. It was approximately 4:30 PM. I was waiting at the traffic light on Edgewood Way and Forest Road when a vehicle traveling south toward West Haven had passed the intersection at an above rate of speed. I turned right into Forest Rd and pursued the vehicle. As I caught up with the vehicle, I checked the speed which was above the posted speed limit of 35 MPH by about 8-10 MPH. I pulled the vehicle over just past Chapel Street. As I approached the vehicle, I observed that a white female was operating. I asked her for her license and registration after identifying myself and giving her the reason I had stopped her. In the back seat were two children, a little girl and a little boy, maybe ages six and eight. I waved and they waved back. As I was checking her license, I noticed the children had their noses pressed against the left rear sidecar window. "Should I give mommy a ticket for speeding kids?" I asked. They both shook their little heads no and gave me that sad look. That look gets me every time. I thought a verbal warning was appropriate seeing that her license and registration was in order. In those days, we did not ask for proof of insurance. I said "Ma'am, I am giving you a break today, thanks to your children. Please obey the posted speed limits in New Haven." As I was returning her license and registration, the little girl said, "I'm telling daddy that you got stopped by a Policeman, mommy. I'm telling, I'm telling." I had to walk away because I was laughing. Policeman have the discretion to write tickets or write warning tickets or give a verbal warning which I did in this case. The lady was polite and she had a good attitude. Her children were also very polite and well behaved. As the lady carefully drove off, using her left signal light, I said to myself, good decision Bob. •

YOUTH DIVISION OPPORTUNITY

Looking back at my career patrolling in Westville, Newhallville and Fair Haven starting in 1962, I fell in love with all the children. From Cooper Place to Conrad Drive to Kohary Drive to Brookside Avenue, then to Newhall Street and eventually Fair Haven. The kids were always important to me. In 1964, a lovely lady with a lot of influence in Westville made me a proposition. "Bob, I am going to get you transferred to the Youth Division. Your love for children will make you a perfect candidate." "Really?" The next day I made a few phone calls. Yes, this lady had the connections to make this happen. "Will I still be able to drive out to Westville and visit my little friends" was one question I asked. "No. Absolutely not. You will be in plain clothes in an unmarked car. You will primarily be assigned to juvenile delinquents and problem children. You will work closely with Juvenile Detention on Orange Street." I sat on this golden opportunity in my career for a couple of days. Talked it over with the most important person in my life, ,my wife, Mary. I reluctantly turned it down. I was so grateful to this woman but after explaining my feelings, she understood. My though was to convey to the children a sense of how important it was to grow up strong and honest and respectful towards others, especially your parents, Teachers and all adult role models. I wanted to be there for the kids before they ended up in juvenile court. My first best decision in my life was to become a New Haven Police Officer. The second best decision I made was to stay close with my little friends. Whether it is patrolling Westville, Newhallville, Dixwell Avenue or Fair Haven. •

It was never a secret that I loved, and still do love, children and cared deeply for their safety and welfare. I got so irritated when a parent would say, "See that cop? If you don't behave, he's going to take you away and we will never see you again." Parents: teach your child that if they are lost or in danger, look for a Policeman. The Policeman is the good guy. Policemen are friends, not the boogey man.

Anyway, this is a story about one of my many little friends. In the mid 60's, I was patrolling on Kohary Drive in Westville. I turned into Stevenson Road and my 7-year-old little friend, Ned, was standing on the sidewalk. I stopped. "Hi Ned." "Hi Bob." Ned asked me if I would give him a ride around the block in my police car. This is just before I got in trouble giving the kids a ride around the block. "Well first Ned, I need permission from your mom." Ned's mom, Shirley, was in the house. I rang the bell. Shirley came to the door and when I asked permission to take Ned around the block in my police car, Shirley said, "Of course Ned can go for a ride with you Bob." I said, "Ned, if I get an emergency call, you will need to jump out of my police car and walk home, okay?" "Okay!" Ned said. "Bob, can Sam come with us too?" Sam was Ned's beagle dog. "Okay Ned. Put him in the back seat." Driving half way around the block, Ned asked me what time it was. "10 minutes to 2:00 Ned." "OH Bob, lets hurry." "Why Ned?" "Because every day at 2:00 o'clock, Sam throws up." "What? He throws up?" "Yep. Every day at 2:00." Red light and siren back to Ned's house. I didn't stick around to see Sam throw up. I left, in a hurry. •

ANNIE'S STORE-GRAND AND JAMES

In the mid 60's, on the 4:00 to 12:00 shift, I always stopped at Annie's for a newspaper or ice cream on the way home. One night, while on duty, I got a complaint from a guy named Glen in the apartments across from Annie's on Grand Avenue between James and Haven. Glen, who also called himself Yvonne when he dressed as a woman, lived on the third floor and liked to dress in woman's clothes. Mini skirt, nylons, the works. He also wore a blond wig. Glen's complaint was that the kids on the second floor would tease him and pinch his butt as he walked up the stairs. Anyway, On Glen's complaint, I spoke to the mother of the kids on the second floor and told her to talk to her kids and stop harassing him. The mother said, "That faggot called the police on my boys?" "Yes, he did." I wrote a full report of the harassment incident. About three nights later, I just got off duty and was on my way home. I stopped at Annie's at about 12:15 AM to get something. I had no reason to lock my car doors. I came out of Annie's and noticed a blond woman sitting in the front passenger seat of my personal car. It was Glen/Yvonne. He didn't recognize me with my civilian coat over my uniform. I opened my car door. "What the hell are you doing in my car Glen? Get your ass out of my car," I said and showed him my badge under my civilian coat. "How do you know my name?" He asked. "Because I was at your apartment the other night when the kids were pinching your ass as you walked up the stairs to your apartment. And you keep that ass out of my car, understand?" "Yes Officer, Sorry. I never proposition an Officer." He walked away toward Blatchley Avenue. I called the Vise Squad and they sent an unmarked car to pick him up before he got in the wrong car and got his ass kicked. You just can't make this stuff up. •

We were getting slammed with home burglaries in the Westville/Boulevard areas in the fall of 1964. One night at midnight, I took an unmarked police car from Station 2. It was a 1960 Chevy Biscayne, two-door, colored green and white. It had a siren with red lights in the front grille. The area I concentrated on was near Connecticut State Teachers College on Crescent Street. This is now Southern Connecticut State University. I was driving slowly east on Crescent Street and had just passed the Boulevard. I was well over to the right side of the road, giving cars behind me plenty of room to pass. Our police cars did not have spotlights in those days, but we had large bright spot lights that we plugged into the cigarette lighter outlet. I was checking back yards and driveways when the vehicle behind me, passed me at a high rate of speed, beeping the horn and spinning the tires. The front passenger leaned out his window, gave me the middle finger and yelled, "Hey asshole. Where did you get your license, Sears & Roebuck?" They picked up speed as they headed toward Goffe Street. I got behind them and hit the siren button and red grille lights. They pulled over just before Goffe Street. I cautiously approached the car. I said, license and registration to the driver. I usually say please but not this time. At this point, all options were on the table, depending upon their attitude toward me. Before I could speak, the driver bragged that his uncle was a Prosecutor with the 6th Circuit Court system. He further states that any ticket that I give him will be fixed by his Uncle. Really? He gave me his Uncle's name. The Prosecutor was a friend of mine, one of the best Prosecutors. Options were now off the table. I started writing the ticket. Unnecessary use of the horn, speeding, following to closely, one windshield wiper was not working so, defective equipment was added. I set a court date for three weeks and told him to be in court and drive carefully. And keep that idiot passenger of yours quiet. I contacted the Prosecutor first thing the next morning. I told him the whole story. He said, "Bob, thank you for bringing this to my attention. I will call his mother who is my sister. I promise that he will pay every cent on that ticket. He earned it and he will pay it." It was almost $200.00 and the kid paid the ticket. •

I can't remember the exact date but it was sometime in the early 1970's. A lady named Kathy (no last names) bought the business. She was a very attractive lady, maybe in her late 40's or early 50's with a daughter named Pat, maybe in her mid-twenties. She kept the same waitresses and chefs and business was good. Her daughter Pat worked there as a part time Waitress. One day I was dispatched to Almar's Diner in regard to a heated Employee dispute. Upon arrival, Kathy was accusing several employees of stealing money from the cash register. She was upset because within a 24-hour period, hundreds of dollars were missing when the cash register was balanced the next morning. I liked Kathy so I got her in the office and said, "Kathy, you can't point your finger at the employees without proof. These people are going to walk out on you." I arranged to set up a hidden camera aimed at the cash register for a 24-hour period. That night we caught the thief, her own daughter, Pat. At 3:00 in the morning, Pat, who was not even scheduled to work, opened the cash register and placed four $10.00 rolls of quarters and an unknown amount of $20.00 bills in her apron front pocket. That morning, the cash register was short $280.00. If you multiplied 30 days times $280.00. That's more than $8000.00 per month. I don't need to paint a picture about what this did to a hard working family. Pat was a drug addict and sometimes drug addicts will steal from their loved ones in a heartbeat. I suggested to Kathy that an apology was in order to all her employees that she accused of stealing from her. Her whole staff was ready to quit when it was discovered that her own daughter was stealing from her. They were insulted and I don't blame them. Even good customers were reluctant to eat there when word got out what happened. This story is real life. It is not meant to embarrass or hurt anyone. If Kathy and even Pat needed me today, I would help them if I could. •

One early afternoon in the summer of 1964, I was dispatched to a home on Knollwood Drive in Westville regarding a home burglar alarm activation. Upon arrival at the home, I observed the double garage door wide open and an audible alarm ringing. Never assuming that it is a false alarm, I called for backup and parked in a safe place where I could observe the home. My backup arrived and the ADT Alarm Company also responded. After a complete and thorough search of the house and garage, we secured it by closing the garage door and resetting the alarm. Approximately three days later, the same alarm went off. Again, responding and waiting for backup and ADT. After a complete search we secured the home. Neighbors reported that the family was in Europe and there were no cell phones in those days to contact people. One week later, the same alarm went off. After going through all the same procedures and having the ADT service man complain that his company was going to charge the customer the next time we are called out on a false alarm. I decided to check the house as often as possible. Even parking in the driveway. Sure enough, three to four days later, while parked in the driveway, the alarm goes off and the double garage door opens. I got out of my police car and noticed about four houses down, a man was pulling into his garage. I caught him just before he closed the garage door. On a hunch, I asked him if I could look at his garage door remote control. Being in full police uniform he handed it to me. I walked out of the driveway and pushed the button. Sure enough the man's garage door closed and so did the house I was investigating. The man was without words and so was I. He said he bought the remote system, something fairly new at Hatry's Electronics. I said, "Mister, please have them re code this one or give you another one." ADT pulled up and I told him I solved the mystery. Yes, maybe I should have been a Detective. •

BAT IN HOUSE

One night around 9:00 PM in the mid 70's, I was dispatched to a large home on Everitt Street just south of East Rock Road. I was told to see the lady who lived there. I arrived to a very large home and knocked on the front door. Two kids came to the door and then a lady. She opened the door and handed me a broom and said, "He's in the study." "Who's in the study?" "The bat." Oh no lady. Wait a minute. I asked permission to use her phone so I could call Station 2. "Sarge. This is Bob M. What's the deal with the bat?" "Kill the damn thing Bob." "How Sarge?" "Shoot the damn thing." "I can't shoot my 38 in the ladies living room or study." "Do your best, Good bye" and he hung up. I took the broom and walked into the study. She closed the door behind me. That really made me feel good. All alone with a killer bat. Her children were outside looking in the windows, cheering me on. One by one I tipped over the overstuffed chairs looking for the bat. Suddenly, it took off circling the room. I aimed the broom and swung but missed. He came around again and this time I nailed him. Splat on the wall and then on the floor. It was dead. The lady gave me a dust pan to pick up the dead bat. I threw the dead bat away in the back yard. The kids were clapping. "Good job Officer." "Thanks kids." Every call is different. I never knew what the next call would be. There are tons of bats in the East Rock area and the lady told me, this was the fourth or fifth bat in her house. •

One Friday night in the late fall of 1963, I took my family to Luigi's Pizza, located on Whalley Avenue near Anthony Street. Terry (RIP) was age eight, Alice was age six, and Bobby was age one. We all loved good pizza and Luigi's was one of the best, except for Pepe's or Sally's. We got there around 7:30 PM. It was crowded but we found a table by the left wall. As I mentioned before, off duty Police Officers are required to carry a badge, a weapon and are subject to enforcing the law, even when off duty, within reason. We placed our pizza order. I waved to Joe, the owner of Luigi's and he waved back. A drunk walks in the front door. He staggers up to the counter. "Sir, can I help you?" asked Joes wife. "Yeah. Rikowski. I ordered a pizza to go." She said, "It's not ready yet. Just a few more minutes." Then he said, raising his voice, "You told me 20 minutes. The next one is mine" and he walked around the counter and approached the oven. Joe, who knew that I was a Police Officer, pleaded with me for help. Mary said, "Mind your own business Bob. You are off duty." Joe called the Police. The man opened the oven. I had to act before someone got seriously hurt. I jumped up and took out my badge. I said, "Mister, you are out of line. Wait your turn." He told me to shove the badge (Cops get that a lot) and took a swing at me. I put him down on the floor. As he went down, he reached for the coat rack and all the coats went flying. My children were crying, except Bobby. At age one he loved seeing daddy in action. I dragged the drunk out the front door to the sidewalk and held him down until backup arrived. He was taken away. Joe thanked me and asked if he could put a fresh pizza in the open. My family was too upset to eat. Just before we left, a Boy Scout Master approached me and said he had a dozen Scouts with him and they loved seeing a Policeman so close in action. They said it was the best pizza party they ever had. Mr. Rikowski was arrested for breach of peace and for intoxication. •

ST. AEDAN'S PRIEST

One Saturday morning, in the spring of 1965, I was dispatched to a one family home on Forest Road between Willard and Fountain Street in regard to a harassing telephone call. A young couple was moving into the house, I think they had two children. I don't really remember. Anyways, the husband met me at the door and he said his wife got a strange call, but that I should talk to her. The wife invited me in and said, "Excuse the mess, we're just moving in." She offered me a seat in the living room. With pen and notebook in my hand, I listened to her. She said, about an hour ago, the phone rang. The phone Company hooked up the phone a couple of days ago. She said hello and a male voice identified himself as a Catholic Priest from St. Aedan's Church. The man asked if they were Catholics and she answered yes. He asked for the names of the family members and their ages. Also, would the children be attending St. Aiden's school? She couldn't answer that yet because they hadn't planned that far. As she spoke to this "Priest", the husband kept busy carrying in boxes and small furniture. After talking to this Priest for almost one hour, his questions because more personal. He asked if they practiced safe sex and approximately how many times they had sex each week. Did they enjoy oral sex? Finally, the husband asked her who she was talking to and took the phone from her. "Hello, who's this?" The male caller hung up. She thought he said Father O' Malley or something like that. The husband looked up St. Aedan's in the phone book and called the parish. No such Priest was assigned there. I called St. Aedan's and got the same answer. As embarrassing as it was, I asked the lady if the caller acted strange or nervous. She said she thought he had a cold because he was having trouble breathing. I had a hard time keeping a straight face. No way of tracing telephone calls in those days. Besides, the lady willingly answered all his questions. I left and did a report of the incident, calling it an annoying telephone call. Just another day. •

ABANDONED AUTO

We all need a cheerful story right about now. In 1964, there was a used car dealer on Columbus Avenue, between White and Arch Streets. It was called Town and Country Auto Exchange. It was owned by a man, Pat Mauro, and his father. When they were on Lafayette Street years before, their reputation was not so good. It was called Jimmy the Gyp. I bought a 1959 Ford station from Pat and it ran very well, so I was in the market for another car for my wife, Mary. I stopped one day and Pat had nothing on his lot but he told me to go over to the Boulevard because he had some cars behind the page fence near the old flee market. I found a 1954 Dodge four-door in real nice condition with no license plates on it. So, I drove back to see Pat. He said, that car was abandoned during a snowstorm and towed to his lot. Pat said, "If you can register that car Bob, it's yours. Free of charge." "Free Pat?" "Yep, if you can find the previous owner, it's yours." I went back and looked in the glove box. Something that anyone could have done. There was a receipt for a new muffler from Midas Mufflers with the name and address of the previous owner on Hudson Street. I drove over to Hudson Street and rang the bell. A man answered and said, "Yes Officer?" "Mister, I am not on official business but I am interested in a car that belonged to you in December that was towed during a snow storm." "Oh, the Dodge?" "Yes sir." "What do you need officer? The title?" "Yes, please." He gave me the title and two sets of keys. Since then, he said, "I bought a new car and we don't need the Dodge any longer." "Can I pay you something?" I asked the man. "No Officer, It's got a new muffler. Please take the car. We don't need it any longer." We shook hands and I thanked him and I drove back to Pat's. I handed Pat the title and the two sets of keys. "Pat, please register this car for me." Pat said, "I could sure use the Dodge as a loaner car." "Pat," I said, "w made a gentleman's agreement." "I know," he said. I don't want to piss off a bunch of cops." "That's true Pat, you don't want to do that." Pat reluctantly registered the car for me and I paid him for the new registration and all the paperwork and time he put into registering the car for me. One of the best cars I have ever owned. Pat Mauro was a good man. A man of his word. His father turned out to be a nice man also. With a few good words from me, his reputation for ripping people off diminished considerably. •

HARASSING PHONE CALLS

This is the story of a guy who was using a pay phone to call and harass a young woman by making repeated harassing and sometimes threatening phone calls to her, usually late at night. She lived on Barnes Avenue near Quinnipiac Avenue. It was in 1969. In those days it was nearly impossible to trace a phone call and it required a court order from a Judge to do so. This young woman was terrified of these calls because the guy would drive by her house and then call her from a nearby telephone and tell her exactly where her car was parked on the street. How many lights were on in her living room. I decided to work with another Policeman and try to outsmart this guy. One morning at about 1:00 AM, I got a complaint to respond to her apartment in regard to harassing phone calls. My partner also responded. As she spoke to the guy, I had my partner stay with her and I drove around the different outside telephone booths that I knew about. At gas station on Quinnipiac and Rt. 80 had an outside telephone booth but it was clear. Then it dawned on me that there was a pay phone outside of Almar's Diner on Middletown Avenue. As I drove into Almar's parking lot, there was a guy on the telephone. I drove past him and parked my police car in front and pretended I was going inside. I walked in one door and came out the other door and snuck up on him. When he saw me, he tried to hang up the telephone but I grabbed it out of his hand and said "Hello?" The girl was on the other end. She said, "Hello Officer?" I said to her, "We got him. Have my partner meet me at Almar's, Okay?" We caught this bastard in the act. I arrested him for making lewd and harassing phone calls. I warned him to never, ever call her again. In those days Policemen could send a message to a punk like this that it's easy to get hurt if you harass a woman. I sent that message to him. After that night, she never had a problem again. Today, everyone has caller I.D. In those days, tracing a telephone call was very, very difficult. You had to keep the person on the phone for about 10-15 minutes and you also had to have a court order, signed by a Judge. If I was a Policeman today, I would probably always be in trouble because I would still do what I could to keep women safe from punks like him. •

THE LADY DRIVER FROM HELL

On Christmas morning in 1965, I was parked at the intersection of Marvelwood Road and Vista Terrace. Because both streets had stop signs, some drivers traveling north on Vista Terrace would ignore the stop sign and proceed right through the intersection without stopping. Sure enough, here comes the lady from hell traveling at approximately 25 MPH go right through the intersection without even slowing down. I even had the Traffic Division erect a large yellow sign stating "*STOP SIGN AHEAD*" months earlier, 100 feet before the stop sign. I pulled her over on Fountain Street. Being Christmas morning, I was prepared to give her a verbal warning. However, when I mentioned that she failed to stop for the stop sign, she replied, "What stop sign?" When I asked for her license and registration, she replied, "I left my license home." Then she said, "For God sakes, it's Christmas morning. Don't you have a heart?" "Yes ma'am, I do but traffic accidents don't take holidays and I wouldn't want to see you get hurt or hurt someone else." I agreed to follow her to her house just ½ block away on W. Prospect Street. She parked in front of her house and as she climbed the porch stairs, with me behind her, I waited outside on her porch for her to return with her license. Instead, she came out with a vicious German Shepard dog and commanded the dog to sic me. I was justified in shooting the dog, but I made one of those instant decisions, that Policeman often make. What if she had children and they were looking out the front windows? I decided to head for the safety of my cruiser and just made it before the dog jumped on the hood. He tried to get to me through the car windshield. With bared teeth and dog saliva. He clawed at the windshield and hood, doing considerable damage to my police car. I will never forget that day. I called for backup including the Dog Warden to respond. The Dog Warden responded immediately and he seized the dog and contained him in the animal control van. The lady came out and was handcuffed and placed in the paddy wagon. I charged her with assault on a police officer, destruction of public property and yes, the stop sign violation. Her husband came out and threatened me so I threw his butt into the other compartment of the paddy wagon and charged him with interfering with a police officer. Christmas Day has never been the same. •

FOUND POCKETBOOK IN STREET

One night in the fall of 1963, I left Station 2 on Sherman Parkway at the end of my 4:00 to 12:00 midnight shift. I was in route to our "new" home in East Haven. We had recently bought this old country home In East Haven. It was so nice to drive through Newhallville and head over to Middletown Avenue to Route 80. As I drove east on Ivy Street just crossing Newhall Street, I observed what looked like a pocketbook just off the sidewalk in the gutter. As I passed it, I decided to turn left into Winchester Avenue and go around the block and check it out. I stopped my vehicle and got out and picked up the pocketbook. It was heavy. My first thought was that it was a child's pocketbook filled with rocks or something. The pocketbook contained about $180.00 in cash and a host of family picture, a picture of a grey haired black lady and so many children's pictures. Priceless pictures of smiling children in braids and different hairstyles. Here I am, all alone, on a dark street after midnight with this cash that amounted to about twi monthly mortgage payments at $95.00 per month in 1963. No one around to question my honesty, only me, a stranger's pocketbook and my conscious. I am a Police Officer and I am held to a much higher standard. My decision was made. I drove straight to Winchester Avenue, turned left, turned left into Bassett Street and then left into Sherman Parkway. I walked into Station 2 and plopped the pocketbook on the front desk. "Sarge. I found this on my way home in the street on Ivy Street." The Sergeant opened the pocketbook, counted the money and looking for ID. A driver's license identified a lady on Ivy Street. He called the lady and she was there in five minutes. She was a grey haired light skinned woman, maybe 70-years-old. She said, "Thank you, thank you so much. I was looking for my pocketbook all day. I have bills to pay including my rent. I was worried sick all day." The lady left clutching her pocketbook. This was Community Relations at its finest. People caring for one another. The Sergeant, whose name was Phil Lang looked at me and said, "Bob. Regardless of whatever happens in the future, I will never doubt your honesty. Someone else might have taken the money and threw the pocketbook out the window. Now go home to your family." •

One Saturday night in the fall of 1966, I was on extra duty at the Jewish Community Center on Chapel Street for a scheduled teenage dance. I had a young rookie Police Officer working with me. There were approximately 100 teens in attendance at the dance. In those days, our biggest problem was cigarette smoking in the rest rooms and youths going to their cars to drink. Once they left the building, they were not permitted to reenter the building. Everything was going smoothly until about 9:30 PM. Suddenly a teen age girl ran out the front door and down the stairs and turned right on the sidewalk, screaming, "They're after me, help!" The rookie said to me, "I think I am in trouble." "What happened?" I asked. "This girl wanted me to put my handcuffs on her wrists, just to see what they felt like. I did and then she ran out the front entrance door before I could stop her. With my handcuffs on her wrists." "Guess you are right. You are in trouble." We had no idea where she went. She was running toward downtown. Soon we got a call from Star Guard Service in the Chapel Mall that the girl was running through the mall with the hand cuffs on her wrists screaming, "Help, the cops are after me." One of the Guards stopped her. She then said it was only a joke and that she came from the Jewish Center. No one was laughing. Especially me. The rookie was called downtown to do an incident report at Headquarters. In my career, I showed dozens of teens and younger children my handcuffs but never put them on anyone's wrists. They are not toys. He had to go see Chief McManus the following week. The girl had red marks on both wrists and her parents were not happy and threatened to sue the City. Not sure of the outcome. He was most likely verbally reprimanded by the Chief. •

DOMESTIC-FLYING TOASTER

One Saturday afternoon in 1966, I was dispatched to the corner of State and Rock Street. Neighbors complained of a loud domestic disturbance coming from the large apartment house. Upon arrival, I observed small household items sprawled on the sidewalk of a three-story apartment house. An ironing board, a television smashed on the sidewalk, books, clothing. As I sat in my police cruiser, relaying to the dispatcher what I have found so far, suddenly, a four-slice toaster bounced off the hood of my police car. A 1966 Ford Custom, almost new police car. "That's it," I said, "send me backup." There was only one window open and that was on the third floor. I climbed the stairs to the third floor and discovered that there was a man and woman, in a heated dispute over possessions. The woman felt that everything that belonged to her, she could do what she wanted with the items. So she started to throw her items out the window – the ironing board, books, television, toaster. The man said, "My wife is nuts." No argument there. The conclusion: I arrested the wife for breach of peace and destruction of Public Property. One big dent on a police car hood. I took her into custody and told the Sergeant to put a high bond on her to keep her in jail until Monday morning court. Give her a chance to cool off. Looking back, I realized that the next item out the window could have been the husband? •

While working a part time job at Chieppo Bus Company in the early 70's, driving a school bus, I was given a special assignment. There was a very mean spirited 14-year-old boy from Sheridan Jr. High that took the Dixwell/Newhall area bus in the afternoon. He lived on Dixwell Avenue between Bassett and Willis Street. He intimidated every driver, male, female, black or white into stopping in front of his house so he wouldn't have to walk from Willis Street, which was the designated bus stop. Buses must stop at certain authorized areas only. I was chosen for this assignment, not because I was a Policeman, but because I would not back down to this 'punk.' After picking up the Dixwell children at Sheridan, I proceeded toward Bassett Street. As I turned right into Dixwell Avenue he yelled out, "Yo driver, stop here man. That's my house, man. Yo what's wrong with you. STOP HERE mother f**ker." I kept right on going. He then called me a 'white mother f**ker' and warned that if I was on the bus tomorrow afternoon, he was going to kick my MF ass. I took this abuse and when I opened the door, he warned me don't be on this bus tomorrow. "Your dead man." A black female bus aide was riding with me sitting just behind me. She witnessed the whole incident. She was on the bus for a reason. This kid was trouble. She said, "You were wonderful. You took all that abuse." She knew that I was an off duty Policeman. We got back to Sheridan and went to the Principals office and did an incident report. This punk's name was Gordon "Mustang" because he liked to steal Ford Mustang's. Because of this incident, he was suspended permanently from riding the school bus. The next afternoon, I was driving the same Dixwell/Newhall bus. I parked in front of Sheridan waiting for the Dixwell students to come out. "Mustang" was seen getting in his mom's car. Almost every kid on that bus thanked me for getting him kicked off the bus. None of the other kids liked Mustang. He was a bully and he was mean. Outsmarting a punk is sometime better than punching him in the face, which I really wanted to do. Just one mean bully can affect the whole school bus. •

RETIRED POLICEMAN ALMOST MUGGING VICTIM

In the summer of 1979, 6 months after I retired from the New Haven Police Department, My wife Mary, was going downtown on a Saturday afternoon to do some shopping. She said, "Bob, want to come with me? Maybe you will bump into some of your old friend's downtown." "Sounds good to me." I answered. I put my 38 police special on my belt and Mary said, "Bob. You are now retired. You don't need that." "Honey, I've seen a lot happening downtown, even in broad daylight. The gun goes with me." We drove from our home in East Haven and arrived on Crown Street between Temple and College and parked in a parking lot. Mary headed toward Church and Chapel and the Mall area and I headed to College Street hoping to see some old friends. Maybe have coffee at the Roger Sherman Spa. As I walked on College toward Chapel, I noticed four or five big young guys heading my way. I sensed trouble and sure enough as they approached me they said, "Hey man, got a cigarette?" I said, "Sorry gentleman, but I don't smoke." Then one of them said, "Hey man, give us your wallet and we'll buy our own cigarettes." They laughed. In any city or state, give us your wallet equates to a street robbery, which is a felony. I pulled out my 38 special Smith and Wesson and pointed it at them. I even cocked back the hammer. Man, did these guys take off in all different directions. I decided to report this incident so I went to the red emergency telephone on Chapel and College and called Headquarters. I identified myself and asked for a Sergeant to meet me there. The Sergeant pulled up and I got in the police car and told him what happened. He said, "Bob, good thing you didn't give them your wallet, they would have beat the crap out of you anyway. It's been happening almost every day downtown." Gangs of youths beating and robbing people. "Did you say you were a Policeman?" "No Sarge. I didn't. Anyway, I'm retired now." "Okay, Bob. I'll file a report of the incident." "Thanks Sarge. Take care." "You too Bob." I did get my coffee at the Roger Sherman Spa and then met Mary at the parking lot. Mary said, "Hi, so how was your afternoon?" "Mary, get in the car. It's a long story." •

GRANDFATHER ACCUSED OF MOLESTATION

Small children are sometimes molested by strangers, sometimes they are molested by close family members or trusted family friends. It's a very touchy subject but cannot be ignored if your child reports something wrong. Please listen to your child but do not act immediately. Accusations that are false can destroy a family. I mean absolutely tear a loving family apart. Accusations from a child that are true can destroy the child if the parents ignore it. Please, seek advice from a Priest, Minister or Rabbi. Calling the Police without actual facts can be a big mistake.

Before I arrested this man, I was very sure that the molestation had occurred. My first concern was for the child. I also was very careful not to put an innocent man in prison. My decision to call in a female Detective was based on the fact that this poor little girl would be more comfortable speaking to a woman, especially if she had just been violated by a man. She would be too afraid to talk to a man. I made the right decision for all parties involved. One day in the late 60's, I was dispatched to a two-family house on Winchester Avenue on the last block just before Sachem Street. A single parent mom lived on the second floor with her two little girls. Ages five and seven. Her 83-year-old father lived on the first floor. The father was the landlord of the house. The young woman was practically hysterical after her 5-year-old daughter accused grandpa of molesting her in the garage, located behind the house. In my humble opinion, anytime a female of any age accuses anyone of molestation or rape, that female should be interviewed by a qualified female police officer or Detective or some other qualified person. After the child was taken to the hospital for the customary examination, she was interviewed by a female Detective. There was overwhelming evidence that the molestation did take place and had been going on for some time. Once I had the confirmation from the female Detective, I did have the pleasure of handcuffing the grandfather and putting him in the paddy wagon. His defense was, "My daughter is behind on her rent and I was going to evict her. It's all a big lie," he said. Months later, he was found guilty by a jury of his peers. I did not follow the case knowing that other inmates hate child molesters. I'm sure justice was served at Sommers Prison, where he was sent. •

POLICEMAN WITH BIG SHOES

After my last depressing story, we all need a funny story. Including me. This incident occurred at about the time in 1967 when I was learning the Spanish language and I was working closely with the Hispanic Community in the Fair Haven section of New Haven. One morning on the 8:00 to 4:00 PM shift, I was driving the Paddy Wagon. My first assignment was to pick up the Inmates at the County Jail on Whalley Avenue and bring them to their 10:00 AM court appearance at the Superior Court located in downtown New Haven. This day, I had fourteen prisoners. I had a long chain with handcuffs attached to the chain. One at a time, I handcuffed the Inmates. There were three Spanish-speaking Inmates. One looked at me and said, "El Policia es Grande!" (I'm big.) Then another said, "El Policia tiene una pistol." (A pistol.) These are acceptable comments. Finally, one of the Inmates said, "El Policia tiene zapatos grande." (I have big shoes.) I am laughing inside at this moment, but I pretended to be angry. I looked right at him and said, "Mira stupido. Yo no tengo zapatos grande, estupido." (I don't have big shoes, stupid.) Well, they all looked on the ground and said, "Lo siento, lo siento Policia." I slammed the paddy wagon rear door and got in the driver's side. I turned on the intercom to hear what was being said. The other eleven Inmates were telling them that the cop was really mad and that they were going to prison for twenty years. When we arrived at Superior Court, I backed in and opened the rear door and assisted the fourteen prisoners, chained together. As the Spanish-speaking Inmates exited the paddy wagon, they were still apologizing to me. I said, "Mira, Olvidelo. No es gran cosa." (Forget about it. It's no big deal.) You just can't make this stuff up. •

In June 1972, I was on duty in the Chapel Street area. On occasion I would use my 30-minute authorized lunch period to take a quick swim at the Jewish Community Center on Chapel Street. Working in Westville in the early 1960's, the kids talked me into joining the Jewish Center. It turned out to be much nicer than the YMCA on Howe Street. Anyway, it was early about 6:00 PM on a Friday night. I parked my police car in the rear yard. I noticed a black Caddy Limo belonging to Hy's Limo Service in West Haven, parked next to me. I was heading toward the pool area when a young man asked me if I was there to escort Tom Jones to the Oakdale Theater. "No, why, is Mr. Jones here?" "Yes, he is in the Men's Club in the sauna." Remember, once I said Policeman in uniform can go just about anywhere? Well, I entered the Men's Club and there he was. Tom Jones. Standing there after getting a massage. I got his autograph for my daughters and respecting his privacy, I thanked him and I left. I determined that Mr. Jones was staying at the Park Plaza and was always welcome at the Jewish Center as a guest. He was performing that night at the Oakdale. I got on the pay phone and called my wife, Mary. When I told her about Tom Jones at the Jewish center, she did not believe me. She said, "He's not Jewish," and I said, "Neither am I but I'm here." Mary still did not believe me, even after I showed her Tom Jones autograph. When she read it in the New Haven Register that Tom Jones was performing at The Oakdale, she began to believe me. Terry and Alice believe me and asked what he looked like. I said, "Well girls, he had a towel around his waist, was bare foot and about 5'9" tall with very curly brown hair." They screamed and said, "Daddy, a towel?" "Yes girls. A towel around his waist. He had just got off the massage table and was getting dressed." They absolutely loved Tom Jones and so did Mary. •

EMPTY MILK TRUCK IN DRIVEWAY

We have been talking about milk and milk deliveries to our homes in the 60's. Well, back in 1967, we had Knudsen Bros. from Hamden deliver our milk to our home in East Haven. In the summer I was working the midnight shift for the New Haven Police Department. From 12:00 until 8:00 AM. I usually came home about 8:20 AM. One morning, pulling in the driveway, I noticed a large puddle of water on my asphalt driveway. It had not rained in a couple of weeks so I checked the garden hose but it was not leaking. Oh well. I entered the back door, took off my uniform and went to bed. I forgot about the puddle of water in my driveway. About three or four days later, I came home to the same thing. A large puddle of water in my driveway. What's going on here? About one week later, I pulled in the driveway and there was a Knudsen milk truck parked in the driveway with the motor off. The truck was empty and there was a large puddle of water under the truck where the ice had melted. That's it, the milkman. I was livid. I barged in the back door and woke up Mary. "Where is he?" I asked. "Where is who?" Mary asked. "The milkman. Where is that sneaky bastard?" Mary said, "Bob, calm down." About 4:00 AM the milkman knocked on the back door and woke her up saying his milk truck stalled in the driveway and he couldn't get it started. He used the phone to call the dairy to send another milk truck. Mary said they made so much noise transferring all the milk bottles from one truck to the other one. I believed her when a tow truck backed in my driveway and towed the disabled milk truck away. That explained the puddles of water in the driveway. As the milk truck sat in my driveway, the melting ice leaked on the driveway. Occasionally I would tease Mary about it by saying things like, "How come we never get a bill for the milk, honey?" After a while, she didn't think it was funny anymore. •

HILLHOUSE FOOTBALL TEAM CHEERLEADERS

One of my part time jobs during my days off as a New Haven Police Officer was driving a bus for Chieppo Bus Company, located on Forbes Avenue. One Saturday morning, in the early 70's, Hillhouse High School ordered two buses. One was to be used to take the football team and the other to transport the cheerleaders to a football game in Bristol, Connecticut. I got the pretty cheerleaders and the other bus driver got the football team with all their equipment. I lucked out. We arrived at the football field in Bristol at about 11:00 AM. Some of our cheerleaders did not have uniforms and some had mismatched uniforms but all had the pom-poms. The football team all had the proper uniforms. They walked in the back gate with no trouble. As soon as our girls tried to enter the field they were stopped and questioned about their uniforms or lack of uniforms. Then some idiot decided to charge all the Hillhouse girls admission to enter the field. I stepped up and said, "I am their bus driver. They are all Hillhouse cheerleaders. I've transported many ball teams to games and never did a cheerleader have to pay admission to the field." I asked if a policeman was on duty and they called for him. I very seldom took out my badge but when he arrived, I showed my badge and introduced myself as a brother policeman from New Haven and stood up for the girls and vouched that they were all Hillhouse cheerleaders. I told the Officer that these gate people wanted to charge them admission. "Which one wanted to charge admission?" he asked. No one answered. He let all the girls in and promised me that they would not be harassed. I felt that it was the right thing to do. Not only did Hillhouse beat this "lilly white" football team. Did I say that? But our cheerleaders were prettier and did a much better job cheerleading. I didn't let the girls see my policeman's badge. They just thought that I was someone important. •

HOME BURGLARY BY RELATIVE

One Saturday morning, in the fall of 1966, I was on patrol in the Grand Avenue/Quinnipiac Avenue area. It was about 10:00 AM when I got a radio call to be on the lookout for a white Ford station wagon with wood grain sides. The call was from the North Haven Police Department. The white male operator was allegedly involved in a house burglary in the area of Shawmut Avenue in North Haven. The Ford was last seen traveling south on Quinnipiac Avenue heading toward New Haven. Taken in the burglary was a cookie jar containing a large amount of cash and a portable television set. I took a position on Quinnipiac and Foxon Hill Road. I waited for a few minutes trying to figure out where Shawmut was in relation the Quinnipiac Avenue. Here comes a white Ford station wagon with wood grain sides operated by a white male. I pulled him over near Barnes Avenue. I immediately recognized him as a man that owned a restaurant in New Haven. On the back seat was a television and on the passenger side floor was a cookie jar. It was full of paper money. I notified the North Haven Police and they requested that I escort the suspect back to the crime scene on Shawmut Avenue. We drove to the address that I was given. As we pulled in the driveway, a woman, who appeared to be the homeowner, approached my police car. She looked at my passenger and said, "S**t. What are you doing in the police car?" Suddenly, it dawned on her that this man, this burglary suspect was her brother. What had happened one week before, this man and his wife were visiting his sister on Shawmut Avenue for coffee. As they sat at the kitchen table, she proudly showed them the full cookie jar that her and her girlfriends were saving for a Bermuda cruise. As I recall, the cookie jar contained about $3000.00 in large bills. Business was bad at the Restaurant so the brother, knowing that his sister was never home on Saturday mornings, went to the house and forced the back door open and stole the cookie jar. To throw off the police, he took the portable television. He also ransacked a few dresser drawers making it look like a home burglary. The sister was devastated and broken hearted. She did press charges against her brother. The first thing that came into my mind was how much I loved my own sister and that I would never, ever do anything like this to her. How could a man do this to his own sister? •

In April 1967, I was patrolling Westville on the 12:00 to 8:00 AM shift. The quietest part of the night is between 3:00 and 4:00 AM. It was a Wednesday morning when I observed an older VW van driving south on Forest Road. The van had no taillights displayed. I pulled the van over on Forest Road just north of Edgewood Avenue. I also noticed the registration tags had expired the month before. The man driving the van could not find his registration. It was a 1962 Volkswagen called a Kombi. A check with the Department of Motor Vehicles revealed that the VW registration had expired in March of 1967. The driver, who turned out to be a well-known orthopedic surgeon, stated that he never received the renewal registration in the mail and he was not aware that the registration had expired. I had no reason not to believe the doctor. That's happened to me on occasion. He said he used the van only to go fishing and he was en-route to meet four more doctors to go out fishing for the day. The other four doctors were waiting for him at a home on upper Chapel Street. There were no cell phones in those days so no way to contact the other doctors. He parked the van on Edgewood Avenue and locked it up with all his fishing equipment in the back. I made a decision to let him go fishing with his doctor friends so I drove him there. The four doctors were surprised to see a police car pull in the driveway with their friend in the front seat. After explaining the situation, the five doctors piled into a Lincoln Continental and headed for the parked Volkswagen van to retrieve the fishing gear. The doctor promised that he would leave the van parked until he could get the registration renewed. All five doctors thanked me and shook my hand. Not all motor vehicle stops result in arrests every time. There are times when discretion and common sense must be applied. Public relations go a long way. Police/Public relations are very important. It promotes respect and good will. I don't see that much anymore. •

DAMAGE TO 1965 CADILLAC

In the spring of 1972, I took my personal car to be washed at the car wash on Amity Road and Fowler Street. My car was a 1965 Cadillac couple Deville that when new belonged to Liberace. I bought this car in 1971 from a man named Barca from Lucy Road, Woodbridge, just over the town line. The car actually belonged to his son, Michael Barker, who was the Director of the Agency of Performing Arts at the Lincoln Center in New York. With a telephone number provided by Mr. Barca, I called Michael, who told me that he often booked Liberace to play at the Lincoln Center and learned that Liberace was trading his 1965 Cadillac for a 1966 model. Michael Barker bought the car for what the dealer was giving Liberace as a trade in. When I bought the car, it had damage to the front grille and the left front fender. I was able to restore the car including a new paint job. For a 7-year-old Cadillac, it looked new. Getting back to the car wash. As my car came out of the car wash, there was a loud noise coming from the engine compartment. The car wash attendant was driving it and apparently stepped on the gas pedal too hard and later I learned that the left side motor mount broke, causing the engine to shift and the fan blade to go through the radiator. Antifreeze was all over the ground and the engine was steaming. My car was not drivable. I got the Manager who was also the owner of the car wash. He was very polite and sympathetic about the damage but he pointed to a sign on the wall that read, "*WE ARE NOT RESPONSIBLE FOR DAMAGE TO VEHICLES*". Everyone there saw the young man floor the gas and cause the damage. As an off duty Police Officer, I had to maintain my composure and dignity. I did not argue. I used a pay phone outside and called the Cadillac dealer up the street. The car was towed there and I called a friend to bring me home. The damage was $840.00. I had no choice but to pay for the damage. I took him to court Five months later and won my case. He offered me 200 free car washes to settle the case. I laughed and said, "Are you serious? The way you treated me and my car? No thank you." •

HUSBAND STABS WIFE TO DEATH

One hot summer night in 1968 at around 9:00 PM, I was dispatched to a domestic fight between a husband and wife on Maltby Place, just a few doors from Grand Avenue. The neighbors had called the police. There was a reported language barrier, so with my knowledge of the Spanish language, I was called to respond with another Policeman. The 33-year-old woman was beaten pretty badly by the intoxicated husband. We separated them, I spoke to the wife and the other Policeman spoke to the husband. I personally have zero respect for any man than hits a woman for any reason. I think they are cowards. Anyway, the woman said, "I have been taking this abuse for years and now I want him arrested. I know he will threaten to kill me but I can't take it anymore. Please, arrest him, please." I put the handcuffs on this guy and as I was escorting him out of the house, he turned around and said to his wife, "When I get out on bond, I will come back and kill you." As he climbed into the paddy wagon, he shouted, "I will be back to kill you bitch." I took him very seriously. So did his wife. I made sure her doors were all locked and warned her to be careful. I kept an eye on her house as much as possible and as time permitted, until getting off duty at midnight. I told my relief about the threat and as time permitted, to keep an eye on the house. I told the Sergeant to please put a high bond on this guy. I went home at 12:00 midnight. At 3:30 AM, my home phone rang and woke me up. It was the Detective Division. "Bob, did you investigate a domestic dispute on Maltby Place?" "Yes, I did." "Well, the guy made bond and went back and kicked in the front door and chased his wife into the street and stabbed her more than thirty times. You need to come in and give a statement." After killing his wife and leaving her body in the street, he sat on the curb, placing the bloody knife on the ground and waited for police to arrive. His only statement was, "I warned the bitch I would kill her if she had me arrested." Thank God the couple had no children. Always take threats seriously. Never say they won't do it. I've seen this happen many times in New Haven and many other places. •

OFFICER SHOT DURING BANK ROBBERY

On May 3, 1974, the day the Black Liberation Army robbed the New Haven Saving Bank in Westville of approximately $10,000.00. I was off duty when the robbery occurred. I was at the Whalley Volkswagen Dealership on Whalley Avenue, just east of Sperry Street purchasing a new engine for my Volkswagen van. Three police cars passed at a high rate of speed traveling in a westerly direction. It was a Friday morning. I called the station to see what was going on. That's when I found out of the robbery and also that at least one Policeman was shot. My Sergeant told me on the telephone not to respond. "Bob," he said, "do not respond." We were required to be armed at all times. I was armed with my off duty snub nosed 38 special. He stated that there were plenty of on duty Officers plus Detectives at the scene or in route. I drove to Station 2 on Sherman Parkway to get an update of the bank robbery. That's when I learned that Officer Willie Bradley had been shot with a shotgun by one of the bank robbers. It was reported that as he lie on the sidewalk, he was shot again, point blank range. The bank robbers got away but were apprehended a short time later somewhere downtown. The money was also recovered. Willie was in intensive care for days but thank God, he survived. Willie was my friend and I would gladly give my life for him and I'm sure he would do the same for me. I just learned today that Willie had passed. Not sure when. God bless Officer William Bradley. One of New Haven's finest and brave Officers. The saddest part of being a Police Officer, black or white in those days, we were called pigs by adults and children alike. There is so much more to this story but I do not have all the facts. My good friend, Inspector Charlie Grady, who was involved in the chase, may be able to provide more details and facts. •

In the late fall of 1965, at about 9:30 PM on a Friday night, I was dispatched to the apartments on Fowler Street just off of Amity Road. The complaint was a loud party. Usually these kinds of complaints did not warrant a backup car so I arrived alone. I knocked on the front door. A young college aged lady answered the door. "Hello Officer. What's wrong?" I told her that I was on a complaint of a noisy party and asked her if this was her apartment. "No, Officer but I will get him for you." She invited me in. There was a party going on but it appeared to be orderly. Maybe a little loud from a stereo playing, but orderly. A man approached me and identified himself as the tenant. I told him a neighbor complained of a noisy party and asked him to tone it down a little. He was polite and agreeable. I spotted a small spinet piano in the living room. I asked what make it was. He said it was a Wurlitzer and asked if I played. "I do," I said. "I have a Baldwin Acrosonic at home." "Would you like to try it?" he asked. "Well," looking at my watch, "just for a minute." I sat down and played a few bars of a Chopin Nocturne. The next thing I heard was that Station 2 was calling me on my car radio. "Calling car 21. Car 21, Call the Station." I used the man's phone. I called Station 2 on Sherman Parkway. Sergeant Lang answered. "Serge. Bob Meyerholz. What's up?" "Where the hell are you Bob?" "On Fowler Street sir, the noise complaint." "Are you playing a piano?" "Yes sir." The lady across the street that made the complaint just called and said the cop was now playing the piano. Causing more noise. "Bob. Get the hell out of there. Get your ass back in your car and get the hell out of there. I sent you on a noise complaint and now you are part of the noise." I couldn't argue with my Sergeant. Guess he was right. I wouldn't consider Chopin piano music as actual noise, but I guess that was a matter of opinion. I got the tenants name, phone number and other needed info. I got in my car and drove away to another location and wrote a noise complaint report. •

OLD GIRLFRIEND (PART ONE)

The following two-part story will probably be the most personal story I ever wrote. In 1953 I was age seventeen. I met a girl named Valerie at Savin Rock. I now had a 1941 green Pontiac, four-door sedan – a step up from my 1936 Chevy, business coupe. Valerie lived at 774 Washington Avenue in West Haven. We fell in love or at least, I fell in love. One Sunday afternoon, Val's mom invited me to Sunday dinner. The first thing Val's mom asked me at the dinner table was, "So what college are you going to when you get out of high school?" "I'm not going to college ma'am. My dad's a Rail Road man who makes a small salary. I want to be a Concert Pianist and I'm trying to do it on my own." Not a word further was discussed at the dinner table. I left and thanked them for dinner. That night Val called me, crying. "I can't see you anymore, Bob." "Why Val?" "Because mom said you are not the boy for me. She wants me to marry a guy with a college education." All my love and respect for this girl meant nothing. A college degree was mother's requirement. The next year, of course, I met my Mary roller skating and we fell in love and got married. My love, respect and devotion to Mary was all that Mary was asking for. Five years later in 1958, I was a married man with two children and working at Nelke Motors located at 226 Whalley Avenue. I was Parts Manager and my uniform was a white shirt and blue tie and blue trousers. It was a Studebaker, Packard, Mercedes-Benz dealership. I drove a beautiful older 1951 black Packard that was my own personal vehicle. One afternoon on my way home from work, I saw Val on Temple Street waiting for a bus. I pulled over to the curb and picked her up and gave her a ride home in my Packard. "Wow," she said, "nice car." She looked at my white shirt that said, Bob and Parts Manager on the other side. "You are doing okay." "Yes Val. Without a college degree. I have a good job, beautiful wife and 2 gorgeous kids. And you Val?" "I'm married and my husband works at Stop and Shop in the produce department as he goes to college." "So nice to see you Val," I said as I dropped her off at 774 Washington Avenue. Still living at mom's house. Through my once broken heart, I still maintained my respect for her. The love was gone and now belonged to my Mary. Years later I met her mom on a bus trip. I will tell that chapter in a little while. •

OLD GIRLFRIEND (PART TWO)

In 1972, while I was a Police Officer with The City of New Haven, I also drove a coach style bus part time for Chieppo Bus Company. One spring morning, I was scheduled to pick up The West Haven Ladies Auxiliary Club on Center Street. My schedule was to pick up 45 ladies and take them to the Gelston House for lunch and then to the Godspeed opera House. I was in my glory with these older ladies on my bus as my love for my mom extended to all ladies. I assisted each one getting on the bus. There she was, Valerie's mother, getting on my bus. Much older, she did not recognize me, but I recognized her. I showed her the same courtesy and respect as I had shown the other ladies. Sometime later, we arrived at the Gelston House. I had some magazines with me to read as I sat on the bus as the ladies enjoyed their day. The last lady off the bus said, "Come on driver. You are having lunch with us." "Really?" I was overwhelmed. Drivers usually wait on their buses. After lunch they had a ticket for me to see an opera. This lady stayed right with me. After the opera they had a ferry boat trip scheduled to go up the Connecticut River as far as Katharine Hepburn's house and back. I was invited. This very nice lady, who was in charge of the trip, sat next to me on the ferry boat. "So, you like driving a bus, she asked?" "Yes ma'am, I do. It's part time. I am a New Haven Police Officer." "You are?" "Yes ma'am." She asked me to call her by her first name, which I now forgot. "Could I tell you a secret?" I asked. "Yes you can." I told her that I had a girl friend named Valerie L. and that her mom was on this bus. "I know her," she said. "Did she recognize you?" "No, that was a long time ago when I was a teenager." I told her the whole story and I asked her not to mention it until after I left all the ladies back in West Haven. I said, "Please tell her that Bob Meyerholz is a respectable Police Officer with a wonderful family whom I love very much. Please tell her I work extra jobs to provide for my family, in spite of my dad's financial inability to send me to college." This brought tears to the lady's eyes and we hugged. She was the last one off my bus and she said, "Let me catch her before she gets in her car. I can't wait to tell her." •

ICE CREAM STORE BURGLARY-COLD CASH

There was an ice cream store, Cumberland Farms, on the southwest corner of Ferry and Peck Street in 1968. In a five week period, someone had broken into the store during the night three times and robbed the cash register. Each time, hundreds of dollars were stolen. One cold night in the winter, I got a call that someone was breaking into the rear door. I sped to the scene silent with no siren or red lights and arrived within minutes of the call but just missed the guy(s) who apparently fled through the back yards. The back door was ripped from the hinges and was lying on the ground. Not sure if someone was still in the store, I called for backup and I entered the store with my Colt 38 police special in my right hand and my flashlight in my left. Unlike in the movies where cops always roam around in the dark, I turned all the store lights on and after a complete search there was no one in the store. The cash register drawer was wide open and empty. I called my dispatcher and waited for the store's owner to respond. It was now 3:00 AM. The owner responded from Guilford. When he arrived he said, "This time the bastards didn't get my money. This time I hid my money." he said. He opened the ice cream freezer and selected from the back row, a half gallon of maple walnut ice cream. The ice cream box was empty except for being full of money. He said the last three times; they smashed the cash register and stole hundreds of dollars in cash and hundreds of dollars more to replace the cash register. I said, "Why don't you deposit the store receipts at night?" He said he was robbed at the bank night deposit box one time before. I realized that the New Haven I grew up in was changing, and not for the better. •

MOTORCYCLE ON SIDEWALK-TOADS PLACE

One Saturday night in 1976, I worked a show at Toad's Place on York Street. With two Officers assigned with me. I was stationed outside. A normal crowd had gathered on the sidewalk waiting to enter. At about 9:00 PM I heard a motorcycle coming from Grove Street. The motorcycle entered a driveway on the north side of the building and drove down the sidewalk and stopped near the front entrance. It appeared to be a new red Harley Davidson. The operator turned the engine off and before I could tell him to get the bike off the sidewalk, he said, "Hey Officer. Can you watch my bike?" "Number one, I am on duty and number two, motor vehicles are not allowed on the sidewalk." Just driving on the sidewalk is illegal. I told him to get the bike off the sidewalk. He said, "Man, that's an $18,000.00 Harley and I'm not parking it on the street." I said, "You are not parking it on the sidewalk either. Get it off the sidewalk now." He looked at me and got on the bike and started the engine. He revved it up then jumped the curb in front of me and drove into the middle of York Street and started doing circles and at the same time, giving me the middle finger. Then he proceeded to drive south on York Street and made a right turn into Broadway. I got on my portable police radio and put out a short broadcast to all units in the area of Broadway to be on the lookout for a red Harley operated recklessly by a white male approximately age twenty to twenty-five. Ten minutes later, a patrol car stopped him in front of Henry's Auto Parts on Whalley Avenue and Sperry Street. Someone from Toad's Place gave me a ride to that location. Once there I identified him and charged him with reckless driving. He mouthed off by saying 'F**k pigs' and was further charged with breach of peace and placed in the paddy wagon. The was a very bad neighborhood to leave a new Harley overnight on the street so I offered to tow his bike for safe keeping. He refused to let me tow his Harley so we left it right there. By Monday morning the Harley was gone. Stolen. Monday afternoon the young man and his mother came to the police station to make a complained against me because the bike was stolen. I told his mom that he refused to let me tow it from a bad neighborhood. She looked at him and whacked him in the face and they both left the police station. The Harley was never recovered. •

Sometime in the late summer of 1966, I was working the 8:00 AM to 4:00 PM shift in Fair Haven. As I approached a red traffic light on Blatchley Avenue and Grand Avenue, I noticed the car in front of me – a Renault Dauphine had a cardboard license plate. The law says if you lose a license plate, first report it to the Motor Vehicle Department and then make a temporary plate out of cardboard with the exact plate numbers on it. Well, this cardboard plate said, 'DC-1 New Haven' on the top and 'Connecticut' on the bottom. I thought to myself, "Something is not right." I pulled alongside of the young operator and told him to pull over when the light turned green, Instead be sped off, while the light was still red and turned left into Grand Avenue. We passed Ferry Street and proceeded east on Grand Avenue, then turned into Clinton Avenue. Another left into Chatham Street toward ferry Street. The low speed chase continued for approximately 20 minutes. Finally we were traveling on Front Street and he turned sharp left into the projects when the car rolled over and landed on its side. This young man climbed out of the broken side window and ran toward the apartments where I tackled him. Turns out that he owned the car, only it was not registered so he made his own cardboard license plate from the brown color of the inside of a Cheerios box. I kept the cardboard plate as evidence for court but I lost it years ago. I made a paper plate from my memory just to show what I saw that day. Connecticut license plates always started with 2 letters and then 3 numbers. Example: 'AV-733' but never 'DC-1.' •

YOUTH TRIED TO RUN DOWN POLICE OFFICER

The following story will be the most serious story I ever told.

In Police Academy, we were warned that there are people out there that would run you down or gun you down to escape. On December 16, 1961, a Saturday night, just after midnight when I came on duty, I noticed a car on Grand Avenue driving recklessly. The car, a 1950 grey Mercury hot rod was stopped for a traffic light on Wallace Street. I cautiously approached the car on foot and motioned to the driver to pull to the curb. Instead, he floored it, spinning the tires and disappeared heading toward downtown. The CT license plate was 455-056. I will never forget that plate. I went to the call box and put out a broadcast for all patrol cars to be on the lookout for this vehicle. Then I learned that the license plate 455-056 on the car was stolen. Monday afternoon December 18th, I was working overtime on Wooster Street in the afternoon. Suddenly, the same car appeared and was heading straight for the Turnpike at the end of Wooster Street. The 19-year-old driver, months later was identified as Joseph Colavolpe, had two other youths with him in the front seat. He got stuck in traffic and I tried to pull him out of the car as he spin his tires on the snow. I had the driver's door open but suddenly, the traffic cleared and Colavolpe slammed the door in my arm and held me there as he sped off. I was dragged for one half block until my arm slid free from the door. I tumbled in the street and almost slid under his car. As I lay in the middle of the street, I pulled out my 38 Colt revolver and took aim at the rear window. Just before I pulled the trigger, I realized that I could possible kill an innocent teen sitting in the front seat. I was justified killing the driver who attempted to kill me, but I was not prepared to kill an innocent teenager. I let the car disappear up the turnpike ramp but vowed that I would get that guy, if it took me the rest of my career. On April 13, 1962, I found the Mercury at Slim's Auto Body on East Street. I got a tip that the car was repainted black but Colavople didn't have the money to pay for the paint job. The stolen license plate 455-056 was found under the front seat. Colavolpe was in the Country Jail for allegedly raping a young woman. I got a warrant for his arrest and served it to him in County Jail. He was shocked that I found him. He was unable to pay the $475.00 fine so he served 180 days in County Jail. •

MEMORIES OF A RETIRED COP

BRAVE NEW YORK POLICE OFFICERS MURDERED

In February 1972, I was working the 8:00 AM to 4:00 PM shift at Station 2 on Sherman Parkway. I remembered it being a Monday morning when the Captain read off at roll call that two New York Police Officers from the 9th Precinct, were shot to death as they emerged from a diner shortly before 11:00 PM. Both Officers were shot in the back. One officer was reportedly still moving while lying on the sidewalk so the cowards shot him again at point blank range and took their police guns. Both Officers were Marine vets and served together in Viet Nam. They were both in their twenties. One Officer was black and the other Officer was white. The Captain was asking for volunteers, who were off that coming Thursday to attend the funeral services for these brave police officers. I was off duty on Thursdays and Fridays that month so I volunteered to show my respect by attending the funeral service. About thirty New Haven Police Officers were available and volunteered. We went to New York that Thursday morning in our converted blue school bus. There were Police Officers from all over the country there: New York, New Jersey, Pennsylvania, Connecticut, Rhode Island, etc. We all formed a close bond that morning with our brothers in blue of the 9th Precinct. Thinking that we had our problems here in New Haven until hearing the horror stories of being a New York Police Officer. The suspects were eventually identified as Black Liberation Army members who killed the Officers in retaliation for the recent death of a Black Panther member. One suspect was killed in a police shootout one month later in Philadelphia, Pennsylvania. The other suspect was still at large. May God bless all the Police Officers and Fire Fighters killed in the line of duty while protecting us and our families. I was so proud to be able to honor these two brave officers who were murdered in cold blood by being shot in the back as they left a diner after their lunch break. •

STOLEN POLICEMAN'S GUN

One warm day in 1974, on a Saturday morning, I was off duty and buying used parts for my own car at Tarducci's Used Auto Parts on Middletown Avenue. John Tarducci was one of the nicest guys. Whatever I needed for my own car, I would bring my toolbox and remove the parts I needed for myself. Then I would stop at the office and tell them what I had and I would pay for them. For small parts, John would tell me to go next door to Almar's Diner and buy the guys working in the yard a hot cup of coffee and bring back a hot coffee black with sugar for him. It was about 10:00 AM. I took a break and walked over to Almar's and purchased coffee and pastries for all the guys working at Tarducci's. It was John Sr., John Jr., Henry, Joey, Arthur and maybe one or two more guys, plus myself. We were in the front office having our coffee when a man walked in the front office door. I had my badge in my pocket. I also had enough back up to stop a small riot. The man pulls out a fully loaded Colt revolver with a 6 inch barrel and places it on the counter. He said, "I'm selling this gun for $50.00 man. Got the bullets in it too." Being in greasy work clothes, the man had no idea that I was an off duty Police Officer. I reached for the revolver, pretending to be interested in buying it. I picked it up, looked it over because it looked familiar. It looked like my on duty service revolver. On the handle it was engraved with 'N.H.P.D.' with the name 'Colt' and a serial number. One year previous, a New Haven Policeman had a burglary to his home and his Colt service revolver was stolen. I pulled out my badge with my greasy hands, and at the same time tackled the man, not giving him a chance to grab the gun. He had no idea what hit him. I was rough because this could be my life if he grabbed the gun. He said, "Man, guess I come to the wrong place." I had no handcuffs with me but the boys held him while I called Headquarters. It was later confirmed that this was the stolen Colt police revolver. The man was charged with possession of stolen property and carrying a pistol without a permit. He said that he bought the Colt revolver, fully loaded on the street from an unidentified man. You just can't make this stuff up. •

DUNKIN DONUT THEFT INCIDENT

In 1968 one Saturday afternoon at about 2:00 PM, I was on patrol in a police car downtown. I got a call of a robbery at Dunkin-Donuts located at Church and Center streets. I proceeded quickly but with caution. I parked a ½ block away and walked to the location. Once I got a visual, business appeared to be normal. Robbery could mean anything – from an actual person with a gun, to a pickpocket, or pocket book snatch. As I entered the front door, I noticed the front of the cigarette machine to the left, was leaning against the wall and assorted cigarette packs and change were on the floor. The manager came out from the kitchen area and stated that five tall teen agers entered through the front door with either a large screwdriver or crow bar and within seconds, pried the front of the cigarette machine off and grabbed as many cigarette packs as they could carry and the change box and walked out the same door and crossed over to the Mall and disappeared. They held up traffic as they crossed the street. The restaurant was packed with Saturday shoppers and families with children. There were plenty of witnesses but none would give statements. One man who was with his family said, "Officer, if you were off duty and had your wife and children with you, would you try to stop them?" My honest answer to him was, "No, especially the one with the large screwdriver in his hands. I would have gone in the kitchen and called for backup. Civilians are not required to do that." The youths split up in the Mall and were never apprehended. They all disappeared in the crowded Mall. Today, cameras would probably have recorded the crime. •

JAMES STREET GUN FIRE

One Saturday afternoon in the summer of 1969, I was dispatched to a house on James Street, between Market and Clay Streets for possible gunshots. It was just after 3:00 PM when I approached the first floor apartment. I also heard gunshots coming from the two family home. It sounded like the first floor. No SWAT teams and no bullet proof vests in those days. We did the best we could. My backup and I climbed the two or three front porch stairs to the front porch. We stood on both sides of the front door and I knocked several times with my nightstick. No answer, so we pushed open the hallway door and found the first floor kitchen door wide open. We entered with guns drawn and discovered two highly intoxicated men sitting at the kitchen table. One was slumped over. There were also two pistols on the kitchen table. One was a 22 caliber JC Higgins 9 shot revolver and the other one was a 25 caliber automatic Beretta. Both guns were empty and still warm to the touch. Both men were searched and then handcuffed. While sitting at the kitchen table, drinking whiskey and beer, they stated they got involved in a heated argument. Both men fired point blank range at each other numerous shots, but every bullet missed its mark. There were bullet holes in the walls, the ceiling and in the floor. Approximately fifteen bullets in all were fired. We originally charged them with intoxication and attempted murder but when the case went to trial, the Judge reduced the charge to attempted assault. He remarked what lousy shots both men were, probably saving their lives. They both got off with a suspended sentence and fifty hours of community service. The guns were confiscated and never returned to them. •

THE DAY I RETIRED

When I retired from the New Haven Police Department on December 10, 1978, we had a retirement dinner at The Laurel View Country Club in Hamden. Eleven Police Officers, including myself, were retiring and were honored that night. One by one each retiring Police Officer's name was called to receive their retirement plaque and a handshake from Officer Arthur Baker for a job well done. Each officer was noted for something that they contributed to as a Police Officer. Some were honored for how many parking tickets they gave out or how many motor vehicle arrests or how many burglars they caught in their career. Mary and I sat there, patiently, waiting for my name to be called. Mary wondered if anyone ever noticed how much I loved children or did anyone ever notice that I taught myself how to speak, read and write Spanish. What are they going to say about me? I was an average officer with an abundance of people skills that were given to me by God. I didn't learn them in school. Love is in your heart, and not in a book. Finally, my name was called. Nervously I walked up to the podium with normal clapping that every officer received before me. Officer Art Baker handed me my retirement plaque and shook my hand. "Here we have Officer Robert Meyerholz, also known as Officer Bob to the Westville kids. To the Hispanic Community, he was known as Bobby El Policia." A few laughs. "Bob did his job well and was an average officer," Art said. "But I will tell you this. I have never known any Police Officer with as much love, compassion and caring for his fellow man than Bob Meyerholz." To me, that meant more than the most parking tickets, the most motor vehicle arrests, who knows the Mayor, who knows the Chief, etc. When I got back to my table, Mary was crying. "Are you okay, honey?" I asked. "Yes, I am so proud of you Bob." That's how I ended my career. The most important person in my life, my Mary, was proud of me. That's all that mattered to me at that moment. I could not ask for a better send off. •

MV ACCIDENT FARREN AND FERRY STREETS

I have a story about a Newspaper Reporter. Most of them are hardworking and decent people that provide a necessary service to citizens. In 1975, I had an incident with a New Haven Register reporter who lacked common sense or just had a heart of stone. It was sometime in the fall of 1975, I was dispatched to the intersection of Farren Avenue and Fulton Street to a very serious automobile accident involving two vehicles and personal injuries. In my earlier career, I was trained in major accident investigation involving personal injuries and major property damage. Someone ran the red light and broadsided another vehicle, causing serious injuries to the female driver. She had to be extracted from her extensively damaged car by the Fire Department, using the Hurst tool. With the assistance of another Officer, we rerouted traffic away from the accident scene. An Ambulance was standing by with the rear door open, to expedite the trip to the hospital. After the woman was freed from the twisted metal of her car, the Ambulance Attendants were rushing her on a stretcher to the ambulance. A New Haven Register Reporter stood by the back door of the ambulance, blocking it while he took his picture of the woman on the stretcher. They had to stop while his guy took his picture. I physically pushed him backward, out of the Ambulance Attendants way. I never put my hands on anyone, but when I saw an ignorant reporter, stand in the path of a severely injured woman, just to get his morning edition picture for the Journal Courier, I had to do something. I was there to assist the injured parties, not to cater to a Reporter. When the ambulance left the scene with red lights and siren blaring, this Reporter approached me as I was investigating the accident scene and said, "I'm reporting you to your Chief. You put your hands on me." I said, "Next time you ever get in the way of an emergency workers way, I will arrest you." I put everything in my accident report, including his name and the fact that I physically pushed him backwards, out of the way to permit the Ambulance Attendants to get the severely injured woman in that ambulance and off to the hospital as quickly as possible. I never heard another word about the incident. I paid the woman a visit three days later. She was doing fine. •

One night in late 1969, maybe November, we were doing radar enforcement on Quinnipiac Avenue near Eastern Street because neighbors were complaining of speeders. I was the chase car. After stopping several speeding cars, I gave some tickets and some written and verbal warnings. I got a call from the radar car that a blue Chevy Nova was preceding at 56 MPH in the posted 35 MPH zone. I got behind the Nova with my blue and white police car and displayed the red lights and finally I hit the siren button when the Nova failed to stop for me. The Nova turned right into Glen Haven Road with me in pursuit and finally pulled into a driveway on Oakridge Road. A lone female got out of the car and ran to the front door and entered the home and closed the door. I called for my partner to meet me there. We knocked on the front door and a man came to the door. I asked to talk to the lady that was driving the Chevy Nova parked in the driveway. The lady came to the door. Here I am with my partner, both in full police uniforms with two blue and white police cars parked in front of her house. "Ma'am, why didn't you stop for my signal, blocks away where I tried to stop you?" Her answer, "My husband told me to never stop for anyone unless I know them." "Lady, I am a uniformed police officer driving a marked police car equipped with red lights and siren." "But, I don't know you and I was doing what my husband told me to do." I asked for her driver's license and car registration and gave her a ticket for exceeding the posted speed limit and failure to obey an officer's signal. I handed her the ticket and said, "My name and badge number is on the ticket, so now, you know me. Have a nice evening ma'am." The husband asked to speak to me in private. We walked to the driveway. He said, "I want to apologize to you officer. I told her to never stop for an unmarked plain car, unless you know the person." There are police impersonators out there, which I totally agreed with him. She probably would have been given a verbal warning, had she stopped for my signal. •

ATTEMPTED RAPE-WEST ROCK PARK

In April 1975, I was on patrol one Saturday night in West Rock Park. It was after midnight at about 1:30 AM. This was just after a young man and woman were shot numerous times by a man with a 22 cal. rifle in West Rock Park. The woman was shot right times and died from her injuries. The man was shot six times and survived. The murder occurred in Hamden, just over the town line at the top of West Rock (Baldwin Drive). We were on very high alert knowing that in any vehicle, parked or in motion, there could be a killer. As I was ascending the long winding road to the top of West Rock, I observed a car in front of me turn left into one of the lover's lanes and then disappear. I was unable to make out the license plate number. Any potential back up was a long way off. I reported my location to my dispatcher. I advised my dispatcher that I would be out of my cruiser on foot, checking on the car that just drove into the lover's lane. I parked my cruiser on the main road. With my flashlight in my left hand and my right hand resting on my 38 special, I walked into the narrow and dark lover's lane. Suddenly. I heard a woman scream. I got on my portable police radio and requested immediate backup, telling the dispatcher my cruiser was parked on the main road. Thank God I left my cruiser on the main road so my backup would know, exactly where I was. As I approached a parked vehicle from behind, I heard a woman scream again. Now, my 38 special was out. In the parked vehicle were three men and one woman. The three men were about to rape the woman. Later, I learned that the three men picked up the intoxicated woman in a local bar and offered her a ride home. In the dark, I announced myself as a Police Officer. I got the girl out of the car first and told her to follow the dirt road and run for my car. One at a time, I got the men out of the car and lined them up. I led them out to the main road at gunpoint and made them lie down on their stomachs on the ground. It was too risky to try to search all three while I was alone, so I waited for my back up to arrive. Within minutes, two or three back up cars arrived. The three men were searched, handcuffed and placed in the back of a squad car. I took the young lady to St. Raphael's Hospital Emergency Room and from there I called her parents. The Detective Division took over my investigation. These three punks never had time to rape her. I was just in the right place at the right time. •

PUERTO RICAN CLUB AMBULANCE CALL

One Saturday night in December 1970, I was working at a dance at the Puerto Rican Club, located at 229 Grand Avenue, second floor. My partner, Officer Richard Kittrell, and I really enjoyed working the dances. The music, the people. Rich and I have been working at the Club for about four years, which is considered extra duty. Most of the people knew us and we knew them. We've both been to Hispanic weddings and birthday parties, all at the invitation of the Hispanic Community. There was a mutual respect there. Richard was working on the first floor at the club entrance door. I was working on the second floor where the dances were held. The bar was also located on the second floor. At about 9:00 PM, twi ladies came to me to report that another female had passed out and was hemorrhaging in the ladies room. Her name was Maria from New York City. Maria had given me a couple of books (novellas) in Spanish to help me practice the language. She was a friend. I entered the ladies room and found Maria lying on the floor in a small pool of blood. I immediately called for an ambulance and alerted Richard as to what was going on. An ambulance arrived and took Maria to Yale New Haven Hospital. The rest of the night was normal for a Saturday night but in the back of my mind, I was very concerned about Maria. The dance ended at 1:00 AM. After we cleared the dance floor I decided to take a ride to Yale New Haven Hospital. Maria was admitted and she was placed in a room on the second floor. I climbed the stairs and went to the Nurses' Station. Policeman in uniform are not restricted to most places. I asked how Maria H****** was doing. The two nurses at the desk started giggling, like two school girls. The Nurse said, "She's in room ***. You can visit her. She's awake. How is she, I asked?" More giggling. "She had a miscarriage." "What? A miscarriage?" Maria was awake and was glad to see me. I was also glad to see she was alright. A little weak but she was okay. I stayed for only five minutes. Very embarrassed, I said to myself, this was a bad idea. As I left, I tried to explain my friendship with Maria, but it was no use. The Nurses, said, "That's none of our business, Officer." More giggling. •

POLICEMAN WAKE UP FIREMAN

In December 1961, I was still a rookie on probation walking the different beats in New Haven. This particular night, I was on the midnight shift from 12:00 to 8:00 AM assigned to Dixwell Avenue, walking from Broadway to Munson Street. It was a bitter cold night. I had a partner, another rookie walking the beat with me. For the first 2 hours, we checked all our doors and windows in the different businesses on our beat to make sure they were completely secure. My older brother, Bill, was a New Haven Fireman stationed at Engine 6 located on Dixwell Avenue, north of Munson Street. Bill told me weeks earlier that if I were ever assigned at night, to a walking beat on Dixwell Avenue that his Battalion Chief said that I could come in out of the cold by using the unlocked back Fire house door. The Battalion Chief said I was welcome to come in as long as I was "quiet", and did not wake up the sleeping Fireman and to leave everything the way I found it. If I wanted a cup of coffee, to rinse out my cup. I remembered what my older brother, Bill, told me. At about 2:30 AM, I told my partner that we could go over to the Firehouse and warm up, rest our legs. Maybe have a cup of hot coffee, but we must be quiet and not wake up any of the Fireman. We walked the short distance to the Firehouse and quietly entered the back door. We decided to get off our feet so we very quietly each sat in the front seat of one of the fire engines that was parked there. All of a sudden, a loud siren was heard. I mean loud. My partner by mistake stepped on the siren button located on the floor of the fire engine. The Firehouse lights went on and the overhead doors opened and the Fireman came sliding down the poles. Before we were thrown out on our ear, we ran out the back door. The Battalion Chief was so angry because we woke up the entire Firehouse, including him. The next day, my brother called me at home. He was so angry. I can't repeat what he said to me. He eventually got over it and so did the Battalion Chief. •

STREET ROBBERY ON BARNETT STREET

In the summer of 1978, on a beautiful warm and sunny Sunday afternoon, I was dispatched to a possibly pocketbook snatch on Barnett Street, a very unusual call for this relatively safe neighborhood just off of Fountain Street. Upon arrival at the Barnett Street Address, I observed an elderly female lying in the street between a parked car and the sidewalk. She was bleeding from her nose. After calling for an ambulance, I administered first aid and provided as much comfort to her as the circumstances allowed. Her 38-year-old daughter, who lived on Barnett Street, stated that the lady was her 83-year-old mother. She had picked up her mother in Hamden and brought her to her house for Sunday dinner. As she was helping her mom get out of her car, two young 'punks' that had double parked a green Chevy next to the ladies car, knocked both woman to the ground and stole their pocketbooks before they fled in the Chevy. A neighbor, who witnessed the assault and robbery, wrote down the license plate number of the green Chevy that they got into along with a vague description. The witness also stated that she had observed the green Chevy double park next to the ladies car and two youths getting out. They walked around the car and attacked the woman. The ambulance arrived and both women were transported to Yale New Haven Hospital. In the mean time I obtained a written statement from the lone witness and ran a license plate check on the number she provided. Unfortunately, the green Chevy was reported stolen that morning from West Haven. I also put out a broadcast for the car and both occupants. Then I drove to Yale New Haven Hospital to check on the condition of both women. The elderly woman was being treated for a broken nose and a broken right hip. Yes, it brought tears to my eyes, looking at this elderly defenseless woman lying on a Hospital stretcher in pain. I cannot describe the anguish and frustration I was feeling. Her pocketbook contained only $6.00. The daughter suffered only a few bruises and she had about $40.00 in her pocketbook. The perpetrators were never caught. The stolen auto was recovered that afternoon in West Haven. People may live in the safest of neighborhoods but criminals drive cars. Sometimes stolen cars so it's imperative that you are always aware of your surroundings. Had these innocent women noticed a car double parking next to their own car, perhaps they would have at least been prepared and facing these two cowardly punks.

Amazingly, a punk will attack a person from behind but think twice if the person is facing and looking at them. I absolutely recommend that women carry a container of mace in their pocketbooks. It is legal to purchase but like any weapon, be absolutely sure you are justified in using it. •

CARNIVAL ON THE BOULEVARD

In 1971, there was a carnival on the Boulevard at the site of the old flea market. It was in the fall and ran from Thursday through Sunday night. I was one of two officers assigned to extra duty. We found out that carnival workers are a tough breed and they take care of their own problems. We were only there because the city had an ordinance that required a carnival of that size to employ two police officers. My partner and I split up as we patrolled the large crowd of people. It was a good, well-behaved crowd with many people patronizing the carnival that we knew. There was a commotion at the Gypsy Fortune Tellers tent. We both responded. What we found was two drunks sprawled out on the ground behind her tent. They made the mistake of insulting the Gypsy Fortune Teller and before we could get there, the carnival workers took care of business. I asked, "Who hit you guys?" "No one. We tripped and fell and now we are leaving." They took off like a bat out of hell. Sunday night the carnival closed at 11:00 PM. My partner and I got paid and we volunteered to work again with them if they ever came back to New Haven. That week, I developed a new found respect and understanding about carnival workers. I learned how hard working they were. Assembling and disassembling all the rides and tents and anything else that required assembly and disassembly. I learned that they were a family and looked out for one another. The next afternoon, they were packed and gone, on the way to Georgia to the next carnival. Never saw them again after that. •

CHANGE MISSING FROM BAR

One Saturday night in 1969, the officers planned to have a men's night out at Gag's Restaurant, located on Whalley Avenue just west of Winthrop Avenue. Gag's was a friendly cop bar, where a Policeman could relax after work among friends and enjoy a cold beer while off duty. There were approximately fourty off duty officers in the bar and restaurant area. We sat down to an excellent meal and then decided to wind down and have a few drinks. I was sitting at the bar with a cold beer in front of me. I had just paid for the beer with a $20.00 bill so my change, approximately $19.25 was on the bar next to my beer. My Sergeant challenged me to a game on the bowling machine. After a couple of games, I went to retrieve my beer and my change on the bar. There was a man sitting in my seat and my beer and change were gone. I said, "Excuse me, did you see my beer and change?" "Nope," he said. "Excuse me, I don't care if you are sitting in my seat and I don't care if you drank my beer but I want my change." "I didn't take your damn beer and change fella." Then he said, "Look, I just got out of prison and I know you guys are mostly cops so here's the money but I didn't take your change." He handed me a $20.00 bill. I said, "Thank you." Just then, two plain clothes Detectives got me aside and said, Bob, that man did not take your money but we know who did." "Who?" I asked. "You've had a few drinks so it's not the time to tell you but that man did not take your money. We'll tell you tomorrow at work, okay?" I gave the man the $20.00 back and apologized to him. I said, "I'm really sorry." We shook hands. The next day at work, the Detectives told me that the Bar Maid, the same woman we all knew and loved took my money. They were officially on duty there investigating numerous complaints from Gag's customers that their change was disappearing as they sat and drank at the bar or at times when they went to the men's room. That next Monday, with a warrant, the two Detectives arrested her for grand larceny. She allegedly stole thousands of dollars from customers. She would wipe off the bar and scoop up the money left on the bar, often, large amounts from the change left on the bar. What really hurt was we all tipped her very well and we all liked her. Some things in life are not what they appear to be. Some people that we like and trust will stab you in the back, if you let them. •

On December 25, 1966, my dad was dying from cancer in a convalescent home in West Haven. It was Christmas day and I was on duty in Fair Haven. I was working the 4:00 PM to 12:00 midnight shift. At about 6:30 PM, I asked my Sergeant for permission to cross the West Haven city line with my police car to visit my dad, using my allowed lunch time. The Sergeant said, "Sorry Bob but I can't give you permission to leave the New Haven area." I understood his concern if I had an accident in West Haven, he would be in big trouble. I absolutely understood that. About one hour later, not admitting to leaving New Haven, the next thing happened, I was driving north on I-91 when the engine blew in my police car. A 1966, three-month-old Ford Custom police car. I coasted off I-91 and rolled down the State Street exit ramp and into the old Connecticut Company property. This is where my assigned beat was. I called my Sergeant on my police radio and gave him my location and told him my police car broke down. He arrived and we opened the hood. There was a large hole in the engine block where a piston broke and came through the block. The Sergeant asked me where this happened. "There sir, on I-91." I said, pointing to the highway, part of my patrol area. There was an engine oil trail from I-91 to where my car finally stopped. He looked at me and said, "Merry Christmas Bob, to you and your family. Let's tow your car to the police garage and let's get you another car. Okay, Bob?" "Yes Sergeant." When the engine blew on I-91 near Trumbull Street, it was like something was pushing my police car off the highway and into my authorized patrol area. Any car with a blown engine just doesn't roll that far. It felt like someone was pushing my car from the back? One month later, on January 29th, 1967 my dad passed away. Not admitting to anything, but glad I got to see you on Christmas Day, Dad. I love you. •

CARELESS VICTIM-STUPID THIEF

This is a story about a careless victim and a stupid thief. One afternoon in the fall of 1973, I was dispatched to the Yale Co-Op on Broadway. Store Security was physically detaining two females for a reported theft. Upon arrival, I spoke to the cashier who was the complainant. She stated that she and another female employee went out to lunch together at approximately 1:00 PM. They walked across the street to a Restaurant for lunch. I believe the Restaurant was called the Yankee Doodle. The other girl was a floor salesperson. They both sat in a booth after hanging up their coats on a coat hook at the end of the booth. The store cashier also hung up her pocketbook with her coat. Bad idea. Anyway, after lunch, the cashier went to retrieve her wallet from her pocketbook to pay for lunch. The pocketbook was still hanging on the hook, but her wallet was missing. A search of the area failed to turn up the wallet. The salesperson paid cash for the meal. Approximately forty-five minutes later, after the two girls returned to work, the cashier was waiting on two ladies. They purchased a small portable battery operated television and some clothing. The customer handed the casher a credit card for the purchase. The credit card had the cashiers name on it. At first, the cashier thought it was a coincidence that the lady had the same name, but then realized it was her own credit card. When last seen, the credit card was in her wallet, which was just stolen less than one hour ago. The cashier kept a cool head and pushed a button to alert store security. She detained the two ladies by telling them she was waiting for approval of the credit card sale. Security arrived and held the two ladies until police arrived. I charged both with being in possession of a stolen credit card and using a stolen credit card to make a purchase under $200.00. After the paddy wagon left the store, I asked the cashier how she lost her wallet. When she told me, she left it hanging on a coat hook at the end of the booth in a Restaurant; I told her that it was a dumb idea to do that. Real dumb. •

ONE AFTERNOON IN JUNE *1966*

One afternoon in June 1966, at approximately 5:00 PM, I was dispatched to a two-family home on Clay Street between Popular Street and Blatchley Avenue, for a reportedly domestic dispute between a husband and wife. I arrived before my backup. I could hear a woman screaming as I pulled up to the house, so I didn't wait. I climbed the stairs to the second floor where the screaming was coming from. I knocked on the door. This mean looking guy opened the door. A woman was crying in the background. The guy said to me that nothing was wrong so you can leave and tried to close the door but I held it open. I walked right past him to the kitchen where the lady was washing her face in the kitchen sink. She was pretty badly beaten up. I asked her who did this to her and she pointed to the guy. She identified the guy as her husband. "Do you want him arrested?" I asked. Note: This was before the domestic violence laws were passed. She said, "Yes, I do." "Are you willing to go to court and testify against him?" I asked. "Yes, I am," she answered. I advised the man that he was under arrest for assaulting his wife. Then I read him his rights. As we were walking down the narrow stairs with the guy in front of me, he spun around and grabbed me and tried to throw me down the stairs. We wrestled on the stairway and I got the best of him and he went down, head first. As he landed at the bottom of the stairway, his head went right through the wall, just under a window in the hallway. A little higher and he would have gone straight through the window. His head was imbedded in the plaster wall, right to his shoulders. Now, finally, my backup arrived. I could not get his head out of the wall. We both tried. I called the Fire Department. The Fireman arrived and broke the wall around his head and pulled him out of the plaster and wood slats used in old houses. He was a mess, but any man that beats a woman deserves nothing less. I called a Sergeant to the scene for my own protection. After explaining that the man tried to throw me down the stairs, he agreed I did the right thing in protecting myself. The Sergeant also observed the lady's face, which was by now starting too blacked from the beating she took from him. The man was not injured outside of plaster in his nose, ears, eyes and mouth. Maybe his pride was hurt. Most woman beaters are no match for a real man. •

In the summer of 1962, I was still a rookie and walking the beat downtown. I finally completed my probation and I was now rotating my shift from days to midnights to the afternoon shift. This particular day, I was working from 8:00 AM to 4:00 PM. Enforcing parking violations was a big part of the day shift. As I walked north on Church Street, between Chapel and Court Streets, I noticed a black limousine double parked in front of a bank. It was not a Cadillac or Lincoln or Chrysler, but a Checker Marathon limo. I've heard of Checker taxicabs but not a Checker Limo. I approached the Chauffer driven vehicle and as I was about to ask the driver to keep moving when a well-dressed gentleman came running out. There was a beautiful Collie sticking his head out the partially opened backside window. He thanked me for being patient and he identified himself as Edwin Pugsley, the retired vice president of Winchester's. He wanted to chat but the vehicle was double-parked and in violation. I instructed the driver to find a parking space across the street. He did and he even put money in the parking meter. I was interested to know more about this Checker Marathon Limo. Mr. Pugsley stated that he had it built special so that his collie dog would have plenty of room in the back. Mr. Pugsley was also an inventor and he had some part in developing the M1 Army rifle. He lived on Leetes Island Road in Guilford. Mr. Pugsley was impressed that I didn't just hand his Chauffer a parking ticket and that I gave him a chance to move the vehicle. He certainly could have afforded to pay for a parking ticket. I explained that if someone is sitting in the driver's seat, with the motor running, I always gave the driver the option to move his car first. Police/Public relations were always a high priority to me. I was invited to the Pugsley home on my next day off. I felt honored to know personally such a fine man. We became friends. Being a Police Officer means using common sense. The enormous authority given to a Police officer was meant to be used wisely. •

GREYHOUND BUS TO NEW YORK

After graduating from Police Academy in March 1961, I was assigned a walking beat downtown on the 4:00 PM to 12:00 AM shift. I met a lot of old time Policeman. One old timer said, "Do you know that you can ride free on most Greyhound buses if you show your police badge? Of course if there is room on the bus. You can also take your family with you. The catch is: if there is trouble on the bus, you must assist the bus driver. A drunk or something like that." "I didn't know that," I said. A few months later on a Sunday morning, I decided to take Mary and my daughter's Terry, age eight, and Alice, age six, to New York. We drove to the Greyhound terminal located on George Street. The New York bus pulled in. I discretely and politely approached the driver and showed him my badge. "How many?" "Four including myself," I answered. He looked at his itinerary and said, "I have four extra seats. Put your family onboard." "Thank you," I said. The girls were so excited. First time on a large bus with a bathroom. They wore a hole in the aisle going back and forth to the bathroom. Mary and I were also excited. After a pleasant trip, we pulled into the Port Authority terminal in New York. After getting off the bus we walked out into the street and flagged down a yellow cab. I got in the front seat with the driver and the girls climbed into the back seat. I told him we were going to the theater district. As we drove, I noticed a picture of an ugly man with a number on his chest on the dashboard. Thinking like a Policeman and remembering studying about mug shots, I said, "What's he wanted for?" The cab suddenly pulled to the curb. "Get out of my cab." I turned around and looked at the driver. That picture was his photo cab license ID. Mary said, "Why did you say that to him?" "I don't know. I'm stupid, I guess. Sorry." Mary said, "Now he's calling all the other cabs to report this and now we won't get a ride from anyone." I did hail the next cab and he took us downtown. The rest of the day was perfect. We saw a moving and had a hot dog and did some shopping. Now we were tired and hungry and broke and we wanted to go home. We walked to the Port Authority and waited for our 9:35 PM bus. The bus pulled in and I showed my badge to the driver. He looked at his itinerary and said, "sorry, no room. My bus is full with paying passengers." "When is the next bus?" I asked. "12:45 AM." We sat down and waited the three hours. •

MEMORIES OF A RETIRED COP

Tired, broke and hungry, we had about three hours until the next bus to New Haven. Mary said, "Wait a minute. I have our checkbook in my pocketbook." "Come on Mary and girls, let's find a restaurant and get something to eat." We walked one block and found a restaurant that wasn't too fancy. We walked in and were seated. I told the waitress that we only had a personal check with us. "Sorry sir, but we absolutely do not accept personal checks." I politely asked for the manager. He was polite but my police badge meant nothing to him. I'''ve heard that story one-hundred times and the badge can be purchased on FOIST (First) Avenue for $5.00." "Please mister, we really need your help. I'm a New Haven, Connecticut Police Officer showing my family a good time." The nanager then said, "If you can find a New York Police Officer to vouch for you, I will accept your personal check." "Wait here," I said to the girls. I took off up 42nd street looking for a cop, I found Officer Murphy. I explained our situation and pleaded with him to help a brother Police Officer. He asked me a few questions that only a Policeman would know. I answered them all. "Come on Ladd. Lets take care of your family." We walked in the restaurant and Officer Murphy spoke to the manager. The manager came over. "I am Mr. Amato. We will accept your personal check. Enjoy your meal." "Thank you sir," we said. We all thanked Officer Murphy. We had a nice meal and then I walked up the cashier with my personal check. "What's this?" the girl said. "We don't accept personal checks." "It was approved by Mr. Amato." "Well, he left for the day. I can't accept this." My daughter's started to cry. Mary was upset. I was upset but I had to control my anger. There was another casher on break. We sat and waited for her to come back. She did come back and said, "Mr. Amato approved this check." She was so nice compared to the rude cashier. "Thank you miss!" I wanted to hug her. "Thank you so much. There are 500 New Haven Policeman that will know about your Restaurant. But, this young lady needs some training in customer relations," I said, pointing to the rude cashier. We caught our bus at 12:45 with plenty of empty seats and headed back home to good old New Haven, Connecticut. •

MAN SHOT OVER SALT & PEPPER DISPUTE

In the summer of 1962, shortly after being assigned to my own police car, I was dispatched to Brown's Restaurant, located at 53 Dixwell Avenue at 2:00 AM. A man had bought a half fried chicken at the Bar-B-Q, located on the corner of Dixwell Avenue and Webster Street. The Bar-B-Q was take-out only so there was nowhere to sit down and eat your food. The man walked one block to Brown's Restaurant with the chicken in the bag. He entered the restaurant, which was open all night, and sat at the counter, asking for a glass of water. Then he opened the bag with the chicken and reached for the salt and pepper. This was too much for Mr. Brown, so he pulled out a pistol and shot the man once in the chest. When I arrived, the man crawled out onto the sidewalk. I called for an ambulance and the man was rushed to Yale New Haven Hospital. The man survived the gunshot wound and Mr. Brown was charged with attempted murder. He felt justified because the man bought food at another restaurant, asked for a glass of free water, and then stole the salt and pepper from Mr. Brown. The courts did not see it that way. Mr. Brown was convicted of attempted murder. Not sure what his punishment was. •

STRANGER ATTEMPTS TO LURE LITTLE BOYS INTO THE WOODS

On September 26, 1964, I received a complaint from a woman on the Boulevard near the entrance to the Edgewood Avenue Park about an incident with a stranger. We had been receiving complaints from parents for weeks that a man was stalking children near the rest rooms. I met with the woman and her 8-year-old son and his friend, about the same age. The boys told me that they were playing on the swings and that they needed to use the rest room. As they emerged from the rest room, a man was standing there and offered them money to go into the woods with him. The boys gave me a good description of the man and they also noticed that he was sitting in a car earlier. The boys described the car as a black station wagon and one of the boys remembered a letter 'C' and a number '7' on the plate. I viewed this complaint as serious. When an adult stalks children, it becomes more than just suspicion. I took the mother and both boys to the Detective Division. I put out a broadcast to all units to be on the lookout for a middle aged white male operating a black station wagon with a partial license plate containing 'C and 7'. I was doing school traffic on Whitney Avenue and Canner Street, crossing children, when I noticed a black station wagon traveling toward me in a northerly direction, toward Hamden on Whitney Avenue. The front license plate read CO-7 Connecticut. I yelled to stop at the white male operator and he pulled over. I made sure no children were in the intersection before leaving the intersection. He denied every being in or near Edgewood Avenue Park on Saturday. I was 100% sure that this was the man so I towed his car and transported him to the Detective Division. The car was registered to a local Florist. I went to the local Florist, hoping that I made the right decision. They showed me delivery records from the past Saturday indicating that the man made a flower delivery in the Edgewood Avenue Park area. Both boys positively identified the man in a police lineup. After the man was booked, I met with the boys and the parents. I commended the boys for doing exactly the right thing. Running from the man, observing what he looked like and getting a partial license plate number of his car. All children should be aware of possible danger from these predators. The man was convicted of risk of injury to a minor and went to prison for a long time and we got a potential dangerous man off the streets. •

MEMORIES OF A RETIRED COP

GRAND AVENUE BRIDGE

In the summer of 1966, I got a call one afternoon from a lady that reported damage to the windshield on her car. The damage occurred as she drove over the Grand Avenue Bridge in an east direction. I met the lady at Durso's Garage on the east side of the bridge. The damage was a cracked windshield on the passenger side. Two days later, a man reported the rear window of his vehicle was shattered as he drove over the bridge in a westerly direction. I called Public Works to have someone come over and check the bridge for possible loose or rusted nuts and bolts that were possibly falling off the bridge to cause the damage. A man from the Bridge Authority responded. He examined the bridge and found nothing. This went on for about one month with numerous complaints of cracked or broken car windows. We assigned a plain clothes Detective with binoculars to stake out the bridge. Finally we caught the culprit. The bridge tender was shooting at pigeons that landed on the bridge with a Crossman model 760-pellet gun. He hit very few pigeons, but hit many cars. All in all, about fifteen windshields were damaged and the city of New Haven was responsible for all the damage. Not sure if the bridge tender lost his job, but if I had to guess, I would say yes. •

RACIAL TENSION AVERTED

Racial equality has always been a part of my life growing up in the Hill section of New Haven. My mom (RIP) taught us that God created us all in his image. We were and still are all the same. Since time began, there are those that do not believe this and they will go out of their way to show their hatred and distain for others that are different than them. Police Officers, in particular, must treat everyone with respect and equality. This story is about a racist who tried to get involved in something that had nothing to do with himself:

On June 17, 1973, at approximately 8:00 PM, I was dispatched to the area of 95 Howard Avenue in regard to a theft complaint. Upon arrival, I spoke to Mr. Cahill who reported that his 12-year-old son and his friend were knocked off their bikes and money stolen from their pockets by two older black boys. The older boys fled on the stolen bikes. I immediately put out a broadcast for the thieves. We were looking for two black teenagers, approximately age sisteen, with a description of the stolen bikes. My partner and I, along with another Officer searched the area and found the two boys riding the stolen bikes a short distance away. The boys were returned to 95 Howard Avenue for identification purposes. The victims and several witnesses identified the two thieves. The bikes and the stolen money were returned to the victims. As we spoke to the thieves, an unidentified white man approached and said we were arresting them solely because they were black. He tried to appeal to some black residents that were in the small crowd, that we were racists and that we should let these two boys go immediately. The black Police Officer, who was my back up, told him that a thief is a thief, regardless of their color and to mind his own business. Only after we threatened to arrest this white man agitator for interfering with police business, did he leave. When we left the scene, black and white residents were in harmony, as good neighbors should be.
•

FIGHT AT THE FRIENDLY BAR

One Friday night in the summer of 1965, I was dispatched to a fight at a bar on the corner of Sylvan Avenue and Asylum Street. Upon arrival, I observed one man lying in a pile of broken glass on the sidewalk. I called for an ambulance. While my partner attended to the injured man, I entered the bar. It was packed. I approached the bartender and asked him what happened. Well, these two guys were arguing at the bar and one guy picks up the other guy and throws him right through the front plate glass window. Another guy jumps in and starts to punch the guy that threw the other guy through the window. Just then, two more guys come from the dining area and start fighting, with a couple more guys. I called for more back up. In the meantime, an ambulance arrives and takes the injured man on the sidewalk to Yale New Haven Hospital. After back up arrives, we cleared out the bar. I spoke to the bartender for information for my report. I needed the name of the guy who threw the other guy through the window. The bartender asked me, "Who's going to pay for my broken window?" "I don't know," I answered. "Who's going to pay for this man's injuries?" I asked him. "When you serve guys to the point of intoxication, you are taking a chance that things like this will happen." The last thing I needed for my report was the name of the bar. The name was written on the plate glass window which was now, all over the sidewalk in pieces. The bartender proudly said, "The name of my bar is called THE FRIENDLY BAR." "What? You got to be kidding me," I answered. •

MISSING WOMAN'S BODY FOUND

One morning in February 1961, while we were in Police Academy on 710 Sherman Parkway, Sergeant Biagio DiLieto came into the classroom and announced that we were all going out on a field trip. Just getting out of the boring classroom sounded good to us. It was a clear but cold day. We had been issued our badges and Colt Police Special revolvers but no uniforms yet. Our blue converted school bus picked us up in front of the Academy. Our destination was Hopkins School. Located on Forest Road. An 84 year old woman had been missing for several days and was last seen walking up the driveway of the school. We had about twenty-two recruits, including four Yale Campus Police recruits. The bus dropped us off in front of the school on Forest Road. We were instructed to fan out and walk through the thick wooded area south of the school. Within the first hour, one of the recruits found the body of the missing woman. The event was just the beginning of our career. It was deeply sad to see someone's loved one lying on the cold ground. At age twenty-five, I immediately felt compassion for this woman's family, knowing that she was someone's mother, grandmother, wife, aunt, or sister. For the first time since becoming a Police Officer, I experienced compassion and genuine sadness for someone else's loved one. A few tears flowed. I wiped my eyes and told the other guys I had chronic hay fever. Sergeant DiLieto thanked us all for our diligence and sent us all back to the Police Academy. No one talked on the ride back. We were all processing our own thoughts. The cause of the lady's death was attributed to exposure to the elements. Later in class, Sergeant DiLieto reminded us that this is just the beginning of what it will be like to be a New Haven Police Officer. He reminded us of the positive side of this tragedy. We, working as a team, brought closure to this family. Many missing people are never found. Then and there I knew that I would always do my very best for all the residents of New Haven. •

STOLEN AUTO RECOVERED

On September 30, 1965, at 12:15 AM, I was dispatched to the Saveway Gas Station on the corner of State Street and Ferry Street in regard to a stolen auto. Upon arrival, a female who had been driving a model 88 Oldsmobile had just filled her gas tank and went inside to pay for her gas. When she came out, her car was gone. I put her in my police car and we drove around in the area to see if we could locate the vehicle. We drove east on Ferry Street and turned right into Lombard Street. I spotted a known car thief walking east on Lombard Street. I continued for one more block and located the Oldsmobile. I then made a U-turn and went back to the young man I suspected of taking the ladies car. I pulled to the curb and called him over to my police car. "Joey, come here." He walked over. If I had asked him if he took the ladies car, he would have said no, so I said, "Joey, why did you take this ladies car?" He said, "I'm sorry. I just needed to get home." I put him in the back seat and took the lady to her car. I knew the young man and his family, so I wasn't concerned that he would run. We checked the ladies car out. No damage and she still had the full tank of gas. I charged Joey with taking a motor vehicle without the owner's permission. The lady was happy to get her car back within twenty minutes of it being stolen. •

ANOTHER STOLEN AND RECOVERD AUTO

The same young man, Joey G****in, had stolen another auto from a lady about one year prior from Ferry and Fox Streets. The lady parked her car on the corner and ran in for grinders, leaving the keys in the ignition (bad idea). I guess Joey must have came along and drove off in her vehicle. When she called the police, I responded. She said, the thief won't get too far. "Why?" I asked. She said she had a bad radiator and the car was leaking anti-freeze. I looked at a puddle of antifreeze on the street and I told her to jump in my car. We followed the anti-freeze trail to Main Street near Market Street. There was her car, overheating with steam billowing out from under the hood and Joey sitting in the driver's seat. I pulled up and put Joey in the back seat of my police car. The lady was sitting in the front. "Joey?" I asked. "Why did you take this ladies car?" "Because the keys were in it." "Really? It's not your car Joey." Joey had the nerve to tell the lady to get her radiator fixed because he got caught because her car overheated. The lady wanted to slap him. Not in my police car lady, take him outside. Anyway, I charged Joey with taking a motor vehicle without the owner's permission that time also. Joey never learned. •

LAUNDROMAT CHEATERS

In the winter of 1975, I was patrolling in the Quinnipiac Avenue and Route 80 area on the 4:00 PM to 12:00 midnight shift. At approximately 7:30 PM, I got a complaint of an abandoned vehicle on a cul-de-sac on Roosevelt Street Extension. Upon arrival, I met with a female who lived on that street. She pointed out a Ford station wagon that had been suspiciously parked there for about one hour ago. She further noticed that the vehicle was unlocked with the driver's window open and a basket of clean laundry was in the rear behind the back seat. She also pointed out that the engine was still warm. With such attention to details, I joked with her that she would make a good Detective. "I think the car is stolen," she remarked. "That's possible," I said. I ran a listing of the vehicle registration. The owner came back to a man living on Melrose Drive. Melrose Drive was a short distance so I drove over to the house. I rang the front doorbell and a man came to the door. I asked him if he owned a Ford station wagon with this license number. "Yes, I do," he answered. "Do you know where your car is now, mister?" "Yes, I do Officer. My wife went to the Laundromat a couple of hours ago." "Oh boy," I said to myself. "Why, did something happen to her?" "I'm not sure mister. Your car is parked on Roosevelt Street Extension, and it appears abandoned." I drove him there with his extra set of keys. As we got out to look in the car, another car drove up but suddenly stopped. The car went in reverse. I stopped the car before it could drive off. His wife was in the passenger side front seat and an unidentified man was driving. After calling for back up, I placed myself between the two men as the lady got out of the car. I obtained ID from the unidentified man before telling him to leave and the wife got into the Ford passenger side. I spoke to the husband and advised him not to do anything stupid. He said he would not and he suspected something for a long time and that they would be okay. "Do you folks have children?" I asked. "No. We don't," the lady answered. If they had children in that house, I would have gone back with them. At this point, it became a private matter between a husband and wife. No further police action was necessary. I wished them both luck and watched them drive off. My back up finally arrived. Glad I didn't need him. I did a complete incident report, just in case something developed later. •

STATE WORKER ENCOURAGES SPEEDING

For years during my career, I drove the major accident patrol car. Among my many other duties and responsibilities as a New Haven Police Officer, I was often dispatched to the most serious motor vehicle accidents involving personal injuries, including deaths and extensive damage to vehicles and property. Over the years, I've learned that excessive speed causes serious injury and also deaths. Two motor vehicles each traveling at 20 MPH that collide may most likely not cause serious injuries or even death but the same two vehicles traveling each at 60 MPH will most likely cause very serious injuries and even deaths. This is not from a scientific study but from my own experience investigating serious motor vehicle accidents. More than I really want to remember, I've gone home with tears in my eyes, thinking about the child that I gave first aid to at an accident scene, because their parents disobeyed a motor vehicle law. Reading about these things is one thing. Being on scene is another. This reminds me of the lady that actually encouraged people to speed:

I was on normal patrol on Forest Road one afternoon, in maybe 1965. Our speed enforcement officers had set up radar on Forest Road, just north of the West Haven city line – a favorite place for speeders. Suddenly, everyone was slowing down just before the radar car. I drove south on Forest Road to the West Haven city line and there was a small black car parked on the west side of Forest Road, facing south, flashing the headlights to northbound oncoming cars, warning them of radar ahead. I alerted the radar car. The Sergeant requested that I check out the car. I was totally shocked as I parked behind this vehicle. It was a black Ford Falcon with State Of Connecticut license plates, similar to State 2-2311. A female was sitting in the driver's seat. I approached her. "Ma'am, are you having car trouble?" "No," she said. "Why are you flashing your headlights?" "My headlight switch is not working so I'm trying to loosen it up," she answered. "The sun is out ma'am." "I know. Maybe I'll be driving tonight." I checked her license and registration. The car was registered to The Department of Welfare, State of Connecticut. I told her that she should be ashamed of herself for warning other drivers about speed enforcement and asked her to leave. She was in an unsafe place to stop. She closed the window on me and drove off. I did a complete and

MEMORIES OF A RETIRED COP

thorough report of the incident and forwarded a copy to her Department. There was nothing that I could charge her with outside of maybe, interfering with a Police Officer but what real proof would I have. My Sergeant agreed that I handled it well. The letter to her Department was my best option. •

MACK MILLER STORE BURGLARY

One Wednesday morning, in the spring of 1964, at about 11:00 AM, I was dispatched to the Mack Miller clothing store on Whalley Avenue. I had always bought that occasional men's suit or blazer from Mack Miller. His dad was an excellent Tailor. Mack and his dad were truly gentlemen in every way. This morning, I was there on official Police business. Mack had explained to me that over the past weekend, someone broke into his store and stole several men's business suits. The burglary occurred when someone forced open the rear door of the store. The burglary was reported that Monday morning when it was discovered by Mack and his dad once they opened the store for business. Mack said to me, "Bob. This morning, about 9:30, a gentleman walked into my store with a men's suit that he claimed he bought here last week. It was my suit with all the tags on it. The hem of the trousers was unfinished and the man said be bought it that way." Mack knew in his own mind that this was one of the stolen suits, but he went along with the man and even apologized about not altering the hem of the suit to the man's own measurements. Mack took the man's measurements, again apologizing to him for the oversight and promised him that the suit would be ready tomorrow. Mack took the man's name, address and telephone number and told him he would call him when the suit was ready. "Mack," I said, "you would definitely make a good Detective." His dad remarked that the guy was a dumb bastard., bringing in a stolen suit and saying we didn't alter it for him. "That's okay Mr. Miller. We will pay him a visit to his house and make things right." I called the Detective Division with added information in regard to the Mack Miller burglary. I said, "We know who did it." "Who," the Detective asked. "I got his name and address here on a piece of paper. Telephone number too." I drove downtown and handed the paper to one of the Detectives. That afternoon, the man was picked up at his home. The same address he had given to Mack Miller. The man was in custody along with another stolen suit he had in his possession, found in the man's home. Yes, the man was a dumb bastard, as Mr. Miller stated. As much as a person may try, you just can't make this stuff up. •

MOTORCYCLE CLUB 4TH OF JULY

In 1973, I was handpicked by Chief DiLieto to be on duty on July 3rd at the Hole in the Wall Club on Forbes Avenue. First I said, "Why me? Out of 500 Policeman in New Haven, can't someone else get stuck with that assignment?" Unofficially, The Hole in the Wall was given special permission to shoot off their large assortment of fireworks in their back yard in celebration of the 4th Of July. Just like Wooster Street always unofficially celebrated the 4th of July. I was bent out of shape to get such a lousy assignment until I was told that Chief DiLieto handpicked me for the assignment. First, because I wouldn't take any crap from the members and second that I would be fair and I would use good judgment in case anything serious happened. He did not want a "hot head" Policeman on duty there and he did not want a Policeman that would take the easy way out and simply look the other way. I was honored to be selected for that assignment, now. I took this assignment very serious and everything went smooth with no incidents. There is always a reason for everything. •

In the summer of 1969, one Saturday afternoon, two men tried to park in the same parking space on Chapel Street, just East of James Street. One guy was backing into a parking space and the other guy was pulling into the parking space from behind. I was not the Officer that responded to this call but after reading the police report, I recognized the name of one of the men. After a heated argument between the two men over the parking space, one man opened his trunk and took out a rifle and shot the other guy in the head, killing him instantly. I had an occasion to speak to the accused murdered. He told me that he was justified in killing the man because he was stealing his parking space. What's so scary is that in his mind, he was justified. There are people out there that actually think this way. To think you can kill someone because they beat you to a parking space is beyond what any reasonable or prudent person would think. Anyone that ever parked in that area to visit the fine restaurants and bars in the area knows that there were always plenty of parking spaces available. Even when there were ball games in the park across the street, there were parking spaces available to everyone. But now, one man is dead and another man going to prison, probably for the rest of his life over a parking space. •

BANK TELLER DOESN'T LIKE POLICEMAN

Just thinking about what ever happened to Whalley Avenue? Al's, Chuck's, Mack Miller? Fox's Deli? My bank was on the northwest corner of Whalley and Sherman. I can't remember the name. Maybe it was Second New Haven National Bank? I pulled in the drive-in with a blue and white marked police car to cash my City of New Haven police check one Friday afternoon. I got a teller that didn't like Policeman. I handed her my work check like I've done since I opened a checking account there one year ago. She looked at my work check, front and rear and asked if I had any ID. "Yes Ms." I opened my wallet and gave her my Connecticut driver's license. She looked that over and said, "Do you have a second ID?" "Yes Ms., I do." Even I have a breaking point, and it was getting very close to breaking. I said, "Ms.," smiling all along, "I will park my authentic blue and white 1967 Ford Custom four-door sedan police car, registered to the city of New Haven, Connecticut and come into your bank and speak to your Supervisor." "OH no, Officer. That's not necessary to cash your work check, sir. Here is your cashed check sir. Please count it sir." I did count it. I said, "Thank you Ms.," and drove off. Either, she definitely got a speeding ticket recently or she just didn't like Policeman or I was on Candid Camera. I did not see Allen Funt anywhere in sight, so Candid Camera was out. That's why I did smile, just in case. I believe she did get some kind of ticket recently. •

DAD AND 13-YEAR-OLD DAUGHTER

One Friday night, in the summer of 1970, I was scheduled to work a teeny dance at the Jewish Community Center on Chapel Street in New Haven. The ages were from nine to about fourteen. The year before, I took my 14-year-old daughter, Terry. with me so this time my 13-year-old daughter, Alice, wanted to go with me. Why not? The Director Stan Sprechmann told me I was welcome anytime to take my daughters with me while I was on official police duty. Alice and I arrived at approximately 6:00 PM for the scheduled 7:00 PM teeny dance. I got Alice comfortable at a table close to me by the front entrance to the dance hall. I knew as the kids came in, Alice would make new friends. I positioned myself at the front door, making sure that the kids paid the small admission charge. Maybe 75 cents? Within a half hour, the tables started to fill up with young kids, anxious to dance and maybe meet new friends. I glanced over at Alice and she had a friend sitting with her – a young boy with large black eye glasses. At first he looked harmless but then he started to move closer to Alice. At that age, I was very shy, but not this young man. Next, he's trying to hold Alice's hand. She looked at me like, Dad, Help. Time to see what's up. I walked over to her and kissed her forehead and asked if she was having a good time. "Dad? This is Barry." I went to shake hands and Barry took off. "Daddy? That boy is so rude. He tried to hold my hand and I told him the Policeman at the door was my father. He just laughed and said. OH sure he is." "Well, Alice. Guess Barry believes you now." Two 14-year-old girls I knew from Westville came over and I introduced them to my daughter, Alice. "Wow, your dad is so cool. We all love him." "Wish my dad was a cop," one said. The girls sat with Alice for the rest of the night until the dance was over at around 10:30 PM. Barry? He never did come back. •

MEMORIES OF A RETIRED COP

A DAY AT WORK WITH DAD –THE POLICEMAN

In the early 60's, Interstate 91 was being built from New Haven to the Massachusetts line. There was plenty of extra traffic duty work for the off duty Police officers that wanted to earn extra money directing traffic for the many dump trucks and other road equipment needed to build the highway. One day, I asked for and was assigned extra duty to direct traffic on Middletown Avenue near Bernhard Road, for the dozens of dump trucks hauling fill as construction progressed on Interstate 91. My three children wanted to come with me. We had a 1957 Ford station wagon with the roll down rear window and tailgate on the back. Mary, anticipating a day off from the kids, packed a lunch for us all. Terry, age nine, Alice, age seven, and Bobby, age two, jumped in the back of the station wagon, just behind the third seat. The kids always called it "the way back". They would say, "Daddy, can we sit in the way back?" It was like their own personal and private space. We arrived at the traffic point on Middletown Avenue near Bernhard Road; it was just before 8:00 AM. Finally, the giant Euclid trucks called 'Euchs' arrived. I rolled the rear tailgate window down so the kids could safely look out the back window as these giant trucks crossed Middletown Avenue. That's when little Bobby yelled, "Look, Daddy, a Fruck," pointing to the giant truck. "Bobby, that's a truck." "Yeah, daddy, a fruck." The girls and I laughed all day. "Look daddy. Another Fruck," Bobby would say. At about 12:00 PM, the trucks stopped rolling for lunch. Now, I was able to put the tailgate down so we could all sit on the tailgate and have our lunch that Mary prepared for us: ham and cheese on white bread and a large bag of potato chips and ice-cold sodas. Nothing fancy just made with love by mom. Mary also packed some fruit and cookies. At 12:30 sharp, the giant 'Euchs' started rolling again. Regardless of what was coming down Middletown Avenue, it was my job to stop all traffic and give the Euclid trucks the right of way. I closed the tailgate and the three kids sat there watching the trucks roll by. Bobby must have said, "Look at the Frucks," a dozen more times before our day ended at 4:30 PM. I was very dusty and tired from all that dirt blowing around but this was one of the best days I ever had with my kids. Bobby is now age fifty-two and he doesn't say Fruck anymore… at least I don't think so.☺ •

PUTTING YOUR FOOT IN YOUR MOUTH

One day while on duty in the summer of 1966, I decided to use my assigned 30-minute lunch period to get a haircut. It was a Saturday afternoon. Our family Barber was Caliendo's on Lamberton Street, between Kimberly Avenue and Howard Avenue. I lived on Greenwich Avenue until joining the New Haven Police Department in 1961. There were no parking spaces available on Lamberton Street so I parked my police cruiser around the corner on Kimberly Avenue and walked around to Caliendo's. I walked in and hung up my police hat on the coat rack and took a seat. Five minutes later I was sitting in the barber chair. Rich Caliendo put the white sheet over my uniform and started to cut my hair with the usual greetings of, "So how are you Bob?" "Good Rich and you?" Just then two men got out of a car in front of Caliendo's, where they were lucky enough to find a parking space. Two ordinary looking neighborhood guys walked in and took a seat and waited their turn. One grabbed the Saturday New Haven Register on the magazine table and started to read a front-page article that read, "New Haven Police Union negotiating for a raise for the rank and file members of the Police Union." Not seeing me dressed in my police uniform because the sheet covered it, one said, "Hey Charlie. These bastards are looking for more money. The bastards are not worth what they are making now." Rich kept poking me and silently laughing. Finally, the haircut was finished and Rich brushes off the hair and removes the sheet. I get up and walk over to the coat rack and put on my police hat and walk out the front door. The two guys sat there with their mouths wide open, like they saw a ghost. I bent over at their front license plate pretending that I was writing down the marker plate number. I walked around the corner and drove off in my police car. One hour later, I came back. I walked in the Barber Shop. Rich, his brother, Bobby, and Mr. Caliendo were laughing their butts off. The two men pleaded with Rich to give them my name so they could send flowers to my wife with an apology note. Mr. Caliendo said, "Let them sweat it out for a few days." •

SHOPLIFTING A 99 CENT BICYCLE TUBE

In the summer of 1968, I was dispatched to King's Department Store on the Boulevard in regard to a shoplifter. Upon arrival, I was directed to the Managers office by one of the Cashier's. As I recall, the office was to the left and being held in there was a 9-year-old Hispanic boy. He was crying his heart out. He did not appear to be a seasoned criminal, but a scared little boy. The stolen item was a 99-cent bicycle tube. The more the boy looked at me, the more he cried. I took him outside so I could talk to him alone. The manager was demanding that I arrest him. I called him son. I said, "Stop crying son. I am not going to put you in Jail. The total for the bicycle tube with tax came to $1.05. A very minor crime. But, it's still against the law to steal," I told him. After he finally stopped crying, he said that his bike had a flat tire for a long time and he just wanted to ride his bike with the other kids. I brought him back into the manager's office. I offered to pay for the bicycle tube. The manager got angry with me and said, "Absolutely not. He is going to learn a lesson. Refer him to Juvenile Court. Take him out of here. I don't want to look at him." I took the boy home. He lived on Truman Street. I spoke to his mom who was very, very upset. I tried to downplay the crime that it was just over $1.00 but still a crime. I told him to never, never steal again or the next time he will go to Juvenile Detention. I wanted that little boy to have that bicycle tube but I decided to leave well enough alone. I even thought of going back and buying the tube but then the manager would be calling the station on me. In my report, I mentioned the fact that the boy cried his heart out and hoped it made a difference with the Judge. Not sure how it ended. •

ATTEMPTED SUICIDE

On November 30, 1977, just after midnight, Officer Robert Coffee and myself were dispatched to the Crown Court Apartments on Park Street. Upon arrival, there was an ambulance and an emergency unit parked outside. The location of the incident was the 8th floor. A 22-year-old female Stone School of Business student was standing on the railing on her balcony of her apartment, threatening to jump. She was holding on to the side of the building while standing on a thin railing. She told everyone to back off or she would jump. It was later learned that this student had been despondent all day. Thinking about my own daughter Theresa, who was age twenty-two at the time, I decided to try and convince her to get off the railing. I said, "Miss, please don't jump. Please get off that railing." She told me to back off. "Please miss; don't jump because you will break my heart." I actually told her that I loved her and that she looked just like my own daughter. I extended my right hand to her. She reached out and took my hand. She got off that railing and we went into her apartment. The President of Stone School of Business was also present in her apartment. She really didn't need all the Firemen or Policemen there. She needed a friend. Someone she could trust. She stated that she was afraid to get into an ambulance so I got permission from my Sergeant to transport her to Yale New Haven Hospital in my police car along with Officer Coffee. Upon arrival at Yale New Haven Emergency Room, I stayed with her until she was examined and finally committed to Middletown State Hospital for a 30-day evaluation period. She agreed to ride in the back of the ambulance to Middletown and wanted me to go with her. I told her that I would love to go with her but I was needed in New Haven and wished her luck and told her everything would be okay. The President of Stone School of Business wrote a beautiful letter to Chief Edward Morrone. The letter is enclosed in the Supplements section at the end of the novel. •

DRUNK SCHOOL BUS DRIVER

In the spring of 1965, at about noon, I was behind a school bus on Fountain Street heading west. I was not on a call so I had some time to just stay behind the bus to see if anyone passed the bus after stopping to let kids on and off. There is always someone that will pass a standing school bus with its emergency flashings lights on and children crossing. We traveled west as far as Seneca Road where the school bus turned right into Seneca Road. As the bus made the turn, the driver almost struck a telephone poll. I decided to check out the driver. I hit my red lights and tapped the siren button. The school bus stopped at the intersection of Fairfield Street. It was not my intention to embarrass the driver, so I used a lot of discretion. As the driver opened the door, I asked him to step out of the bus for a minute, making it look like we were friends. The driver could not get off his seat. He was intoxicated. I turned the engine off and took the keys and set the emergency brake. I called the Bus Service to send another driver. I put the driver in the back seat of my police car. The children were all kindergarten age so they had absolutely no knowledge of what was going on. Seemed like fun to them that a Policeman was on their bus. An empty pint bottle of vodka was under the driver's seat. I arrested the bus driver for operating a motor vehicle while under the influence of alcohol or drugs. Again, using discretion. I did not want the children to be upset, knowing that they were in danger. I did not put him in a paddy wagon. After the relief bus driver arrived. I took the intoxicated driver to Sherman Avenue and booked him. I sent the Bus Company owner a complete copy of the incident and my motor vehicle arrest of the bus driver. Thank God I had some time on my hands this day. I'm sure this bus would have eventually struck something of someone. We did not measure blood alcohol like we do today. He was too drunk to blow into the breathalyzer that was the tool we used in those days. •

FEMALE POLICE OFFICERS

My next true story is in honor of the many brave female Law Enforcement Police Officers currently serving the public, in Police Academy, or has aspirations of becoming a Police Officer:

Sometime in the summer of 1977, I was assigned to the Dixwell Avenue area of New Haven. One afternoon, I reported for duty at 3:45 PM at 710 Sherman Parkway for the 4:00 PM shift. Something was different this day. There was a young black female uniformed Police Officer getting ready for inspection. Just then, my Captain called me to the side between the lockers and said, "Bob, will you take the new recruit with you and train her?" "Absolutely Captain." "Thank you Bob," he said. I introduced myself to her and told her she is riding with me tonight. Her initials were B C. She was maybe 5'1" and 110 lbs., but that 38 Colt police special on her belt made her look much bigger. As we drove out of the driveway, heading to Dixwell Avenue area, a few negative comments were heard. Mostly from ignorance. New Haven has always had fine black Police Officers, but it was the fact that she was a female. We had eight hours to go to, let's see what happens. We were out for maybe fifteen minutes when we got a call. Signal 11 (go to) the Dixwell Plaza and break up the loitering. Upon arrival, there were approximately 40-50 men just loitering, drinking from brown paper bags and yes, urinating wherever they wanted. This behavior was very bad for business. I parked my police car and we both got out with nightsticks in hand. I left the motor running. As we approached the crowd, B C returned to my police car and removed the ignition keys. She said, "Sir, you forgot your keys," and handed them to me. "Who's training whom?" I asked myself. As we approached the large crowd, I made the announcement I've made 100's of times before: "Okay guys, break it up. Let's go. No loitering." One big mouth looked at B C and said, "Look at what we have here? My. My, my." B C said, "You are looking at a New Haven Police Officer that will lock up your ass in a minute, so keep moving. You have one minute to disperse." They all took off. The rest of the night went just as well and the rest is history. I retired one year later in 1978 but I've heard that B C made a career for herself. I would trust my life to any female Police Officer. They show courage and would take a bullet for their partner. •

MEMORIES OF A RETIRED COP

BELLEVUE ROAD HOME INVASION BURGLARY

In 1974, in the winter months, I was dispatched to a home on Bellevue Road in regard to a home invasion burglary. It was approximately 2:00 AM. Upon arrival, the homeowner met me at the front door. He was a well-known New Haven Attorney whom I knew on a first name basis. Steven stated that he and his wife went to bed at approximately 1:00 AM. Steven stated that he was angry with himself because he forgot to set his burglar alarm. At approximately 1:45, he observed a large man going through his jewelry on his dresser. The man actually selected his Rolex watch and put it on his wrist. Steven said he yelled at the man, screaming, "Get your F'n hands off my watch!" The man fled down the stairs with the watch on his wrist and out the front door that was open. Steven chased him out of sight and returned to call the police. As Steven was inspecting the broken rear kitchen door glass window, he heard a car start in his driveway. He went to the front door and watched his 1973 cream colored Oldsmobile convertible disappear down Bellevue Road. The burglar apparently stole the car keys off the dresser along with the Rolex watch. Steven also noticed his large table model television was missing from the living room. Steven was livid. If I caught that bastard, I would have beaten his ass. I put out a general broadcast for the Oldsmobile Convertible and a description of the burglar who was described as a tall black male, dressed in dark clothing. One feature Steve remembers was that he was wearing pure white sneakers. I contacted the Detective Bureau. I left Steve's house and commenced to search for the Olds. At approximately 7:00 AM, I observed a tall black male dressed in dark clothing, riding a bike in an easterly direction down Whalley Avenue passing Ramsdell Street. He was wearing pure white sneakers. I stopped him near Anthony Street. He had a screwdriver and a flashlight sticking out of both rear pockets. He was also wearing a $10,000.00 Rolex watch. Within five minutes of questioning him after reading him his rights, he admitted to the burglary. He also said he ditched the Olds somewhere in Woodbridge and then he stole the bike from an unlocked garage. For my safety, I cuffed his hands behind his back. The stolen television was in the back seat, along with some expensive antiques, later reported stolen from another home burglary. I called Steven to give him the good news. Everything was recovered with no apparent damage. •

HOME INVASION NIGHT BURGLAR

On April 15, 1977, at approximately 1:30 AM, I was on patrol in the Westville area of Forest Road, Fountain Street, Chapel Street, etc. We had been plagued with home invasion burglaries as families slept in their beds. I received a radio call that a burglary was in progress and that a burglar was in an occupied home on 81 Marvel Road while the family was sleeping. This is the most serious of all burglaries when family members are home alone with a potential killer; a call that every Policeman uses every means to his disposal to get there as fast as possible. I arrived in minutes to observe the burglar driving off and the complainant standing on the front porch, pointing to his car as he sped off. He had a head start and was almost out of sight. I radioed a vague description of the car and direction of travel and gave chase. Seconds later, Officer Terry Heffernan picked up the pursuit on Fountain Street, traveling west on Fountain at very high speeds. The suspect crashed his car somewhere near Barnett Street and fled on foot. Officer Heffernan got a good look at the suspect and radioed a detailed description of him and the approximate area where he was last seen. We searched the back yards on Fountain Street near Barnett Street where I eventually found and tackled him to the ground. I cuffed him and after searching him, I found that he was in possession of burglary tools. He later admitted to Detective Otha Buffaloe to at least right more home invasion burglaries in the Westville area. The thorough and complete investigation by our Detective Division recovered thousands of dollars worth of stolen items from more home burglaries than we first thought. This was a major bust and I was so proud to be a part of it. Officer Terry Heffernan and Detective Otha Buffaloe and so many other members of the New Haven Police Department did an outstanding job of stopping this brazen night burglar. •

MOTORIST MOTOR VEHICLE EXCUSES

I would like to share some excuses I've heard from people that have been stopped by me for motor vehicle violations.

One lady was stopped for speeding. She said, "I'm in a hurry because I need to pee real bad and I gotta get home quick. I can't hold it." Checking her driver's license, she lived in Hartford, CT, 45 miles from New Haven, CT.

A man was stopped for swerving all over the road. His excuse, "My right leg was paralyzed in an accident," he said, "so I sometime hit the gas pedal instead of the brake pedal." I asked him to get out of the car. He was limping on his left leg. "Oh," he said, "I'm nervous. Did I say the right leg?" "Yes you did mister. I meant the left leg." As he was trying to make up his mind which leg was paralyzed, I wrote him a ticket for reckless driving. He got back in the car with the ticket in his hand without limping at all. Guess I cured the limp.

Another man was stopped for speeding and he had the peeing excuse. "Did you come from a bar and drink a lot of beer? That's why you need to pee?" "No, Officer. I don't drink." "Oh, I see. Then how come you can't hold it?" Well, if you drank six beers, wouldn't you need to pee too?" "I thought you just said, you don't drink?" "Well, not every day."

The best one was the man driving 22 MPH in a 45 MPH zone. It took me ten minutes to stop him. I approached his car and with his best impression of a sober man, he said to me, "Hi pal. Howdy pal." Sober people never call a Police Officer pal. I asked him if he had been drinking tonight. He said, "I beg your pardon occifer, uh office sir." I asked him again. "Mister, have you been drinking tonight?" He thought really hard about the question and said, "Damn right. Look at me occifer. I am in no shape to walk. I keep falling down so I took the car. Does that answer your question occifer, sir?" "How much have you had to drink tonight mister? Bottles, cans or kegs?" "If you had a wife like mine, you would drink too. That's all I got to say. Lock my ass up now. I don't care. Lock me up now." "Okay, mister." I towed his car and put him in a waiting paddy wagon. •

During my days in the Police Academy from January 9, 1961 to March 3, 1961, as Sergeant Biagio DiLieto put it, we have a special guest coming tomorrow morning. This occurred sometime in early February 1961. An FBI Agent arrived to teach us basic come along holds and also self-defense. Policemen are trained to never hurt people but to defend themselves and then to defend others. He was about 5'8" and maybe 180 lbs., I was 6'1" and maybe 210 lbs. Anyway, the course was very interesting. He taught us that hitting a person in the head with our night stick would in most cases, only make that person real mad and it would only dull their senses and they would come at you like a freight train. Wish I had remembered that during the riots. (That's for another story). He taught us a way to stop a person cold – take any one of their fingers and bend it back and break it. They will immediately stop fighting you. Sounds cruel, but there will be people out there that would kill you without conscious and get a good night's sleep that same night. Anyways, getting back to what happened to me. The FBI Agent turned his back to me and said, "Grab me and throw me down on the floor." "What? You want me the grab you from behind and throw you to the floor?" "Yes." I didn't want to hurt an FBI Agent, but reluctantly I grabbed him from behind and found myself sailing over his head and landing on the my back on the mat. My back was okay, but my wristwatch broken. "Aw kid, are you okay?" he asked. "Yes sir, but my wristwatch broke, sir." He looked at the wristwatch and said he would replace it with a new one. The Government has insurance you know. Two days later he came to class with four new wristwatches. Three were of the same quality as mine and one was very expensive. I chose one of equal value. He smiled and said, "Most people would automatically have chosen the expensive one. You will be a fine Officer. Honesty is high up there with courage." •

DECISIONS POLICEMAN MAKE

In the fall of 1961, half the graduating class of eighteen Police Officers rotated our shift from 4:00-12:00 AM to the12:00-8:00 AM shift. This was our 12-month probationary period. Among so many other things, we were trained to treat everyone equal. Treat everyone with dignity and respect. Never show favoritism in regard to race, religion, political views, etc. This one night, I was walking the beat on State Street from Grove Street to Bishop Street. Hardly a time to find any parking violations, but as a walked past Saint Stanislaus Church on State Street and Eld Street at 7:00 AM I had observed several parking violations. *NO PARKING HERE TO CORNER* on State Street and on Eld Street, *NO PARKING THIS SIDE OF STREET*. Let me point out that I am a Catholic, but I am also a Policeman so religion has nothing to do with the way I perform my duties, right? That's what I was taught. Can I walk into the church and yell out, move your cars? Of course not. In my own mind, if I walked past these parking violations, I would not be doing my job. The very job I was being paid to do. The very job I was trained for, so I got out my ticket book and wrote out maybe eight parking tickets and then continued to walk my beat. At 8:00 AM, I was signing off duty and handed in my parking ticket stubs. My Captain observed my badge number 267. "Officer, I want to see you in my office, now." He appeared upset. Why was he so angry with me? I walked all night and did my job as I was trained to do. "Officer? Why did you ticket people going to church on a Sunday morning?" "Sir, because they were in violation, sir." "Get your ass over to St. Stan's Church and see the Priest. Bring those tickets back to me. They will all be excused. Use more common sense in the future. Now, go home." Sometime, a Policeman can never please everyone. Only the beginning of a career that regardless of what decision I make or of what I learned In Police Academy, I will never make everyone happy. I went home feeling pretty bad that morning, trying my best to be a good Policeman. If churches are exempt from parking violations, then why are there no parking signs on the street? Looking back at the way I treated and respected every one, I hold my head high and know in my heart I did my best. •

I have one more parking ticket story. In 1965, I was on the 4:00 PM to 12:00 midnight shift in Westville. At approximately 6:30 PM, I received a complaint of several illegally parked cars on Forest Rd, causing a traffic hazard. The illegally parked cars were on the west side of Forest Road in a *NO PARKING ANYTIME* area. The four or five illegally parked cars were in front of a known Police Captains home. There is such a thing as professional courtesy, so I rang the bell. The Captains wife came to the door and I greeted her with my name and told her about the illegally parked cars in front of her home and I also told her I was responding to a complaint. She was so apologetic and stated that she was having a Tupperware party. She asked the women there to move their cars. Everyone thanked me for not giving them a ticket. Again, professional courtesy is important. All cars were moved to Willard Street, a side street off of Forest Road, where parking was not only legal, but safe. Again, the Captain's wife waved to me as I drove away. The next day, I reported for duty at 3:45 PM. I had a message to go see the Captain, the same one who lived in that house. What was I thinking? That he was going to thank me for showing courtesy and consideration for his rank? Wrong. I walked in his office. He began to berate me and called me an overzealous cop, while having his feet on his desk, to me showing total disrespect to his position and at the same time, looking down his nose at me. I listened to him telling me what nerve a uniformed cop had to come to a Captain's house to have his guest's move their cars. "You have a lot of nerve mister. Just who do you think you are?" he said. When he got finished insulting me, it was my turn. My whole career was on the line but I expected the same respect that I showed to his position. "Maybe I am just a cop, but I risk my life every day just like he does. I did nothing wrong." I said "Captain; I would welcome the chance to finish this discussion in the Chief's office now, sir. I am willing to go to the Chief's office with you right now. If I did something wrong, I want the Chief to tell me, not you sir." He threw me out of his office. He was so angry that other Officers left the room. •

AIRPLANE CRASH

On June 7, 1971, at approximately 10:00 AM, I was assigned to escort a large funeral procession from Chapel Street near Chestnut Street. I can't remember the name of the Funeral Home but it was near the corner of Chapel and Chestnut Street. Suddenly, my dispatcher called me to immediately abort the funeral procession and head for South End Road and the East Haven town line in regard to a possible airplane crash. I got on the CT Turnpike from Wooster Street to save time. As I was approaching Lighthouse Road, the dispatcher confirmed that it was in fact an Allegheny airliner that struck several cottages in East Haven and was now on fire. At this point, it was determined that the crash was the jurisdiction of the East Haven Fire and Police Departments but we were to assist them in every way possible. I set up a traffic point on South End Road and Meadow View Road and stopped all traffic going into East Haven. I allowed at least ten ambulances to proceed. Apparently, the news of the airplane crash got out and dozens of cars attempted to enter the crash site via South End Road, some with small children hanging out of the windows. I would not want my small children to see a grizzly scene like I Imagined it to be, and in fact, it was a horrible scene. Off duty Fireman from all over also attempted to enter the crash site. East Haven Police requested to stop all unnecessary traffic and only allow those actually involve to proceed. Because so much traffic got to the scene before I was able to stop the traffic, emergency vehicles were unable to get close to the scene. Eventually all the ambulances returned empty and headed back to their designated companies. By early afternoon, at least 15-20 black Hearst's passed me heading to the accident scene. It was a horrible and sad site. Later I learned that at least 26 people perished and possible 28. The final count I believe was 28 confirmed dead. •

FIGHT IN YELLOW LANTERN BAR

One warm summer night in June 1961, I was assigned to a walking beat on Dixwell Avenue, from Broadway to Munson Street. I left Headquarters on Court Street at 4:00 PM and I was transported to Dixwell Avenue and Webster Street via police car. The patrol car Officer dropped me off and said he would pick me up at 11:45 PM after our shift ended. I was alone but felt confident that I would be okay. I had walked the same beat several other nights before since I graduated from police academy in March 1961. I was becoming familiar with the neighborhood and the residents that lived in the area. I was never afraid because I had my Department issued equipment consisted of my Colt 38 special police revolver, 12 extra 38 caliber bullets, a nightstick, black jack, the claw, Peerless brand handcuffs, etc. There were no portable radios in those days, just the emergency red phones on certain corners were the way to communicate with Headquarters. As I walked the beat, all of a sudden, this lady comes running from the Yellow Lantern Restaurant/Bar then located at 144 Dixwell Avenue and yells, "There is a fight in my bar and they are breaking up the place." We were trained to never run to a fight because by the time we get there, we will be all out of breath and not good to anyone. Secondly, to call for backup before proceeding. I told her, "I'll be right there." I picked up the emergency red phone on the corner of Dixwell and Webster. I told the Captain that this was Officer Meyerholz and that I had a report of a fight at the Yellow Lantern and to send back up. The Captain said that he had no one available and to do the best I could alone. I walked briskly to the Yellow Lantern. I walked in the front door and announced, Police. Break it up now. I had my nightstick in my right hand. Someone yanked it from my hand. Then I got punched in the face. I tasted my own blood from a cut on my lower lip. That did it. I started swinging back. Without a nightstick I only had my black jack and my fists. I used both. I rounded up four men and escorted them outside. I marched them single file to the call box on Dixwell and Webster. Told them not to move an inch. I picked up the red phone and called the same Captain who answered, "Headquarters." "Captain, this is Officer Meyerholz again." "What do you want Ladd?" "Captain, send the paddy wagon; I got four prisoners from that fight at the Yellow Lantern, sir." "What Ladd? You got four prisoners?" "Yes sir. I'm holding them at Dixwell and Webster."

MEMORIES OF A RETIRED COP

The paddy wagon pulls up and I put the prisoners in the back and told the paddy wagon driver to book them to me. The rest of the night went well. Later that night he same lady from the Yellow Lantern came looking for me and handed me my nightstick which was found under a table. She thanked me. The next night at 4:00 PM, I was dropped off on the same beat. As I walked past the Yellow Lantern, a group of men standing on the sidewalk, looked at me and said to the others, "Don't f**k with that cop. He is one m**her f**ker." I made a reputation for myself that night. •

After graduating from Police Academy on March 3, 1961, half the class of eighteen new Probationary Police Officers were assigned to squad B (4:00 PM to 12:00 AM) and the other half to squad C (12:00 AM to 8:00 AM. I worked the first six months in squad B and then changed to squad C in September. From 12:00 until 2:00 AM we were busy checking all our doors and windows of every store and building on our beat. We also looked out for vagrants and wine-o's sleeping under the bridges and in abandoned cars and trucks along State Street. Today some vagrants are called homeless people. After that the rest of the night dragged and we were mostly bored. We found things to do to pass the time. I had beat 9 and my partner Vinnie had beat 17. Those two beats ran on State Street from Grove Street to South Water Street and one block either way. Beat 9 had the west side of State Street and beat 17 had the east side of State Street. This is one story about my partner Vinnie and I. One morning just after 2:00 AM we decided to enforce some motor vehicle violations on foot. How do you do that without a police car? Vinnie and I found a way. Vinnie stood on the North West corner of Chapel and State and I stood on the North East corner of Chapel and Orange. If a motor vehicle passed Vinnie heading west toward the vehicle and me had one taillight or no taillights on, he would flash his flashlight once. If the vehicle had no license plate lights displayed, he would flash his flashlight twice. I would cautiously step off the curb if the vehicle had to stop for the red light at Chapel and Orange and approach the driver. I would ask him/her for their license and registration telling them that they had either one or no taillights or no marker lights displayed. They would be amazed that I knew that from the front of the car. I would say, "We are highly trained to look around corners." In most cases I would let them go with a verbal warning. Occasionally, I would stop a car with either a drunk driver or someone who was driving under suspension or without a license. In one case a 13-year-old that stole his grandma's car. It helped us pass the time and impressed the hell out of the desk Sergeant. •

STUFFED BEAR ATTRACTS ATTENTION OF OFFICER

I have another story about my partner Vinnie and I during the time we took our turn working the midnight shifts while we were still on probation. It was in January of 1962. We both left headquarters then located on 165 Court Street at 12:00 midnight. We were assigned to walking beats number 9 and beat 17 on State Street from Grove Street to South Water Street. We started on Grove Street by the old New Haven Arena checking all our doors and windows to make sure they were all secure. We walked south. I had the west side of State Street and Vinnie had the east side of State Street. For some reason Vinnie was way ahead of me. By the time I reached Chapel Street Vinnie was at Crown Street. All of a sudden a marked police car sped by me heading south on State Street with red lights on but no siren. Then another police car sped by and yet another one came from Crown Street. They all stopped on State Street just south of Crown Street in front of the Acme Furniture Store. Acme had a large stuffed grizzly bear on wheels that would be on the sidewalk during the day and at night they would wheel it inside and leave it in the window. Vinnie decided to draw his Colt 38 special and aim his weapon at the bear. At the same time, our Lieutenant, drove by in car 9, an unmarked black Chevy station wagon and observed officer Vinnie with his weapon pointing at the store window. Thinking the Officer was holding someone at gunpoint, the Lieutenant radioed for backup, stating that an Officer was holding someone at gunpoint. I arrived on foot after walking briskly the long block to Acme Furniture. After I found out that Vinnie was playing bang, bang your dead, with the bear, I kept my distance because the Lieutenant was pretty angry for making a fool of himself by calling for backup, thinking the Officer was in trouble. The Lieutenant was one of our best Lieutenants who would always assist an Officer in trouble, especially a rookie just learning the job. To this day, I have the highest regard and respect for the Lieutenant. He took a little ribbing from the guy's right after the incident. Officer Vinnie was given a few days off without pay for conduct unbecoming an Officer. Never, ever draw your weapon unless you are prepared to use it. That's just common sense. Before we completed our 12-month probation period, Officer Vinnie was terminated for yet another stupid thing he got himself into. •

In December 1961, I was on my second 6 months of probation. Working the first six months on the 4:00 PM to 12:00 Midnight shift, I was now on the 12:00 AM to 8:00 AM shift. I had been on beat 9, which was State Street from Grove Street to South Water Street most nights. My partner Vinnie had beat 17, which was the opposite side of State Street from beat 9. We usually left headquarters a few minutes after midnight, depending how long roll call was. We would walk east on Court Street and either walk north or south on State Street, never using a stead routine. I'm sure a good burglar studies how Policeman walk the beat so we would throw them off by not walking the same way twice in a row. This night we started on Court Street and walked north checking all our doors and windows, including alleys and back yards. At about 3:15 AM Vinnie and I decided to walk into the alley of Shartenberg's Department Store on Chapel Street. The alley was off of State Street. There were three furniture delivery trucks backed up to Shartenberg's loading platform. In those days, most delivery trucks had a canvass on the back of the truck just above the tailgate. Unlike the modern trucks with double steel locking doors. Vinnie and I jumped up on the loading platform and checked each truck for sleeping vagrants who sometime slept in the back of these trucks at night. All 3 trucks were empty except the middle one. It had an old couch that was probably a trade in. Vinnie asked me if I would mind if he took a short nap on that couch. He said he was working an extra job at 8:00 AM. Traffic duty in the street. I wasn't pleased with his decision to sleep on the job but I was not his boss. I was a rookie just like him. I said, Ok. He reminded me to wake him in a few hours. I said don't worry. I will. I came back just after 7:00 AM to wake Vinnie. The middle truck was gone. The other two trucks were still backed up to the loading platform. I looked everywhere including the front of the store on Chapel Street. No truck and no Vinnie. I signed off duty at 8:00 AM and the Captain asked if I saw Vinnie. Not since 3:15 sir. Which was the truth. I went home at 8:00 AM. No cell phones, no texting. No way to find out what happened. That night Vinnie was at roll call. "What happened to you Vinnie?" "I'll tell you later," he said. Vinnie said he woke up on the Bruckner Boulevard in New York from the rough cobble stone road. No Ct. Turnpike in those days. Only RI 1 (Post Road) to New York.

Somehow, Shartenberg's driver and helper discovered him on the back of the truck and brought him back to New Haven. Telling the Captain that they found him sick or unconscious in the back of the truck. Not sure and didn't want to know. Months later, Vinnie was gone. Only a matter of time, too many stupid things happening to one person. •

ILLEGALLY PARKED IRATE MOTORIST

On February 12, 1962 I was finally off my 12-month probationary period. I was doing very well. Still walking the beat but possibly would be transferring to Station Two on Sherman Parkway soon. There, I would have my own police car and maybe see some other parts of New Haven beside downtown every day. In the meantime, I was on the 4:00 PM to 12:00 AM shift downtown. On February 27, 1962, I was assigned to traffic duty at Chapel and State Street. At 4:00 PM I turned off the traffic light and got in the intersection to do hand traffic for 2 hours. Traffic was heavy, but I was now confident and had almost one year of experience doing hand traffic. I suddenly hear horns beeping in the direction of Orange Street. A car was parked at the curb in front of a candy store causing other cars and buses to swerve around him. *NO STANDING* 4:00 to 6:00 PM signs were posted along both sides of the street. All 4 lanes are needed between those hours to accommodate the heavy traffic. One illegally parked car can cause traffic jams and also cause accidents. I tried to get his attention to move his car, but he ignored me. Finally, I had no choice but to turn the traffic light back on and walk over to his illegally parked car. I walked up to his car and I asked for his license and registration. He only had one license plate on the back of his car, a violation in Connecticut. He said he lost it months ago. I issued a written warning ticket for the license plate violation. Just then, a lady came out of the candy store and got in the car. He drove off in a huff. I returned to the intersection and resumed traffic duty. One week later, I was called into Chief McManus's office. The man wrote a nasty letter to Chief McManus stating that I was rude to him and that I cursed at him. I was very authoritative but not rude to him I told the Chief. He also enclosed the written warning ticket that I issued, asking the Chief to excuse it. Chief McManus heard my side of the story. The Chief said to me, "Robert. You made one big mistake that day. You were actually too nice to him. You should have arrested him for obstructing traffic, failure to display two license plates and failure to obey an Officers signal. Otherwise, you did a fine job and you are not in any trouble. When I get letters like this one, I know my Officers are out there doing their jobs. Carry on and be careful out there Robert." I shook the Chief's hand and thanked him for being fair with me. •

MEMORIES OF A RETIRED COP

On August 19, 1967, a civil disobedience occurred in the city of New Haven, Connecticut. I was on extra duty at a teenage dance at the Jewish Community Center on Chapel Street. Shortly before 10:00 PM, Officer Al Gambardella came to the Jewish Community Center and stated to me that a serious incident had occurred on Congress Avenue and that all police personnel were being recalled to report to Station Two, located at 710 Sherman Parkway for further instructions. The dance was not scheduled to end until 11:00 PM so in an orderly fashion, I arranged for all the teenagers to call their parents to pick them up as soon as possible and that the dance has ended. There were approximately six telephones in the offices at the Jewish Center for the teens to use to call their parents. It took approximately 30-45 minutes to clear the dance hall and building. Once everyone was safely out of the building, I headed to Station 2. Upon arrival, I was handed an unloaded Winchester 12 gauge riot shot gun and shot gun shells with instructions not to load the weapon until instructed to do so. We were put into several police cars and driven to Congress and Howard Avenues where we assembled and waited for further instructions. We were told that a very large and angry crowd had gathered at Congress Avenue and Kossuth Street. People's Market was on fire and that there was also looting of several businesses in the immediate area. After we were instructed to load our Winchester 12 gauge shot guns, we formed a police line and walked from Congress and Howard Avenues to Congress and Kossuth Street. Upon arrival, it was determined that the New Haven Fire Department was under attack from the crowd that were throwing rocks, bottles and bricks at the Fireman trying to put out the fires. It was a battle zone and extremely dangerous for anyone on the street. I not only feared for my own safety but for the safety of all the police and fire personnel as well as residents. We all exercised extreme patience and determination to keep the situation under control. After numerous warnings to clear the streets, we were given the command to arrest anyone not complying. Dozens of residents were arrested and placed in waiting paddy wagons. The Salvation Army arrived with hot coffee and sandwiches. We stayed awake all night and all day Sunday until some of us got a break and were taken to the Park Plaza for hot showers and some rest. I arrived at about 2:00 PM and took a shower and just got into bed when the telephone rang. "Be ready in 5 minutes to return to Congress Avenue," the Sergeant said and hung up the telephone. Connecticut State Police as well as the National Guard arrived Sunday afternoon to give us much-needed backup. We remained on 12 hour per day shifts with no days off for weeks until things quieted down. I did not see my family for several days. They of course were worrying about me. I was worried about them as well. The rest is history. •

ELDERLY WOMAN SWINDLED

In the spring of 1962, I was on the 8:00 AM to 4:00 PM shift patrolling downtown on foot in New Haven. I answered the Emergency Red Telephone on Church and Chapel Streets. The desk Sergeant instructed me to come to Headquarters and speak to an elderly woman who was making a complaint about two other women that swindled her out of some money. I arrived at headquarters and met with an elderly lady. I escorted her into the squad room where we could sit down and talk. I can't remember the name of the Bank next to the Post office on Church Street between Chapel and Court Street, but the lady stated to me that she entered her bank to make a deposit to her savings account. As she was leaving the bank, she was approached by two well-dressed women who had a financial proposition for her. They crossed the street and sat on a park bench in the green. They told this naive lady that they were investment bankers and they were impressed with her and said they knew that she was a woman of quality. By the way she was dressed and also by her mannerisms. I believe this compliment was part of the scheme to impress her and maybe let her guard down. They told her that if she withdrew $3000.00 in cash to show good faith, they would invest her money and double it within one hour. They also showed her a large amount of cash which they claimed was their own money which they were using to double their own money. The lady fell for it and entered her bank and came out with the $3000.00 in cash and handed it to the 2 women who were still waiting for her across the street on the bench. They showed her their driver's licenses and a few credit cards to prove who they were. The elderly woman, whom was impeccably dressed, ran a few errands to pass the time and returned to the park bench in one hour. She waited for another hour and finally realized that she was taken for a ride so she went to the Police Station to report it. She gave me a pretty good description of the woman and I put out a general police broadcast to be on the lookout for these women. They were never located. My Sergeant reminded me that these criminals seek out individuals that look like they are also looking for something for nothing. I'm not saying that the victim was one of those people, but no one will double your money in one hour unless there is a catch to it. Obviously there was a big catch to it. •

In the spring of 1968, I took my family to New Hampshire for a one-week vacation. We came back very late on a Saturday night because I was due back to work that Monday morning. Sunday afternoon I decided to take a ride over to the Puerto Rican Social Club, located on 229 Grand Avenue second floor. I had been one of the two Police Officers that worked there on the weekends when I was available so I was well known and as far as I knew, well liked. The feelings were mutual. I was known as "Bobby El Policia". My kids wanted to go with me so I took Terry, age thirteen, Alice, age eleven, and Bobby Jr. age six. We got there about 2:00 PM. We walked up the stairs and I greeted my friend Wilson who was the President of the P.R. Club. I think his wife Felicia was also there. I ordered a cold beer (una cerveza, bien fria) and three sodas for the kids. As I sat at a table with my kids, I felt that something was very wrong. Some men in the Club seemed angry for some reason. I had no fear for myself, but I started to worry about my kids. I was armed with a 38 Police Special revolver and everyone there knew that I was a Policeman. Then, four men approached my table. One had bandages on his head. They were angry with the Police in general because last night, there was a big fight at the Club and several people were arrested and injured, including the man with the bandages on his head. They vented on me and told me how much they hated the police. I let them talk and get off whatever was on their minds and when they were finished, I had my opportunity to speak. I was completely surrounded by angry men and I didn't like it. My children were crying and they said, "Daddy, let's go home please." I did not want anyone there to think I didn't care about the Hispanic people or The Hispanic Community, because I did. I cared about everyone and how the police treated them. That had always been on my mind, but this incident had nothing to do with me. I was on a well-deserved vacation with my family away from New Haven. I believe that if I was on duty that Saturday night, this would never have happened. I told this group of angry men that if I didn't care, I would not be there visiting with my children as a friend. I would not be sitting amongst friends, socializing. Wilson Morales came over and said the same thing to the group of angry men. He said, "Bobby," (that's what people called me), "is a friend of the Spanish people and he would never let this happen, if he was on duty last night." The tension eased up a bit and there were handshakes and apologies but I stayed alert for any possibility of anything happening, especially with my children present. Alone, I could handle it, but not with my children in possible danger. I did not finish my beer. I did not want my mind clouded or my guard to be dropped. This to me was a very serious matter. Anything could happen. When performing my official duties as a Police Officer, I would risk my life but not when off duty with my children present. I've seen people shot dead for less. This was months after the riots broke out in New Haven and there was still tension in the air. This day was a turning point in my life where I knew that the old days of socializing in New Haven were over and it was too dangerous. I continued to work at the Puerto Rican Social Club as a Policeman and friend of the people, but I also knew times were changing in New Haven and not for the better. •

ROOKIES FIRST TIME IN POLICE CAR

One week before we graduated from the Police Academy in March 1961, the whole class was assigned to ride an eight-hour shift with a seasoned Police Officer. We were told to report at 1600 hours (4:00 PM) the next day and wear the complete uniform including all the equipment that was assigned to us. Ticket books, everything. We will actually do everything a Police Officer does. We were all excited. Fights, accidents, maybe a shootout with criminals with guns? Everything we imagined and seen on television would happen on the street. The next afternoon, I couldn't wait to go on duty. I read the schedule on the wall in the squad room. *Officer R. Meyerholz will ride with Officer G. Carey in radio car 24.* I looked for Officer Carey in the squad room. I found him. I introduced myself. "I'm riding with you tonight sir." "Oh, really?" "Yes sir." "That's just great. A rookie with me for eight hours. Don't ask to drive." "I won't sir." After roll call we walked outside to a line of black police cars. All Chevy two-door Biscayne's. "This one is ours," he said, pointing to one of the identical police cars. I got in the passenger side and got comfortable. Motorola 2 way radio. 4 channels. Siren switch. Overhead red lights switch. I was age 25 but I felt like a kid. My dream of becoming a Police Officer was real. I wanted to save people. I wanted to make a difference. As we drove south on Sherman Parkway, Officer Carey observed a car run the red light on Whalley and Sherman. He gave chase and put on the overhead lights and switched the siren button so it would operate if he pushed on the horn button. This way, he explained that when in pursuit, your hands are always on the steering wheel. Wow. That made sense. I sat in the car and observed Officer Carey give the man a ticket for the red light violation. Then he went to a red call box and called the Record Division to report the motor vehicle arrest. "Now, you have traffic duty at 4:30 PM." "Where?" "Berger Bros. on Derby Avenue." We drove to Berger Bros. I got out of the car and waited for the shop workers to come out of the side door and get in their cars or cross the street on foot. I stood in the street for thirty minutes and directed traffic until everyone was out and had left the shop. I got back in the car. Now we will do some patrolling. Look for motor vehicle violations and parking violations. We tagged a few cars on the sidewalk in front of Al's Restaurant on Whalley and Winthrop. We heard some complaints that they were only in the

Restaurant for five minutes. Officer Carey says never argue with them; either give them a break and void the ticket or drive away. About 6:30 PM the dispatcher called our car. "Calling car 24." "Answer the radio, Bob." "This is car 24." "Signal 13 and call your station, right away." "Go ahead, Bob. Pick up that red phone and call station Two." "Yes sir." I got out of the car on Whalley and the Boulevard and called Station Two. "Hello. This is Station Two." "Sir, car 24, sir. You called us?" "Yeah kid? Go over to Chuck's and pick up 2 regular coffees and one black. Got that kid?" "Yes sir." We had two minor domestic calls all night and that was it. I was very disappointed. But later in years, I had wished it had stayed that quiet. •

GREEK SOCIAL CLUB ROBBERY

In 1969, there was a robbery at the Greek Social Club, then located on South Orange Street in New Haven. One of the robbers was shot by one of our Detectives. Maybe someone can confirm the accuracy of the date this occurred. The robber was taken to St. Raphael's Hospital where he was treated for his injuries and then admitted. Because of the serious nature of the crime, the robber was being guarded 24/7 by the New Haven Police Department. The following night I was working the 12:00 midnight to 8:00 AM shift. I was assigned to guard the prisoner and was sent to St. Raphael's to relieve the 4:00 to 12:00 shift Officer. I arrived at about 12:10 AM. I went up to the third floor where the prisoner was confined to a room. The Officer filled me in and showed me the room and the prisoner who was sleeping at the time. He also showed me the handcuffs attached to the prisoner's wrist and the other end to the hospital bed, making escape practically impossible. There was a chair in the hallway facing the prisoner's room and a pile of books and newspapers on the floor. I settled in for the night and the other Officer went home. Police and Nurses usually always get along very well. I like Nurses. The Nurses would bring me coffee or food because I could not leave the prisoner unattended. He was facing some pretty serious charges. After reading for about two hours, I got sleepy and apparently dozed off. Like I said, Nurses and Policeman usually get along. So, instead of waking me up, the Nurses decided to play a joke on me. One of the Nurses shook me awake and said, "Bob, Bob. Wake up. Your prisoner just ran down the hall and into the stairway and down the stairs." Instead of checking his room, I ran down the hall in that direction before the Nurse could stop me to tell me it was only a joke. I ran all the way down the stairs to the street level and outside the Hospital on the Chapel Street side. Looking both ways, nothing was in sight. In my own mind, the prisoner had escaped on my watch. Nothing more to do now but to call the station and report that my prisoner had escaped and maybe get suspended or worse. I walked back to the third floor and went to the Nurses' Station to use the telephone. The night Nurse in charge, who was in on the joke asked me, "What are you doing?" "Calling the station." "For what?" "Because my prisoner escaped." "Did you check his bed?" "No." "Well check the room," she said. The guy was sound asleep and snoring and still cuffed to his hospital bed. I said, "Where are those

Nurses?" "They are hiding from you." "They better hide," I said. I was wrong for dozing off but that was a dirty trick and I swore to get even with them. I'm laughing now and still looking for them, forty-five years later.

PS: I still like Nurses. •

OFF DUTY POLICEMAN IN HOSPITAL PAJAMAS

Not sure of the exact date but sometime in early in 1966, I was at St. Raphael's for minor surgery. One week before, I was collecting the drunks from the lower green on Temple Street. This real heavy guy was sprawled out on his back so drunk that he could not stand. The paddy wagon was standing by. I picked him up under his arms and my partner picked up his legs. I had the heavy end. As I lifted, I felt a strain in my groin area. I ended up with a hernia, which required surgery. I had a private room on the second floor on the Sherman Avenue side. The surgery was job related from the hernia so the PD made sure I had a private room at St. Raphael's. At about 8:00 PM, the telephone in my room rang. The desk Sergeant from Headquarters received a complaint from a visitor on the second floor at St. Raphael's. The complaint was that a man in pajamas and a police badge pinned to his pajamas was threatened to arrest him if he didn't leave because visiting hours were over. "Serge. That wasn't me sir," I said. "I know that Bob, but go out in the hallway and see if some idiot is walking around with a badge threatening to arrest people." "Okay Serge. I'll call you right back." "And Bob. If you find him, take that GD badge away from him, okay?" "Yes sir." I walked out in the hall and sure enough, there was a young man with a New Haven Police badge on the front of his PJ's telling people that visiting hours were over and to leave now. This was 8:20 PM. I approached him and asked what he was doing? "Who are you?" he asked. "Officer Meyerholz. Per orders from Headquarters, give me your badge. Some citizen lodged a complaint against you," I told him. "There is Hospital Security to do that." He gave me his badge and asked if he was in trouble. "Not sure," I said, "but don't get involved in Hospital business." "What are you here for?" I asked him. "Tonsils." Ouch. I felt sorry for the kid. He's only been on the force for three months. He was just showing off his badge. I called the Sergeant and told him I had the rookie's badge. "What's the number on it?" I gave him the number. "Thanks Bob. Give it to Hospital Security and I'll send a car for it." "Serge," I said, "as rookies, we all do some stupid things. Is the kid in trouble?" "No, but I'm teaching him a lesson. Let him sweat it out." "Thanks Serge." •

STRANDED TEENS AT NEW HAVEN COLISEUM

In the fall of 1974, I worked a concert at the New Haven Coliseum when Three Dog Night group was playing. We had approximately 45 New Haven Police Officers on duty. We expected a large crowd and we got a large crowd. The concert started at 9:00 PM and broke at approximately 11:45 PM. After the concert I was assigned traffic duty at the exit of the parking garage. By the time people reached the top levels of the garage and got in their cars, it was about 12:00 AM when the cars started to leave the garage and come down that spiral ramp. I allowed as many cars as possible to exit the garage before stopping them and allowing cars on South Orange Street to proceed. With all the noise from the traffic I heard someone saying, "Officer, Officer!" On the sidewalk there were two teenage girls. They were trying to get my attention. Unable to leave my traffic post and unable to hear a word they were saying, I motioned to them to wait for me. They stood there patiently doing a little dance from the cold chill in the air. Finally at about 12:30 AM, I was able to leave my traffic post. I walked over to them and asked what I could do for them. They were driving a 1965-66 Ford Mustang. Their car was parked on the top lever and it wouldn't start. My personal car, a Volkswagen van, was parked on the lower lever. We took the escalator up and reached the top level. The girls were Betty, 20 from South Windsor, Connecticut, and Cathy, 18 from Massapequa Park, New York. It was Betty's car, so I had her open the hood. With my flashlight I discovered that the battery was loose from broken battery hold down bolts and it had a large hole in the side of it. All of the battery acid had leaked out. I said, "Girls, you are not going anywhere with that broken battery." Betty told me, coming in from Long Island; she jammed on her brakes due to heavy traffic on Long Wharf and heard a loud noise coming from the engine compartment. The battery apparently shifted and struck the cooling fan, putting a large hole in the side of the battery. They both started to cry. My own daughters were that age. I couldn't leave them there alone in the cold and dark so I put them in my VW. We drove around looking to buy a battery. The few gas stations open had their parts locked up until morning. I found a gas station open on Congress near Howard. No new batteries but the attendant said I could look for an old battery behind the building to put in and jump it to get them home. I found a Ford battery and he gave it to us. I thanked him and we went back to the Coliseum. With the tools I had in my car, I changed the battery and used an old coat hanger to tie it in. I jumped the battery and the car started. The girls were very happy and I got two big hugs. My hands were so greasy and I got grease on my blue shirt. They were in route to Springfield, Massachusetts, following the Three Dog Night group. I got them on I-91 to Hartford. We were pen pals for several years afterwards. I was very late coming home and Mary was angry. After telling the story about the two stranded girls and seeing my greasy hands, she calmed down. Betty and I are still friends. •

After getting Betty's Mustang running, the girls asked me for the route to Springfield, Massachusetts. They were following the Three Dog Night group. I said follow me girls. We exited the same spiral ramp that I had been doing hand traffic earlier. I got on the Oak Street connector and then on to I-91 northbound. I told them that I was getting off at exit 8 and to continue on 91 all the way to Springfield. We waved at each other as we went our separate ways. Two weeks later, I received letters from both girls thanking me and telling me their parents were writing letters to the Chief. A year later Betty's dad died and she wrote to me, telling me the sad news. I drove to South Windsor to pay my respects to her and her family. Months later, Cathy wrote to me and said her father was a Policeman and he wanted to meet me. The next Saturday I was off. I asked Mary if she wanted to take a ride with me to Massapequa Park. "No," she said, "that's too far. You go alone and be careful and behave yourself." "I will honey." Cathy gave me her phone number so I called her the night before. "Is tomorrow okay, Cathy?" "Yes. See you then. Daddy wants to meet you." Next morning I headed to Lake Shore Drive, Massapequa Park, New York. No GPS, no cell phones in those days, just a map to the Southern State Parkway… a very long drive from New Haven. Finally arriving in Massapequa Park to the address I had been writing to, I pulled into a circular driveway and noticed a black Ford unmarked police car with five more antennas than I had on my police car. I rang the bell and a maid came to the door. "Wait," I said to myself, "Daddy's a Policeman? Must be the wrong house." "Hello. You must be Bob? I'm Martha. Come in. Cathy is expecting you." I looked around. Daddy is a Policeman? What am I doing wrong? Just then Cathy comes running down a long staircase. I brought a gift for her. A hat. After a big hug, her father comes down the same staircase, dressed in a T-shirt and jeans. He was about my size, 6' 1", 220 lbs. We shook hands and sat in the kitchen. Martha served us coffee. "Thanks for taking care of my daughter. I wrote to your Chief." Cathy's father was a Deputy Police Chief with the New York Transit Authority Police Department. That explains all the antennas on his car. He asked if I liked horses. "Yes, but I don't own one." He owned a riding stable in Huntington, Long Island so we drove to Huntington and looked at some beautiful horses, including one that Cathy owned. Back to the house

Martha served lunch and then I said my good byes and left for home. A very long day for me but I will never forget Betty and Cathy and their families. I am in touch with Betty via Facebook but I can't locate Cathy. Her last name, as I can remember it was Christy or Christi. •

GOOD SAMARITAN THIEF

In 1975, the New Haven Police Department was having a big problem with parked cars being broken into every time The New Haven Coliseum had a concert or any other event including hockey games. Just behind the Coliseum on State Street there was a large building designated 1 State Street, which is still there. The Coliseum is gone, but 1 State Street is still there. Just behind 1 State Street there is a small one-way street that has been renamed State Street North. To save the $5.00 parking fee charged by the Parking Authority, some people would take a chance and park on this dark and deserted street. The street was littered with broken glass from thieves breaking the windows of parked cars and stealing anything valuable in the vehicles: coats, cameras, pocketbooks and even AM/FM stereo radios and 8-track players. One night on the 4:00 to 12:00 shift, I was assigned to that area. I drove an unmarked police car in hopes of catching some of these thieves. Just after dark I slowly circled this street in my unmarked police car, looking for any suspicious activity. After maybe the 10th time circling the area, I noticed brake lights flickering on and off on one of the parked cars. That meant that someone was in that parked car. Could have been someone sleeping who stepped on the brake pedal or a couple of lovers sitting in the car. Anything was possible. I pulled around the corner on Fair Street and parked my police car and got out. I slowly walked back to the parked car. The first thing I noticed was the driver's window was smashed with broken glass all over the sidewalk. I shone my flashlight in the car. There was a young man with his head under the dash board and his legs over the front seat. His right shoulder was on the brake pedal, he was removing the stereo radio from under the dash board. I announced myself as a police officer and ordered the young man out of the car. He was a young black male maybe age eighteen. He climbed out the driver's side and told me he had just chased three or four white boys from the car who were trying to steal the man's radio. He was being a Good Samaritan and he was putting the radio back. "What?" I said. "You were putting the radio back?" "Yeah man." I searched and handcuffed the young man and charged him with tampering with a motor vehicle and destruction of property (broken window) and attempted theft. I warned him not to tell the Judge that ridiculous story about chasing other boys. "You were caught fair and square. Deal with it," I advised him. Five weeks later the case came to the 6th circuit court and I was there to testify. When his name was called, he approached the bench and pleaded not guilty. He had a Public Defender. He told the Judge the story of his innocence and that he was a Good Samaritan and how he chased the real thieves and tried to put the radio back in the car. The Judge had to clear the courtroom because everyone was laughing, except me. I knew better. After six or seven continuances, he was found guilty on all charges and paid a fine to avoid jail time. •

OFF DUTY POLICEMAN WAS VICTIM

In May1972, one Sunday afternoon, I was driving my personal 1965 Cadillac Coupe Deville. I was off duty and I decided to visit one of my favorite Spanish Restaurants on Washington Avenue. My 7-year-old car had all the latest accessories including an AM-FM stereo radio and separate 8-track player, all factory built into the dash. The restaurant was located on Washington Avenue between 6 Corners and Daggott Street, near Leon's Restaurant. I parked my Caddy ½ block away toward the 6 Corners and locked the doors. I entered the restaurant and sat at the counter. We exchanged greetings in Spanish. I said, "Buenas tardes amigos. Tengo hambre." (Good afternoon friends. I'm hungry.) Everyone knew me and knew that I was a Policeman, a friend to the Spanish Community, a Policeman to trust and who cared. I ordered one of my favorites meals. Arroz y alubias con chuletas (rice and beans with pork chops.) I was there for maybe 20 minutes when a guy opened the front door and asked if anyone owned a blue Caddy parked down the street. "That's my car, why?" "Some kids broke your window and stole something." I ran out of the restaurant, followed my some of my friends, to find my passenger side window smashed, with glass all over the front leather seat. Ripped from the dash was my 8-track player. The damage done to my car was incredible. I was very hurt and angry at the same time. I went back to the restaurant and paid for my meal and went home. I obviously lost my appetite. That day, I realized that the New Haven where I was born and grew up in had changed. If an off duty Policeman who was friendly and helpful and kind to the community could be a victim, then no one was safe in New Haven or anywhere else. To add insult to injury, a few days later, one of my friends told me he knew where my 8-track was. A boy from White Street had it and I can get it back for $50.00. I told him to tell the boy what to do with the 8-track. To pay to get my own property back was outrageous. "That stolen 8-track will bring him only bad luck," I said. Months later, he was arrested with thousands of dollars worth of stolen auto accessories in his home. My 8-track was not part of it but he did admit to stealing it. •

ESCAPED HOSPITAL PATIENT HAVING A BEER

One day in 1972, I was working the day shift. 8:00 to 4:00 PM. I was patrolling in Westville. I got a call that a patient from St. Raphael's Hospital was missing. He was described as a white male, 5'8" tall, age forty-five, last seen wearing blue pajamas. The male patient was scheduled for major surgery the next morning. While Hospital Security searched the Hospital interior, I drove around the perimeter of the Hospital. George Street to Orchard, Orchard to Chapel. Then Chapel to Sherman Avenue. Nothing. I had the dispatcher call Hospital Security to see if they located him yet. Then I got a hunch. Being a moderate drinking man myself at the time, I decided to check a local bar that I remembered being on Sherman Avenue and the corner of Scranton Street. My wife, Mary, just told me it was called The Beacon. I parked outside the bar and walked in the front door of the bar. About six men were seated at the bar, sipping beer and whiskey. One guy in the middle was dressed in blue pajamas, it was like they were hiding him. That was my first clue that I found my escaped patient. I approached him and before I could ask him anything, he offered to buy me a beer. "I'm on duty mister but I think you are playing hooky from St. Raphael's, right?" "Yeah, Big day tomorrow so I thought I would have a couple of beers today." I did let him finish his beer and then notified my dispatcher that I located the missing patient and was in route back to the hospital with him. I pulled in the Emergency Room driveway and Security was waiting. It was really comical to see a guy sitting at a bar in pajamas. One of those moments where wish I took a picture of this. •

POLICEMANS WIFE RIPPED OFF

The following story is true. It happened in 1974-75 while I was on duty at the then new Police Station at 1 Union Avenue in New Haven, Connecticut. I was working the 4:00 to 12:00 midnight shift. My general area of car patrol was downtown. From 4:00 to 6:00 PM I was assigned to Detention or prisoner lock up. I would book in new arrestees and assist the desk Sergeant. This day at about 4:30 PM, the Sergeants wife called him. I handed him the phone. Next thing, he's saying to her, "What do you mean $450.00? I sent you there for two front tires. That's all." When he got off the phone he was very upset. He told me that he sent his wife to a tire store in the area for two badly needed front tires. They sold her two front shock absorbers, rear brakes, two front upper ball joints, etc. The store is still in business so I will not name the store. She drove in for two new tires and had her children with her. As she sat in the waiting room with the children, the Service Manager came out and said to her, "You need all these additional parts and service." She said, "I'll tell my husband." He looked at the children and said, "Are they your kids?" "Yes." "You would endanger their lives driving an unsafe car?" A mother's protective instinct kicked in and she authorized the extra parts and service, knowing her husband would be furious. I said, "Serge. You are mad at the wrong person. It's not your wife. It's the Service Manager." We had two other Police Officer's relieve us at Detention and we drove over to the auto center, just blocks away. We walked in the front door. The Service Manager greeted us with a big smile. I did the talking. "Hello. The Sergeant's wife just left here with all these new parts and services." He stopped smiling. "The lady with the cute kids? Remember?" "Yes." "I want to see the old parts. The front shocks, the rear brake shoes, the front upper ball joints, etc." "Well, we threw them away. She didn't ask to save them." "Where are they?" "In the rear of my building." We walked outside. There was a pile of old shock absorbers five feet tall. Not one shock absorber was leaking hydraulic fluid. General Motors Delco shocks are gold and red. Ford has blue. I tested dozens of them. I have a mechanical background so I knew what I was talking about. The Service Manager said nothing in his defense. He took my Sergeant's credit card and gave him credit for everything except the two front new tires, mounting and balancing. That amounted to under $100.00. He received credit for more than $300.00. I still reported it to the Connecticut Motor Vehicle Department, Dealers and Repairers Section. I told them that they made restitution after they got caught. It was a down right rip off to a nice lady with adorable children. Almost every auto repair shop works on commission. The Service Manager and the Mechanics. You go in for an oil change or some minor repair and they try to sell you shocks, struts, brake shoes and pads, etc. all to make more money on commission. It's dishonest and downright wrong. That day, the good guys won. •

8-YEAR-OLD FALLS WHILE ICE SKATING

On August 4, 1965, I was on police car patrol in the New Haven downtown area. At Approximately 1:00 PM, I was dispatched to the New Haven Arena in regard to an injured child. Officer Robert Forbes was on duty at the Arena. Officer Forbes called for an ambulance and also for a police car to respond. An 8-year-old girl took a terrible fall on the ice, causing an injury to her head. Rather than wait for the ambulance, I took her and her mom to Yale New Haven Hospital for treatment. Normally, sick or injured people are transported via ambulance. Because of the severity of the injury and also because it was a child who was frightened of ambulance's, I decided to transport Katy and her mom in my police car to the Hospital. One week later, I was notified that Katy's mom wrote a nice letter to Chief McManus. •

POLICEMAN SHOOTS RABID RACOON

In the spring of 1965, one Saturday afternoon, I got a call to respond to a home on Englewood Drive. The report was that a rabid raccoon was chasing children in the back yard. Upon my arrival, the lady of the house met me at the front door. The lady informed me that there was a raccoon in her back yard that came out of the woods and started chasing the children who were playing in the yard. I cautiously walked around the driveway side of the house and as I entered the yard, a raccoon came running out of the woods and started to chase me. It was not foaming at the mouth but it was aggressive and showing its teeth. There was a Bilco style metal basement door attached to the house so I climbed on the door to get away from the raccoon, assuming it was sick otherwise it would not be acting so aggressively in broad daylight. This raccoon attempted to bite my legs as I was standing at the top end of the Bilco door. I had no choice but to un-holster my weapon and shoot this creature once with my Colt 38 caliber police revolver. The bullet went right through the animal and also through the Bilco metal door, leaving a nice round hole. The animal was dead. My first thought was, "How will this affect the children?" who were in the house watching me through the window and second, "Will the lady be angry that I put a hole in her Bilco basement door?" The kids came running out the front door with the lady. "I'm sorry ma'am. I had no choice but to shoot the raccoon, as it was attempting to bite me." I told her the city of New Haven would pay for the damage to the door. "Oh no, Officer. That's a conversation piece. Leave it alone. I love that bullet hole. Please leave it like that." The kids were not traumatized. They were thrilled, watching a Policeman shoot a "dangerous" animal right there in the yard. I had the Animal Shelter pick up the dead raccoon. They sent the animal carcass to Hartford and it was confirmed that the raccoon was in fact rabid. All and all, everything turned out okay, just one happy lady and a bunch of kids with a story to tell Monday when they go back to school. •

No other job in the world gets a person into the intimate lives of other people like a Policeman's job. No other job in the world can you see, firsthand, the good and the bad in all nationalities, skin colors, religions, sexual preferences, than a Policeman's job. I have seen it all and I have heard it all. Sergeant DiLieto once said in the Police Academy that we would meet people face to face that would put a bullet in our head and then get a good night's sleep without even giving it a second thought.

I have been in homes so filthy that when I went home that night, I would thank God for having a wife who left a dish or 2 in the sink. I would kiss my children as they slept in clean and warm beds.

I would also think of the poor family on Downing Street in the projects who fed their children dog food, because it was eight cans for one dollar.

I would think about the apartment on Haven Street where I was sent to a domestic fight that had so many cockroaches in the kitchen that after I realized they were crawling on my uniform pants leg, I retreated to the front porch and told the lady I would not stay in her kitchen and that I would talk to her outside. I refused to reenter that house. She refused to come outside saying, "I pay your salary." My Sergeant was sent to the apartment. When my Sergeant arrived he said, "What's the problem Bob?" "Serge," I said, "the apartment is crawling with cockroaches." My Sergeant walked in and came right out. He told the lady that his Policeman would not enter a roach infested apartment like hers. She slammed the door and called us m*****f**fers.

I recall the wealthy doctor downtown that called to report that his heroin-addicted wife stole his Cadillac and was trying to sell it for $200.00 on Park Street at a Drug Rehab Center.

Being a Police Officer makes you so appreciate what you have and makes you love and appreciate your family more. There is so much more evil in this world today than in 1961, but look around and still see all the good there is in this world. As a little boy growing up on Arthur Street in New

Haven with 3 siblings (RIP, all three are gone), my mom would tuck us in bed at night and she would always say as she kissed our foreheads, "Good night, God bless you, I love you." We would repeat the same words back to her. I will never be ashamed to say, I love you to a family member or a friend. I will never be ashamed to say God bless you. We all need more love and hugs and more of God in our lives. •

POLICEMEN WORK WITH HISPANIC COMMUNITY

I remember my first night working at the Puerto Rican Club on Grand Avenue. It was sometime in the winter of 1965, the Club had a reputation as a trouble spot with many fights. When you mix alcohol with beautiful woman, that's to be expected. I was told to be there at 7:00 PM for the 9:00 PM dance. My partner Officer Richard Kittrell was there ahead of me. Rich would work the front door and I would work the second floor where the dance hall and bar were located. Rich was well liked and respected in the Hispanic community. He also rode a police motorcycle. I introduced myself to the President of the Club, Wilson Morales and his lovely wife, Felicia. They gave me the name of Bobby El Policia. I had no knowledge of the Spanish language. The dance started on time. I mingled with the crowd. I tried to balance myself with authority but also as a friend. I wanted to be respected but also I wanted to be liked. It worked. A genuine smile does a lot. Anyway, at about 10:30, they played a song called El Corazon Herido. It was a bolero, aslow dance. Wilson said, "Bobby, that girl wants to dance with you." I did not want to offend her but I was not sure I could do this while on duty. I called Station 2 and spoke to my Sergeant. He said, "Well, why not. Bob, no drinking and keep your full uniform on, okay?" "Yes Sergeant." I danced with this very pretty girl from New York. I thanked her in English and she thanked me in Spanish. Late Richard also danced as I covered the front door. Public relations were a high priority in those days. A short while later the girl requested to dance with me again. Again not to offend anyone, I danced with her. But at the same time being alert of any possible trouble. Just before the dance, some men that I met wrote down something on a piece of paper. It was a Spanish lesson for me. They said tell the girl you are honored to dance with her only in Spanish, so she will understand your good intentions. Ok guys. Thanks. It said, "Con mucho gusto estoy interesado en usted." What I didn't know was, it was a joke on me. I was telling this young lady that I was interested in her. I told Richard about this and he said, "They got you too, huh?" Wilson took care of things so there were no misunderstandings. No more jokes guys, I said. It is so hard to maintain a balance of authority and of friendship. Some people mistake friendship and kindness with weakness. All and all this genuine friendship

I showed helped the Spanish Community to know that the Police are also friends. •

LADY WITHOUT HEAT IN JANUARY

In the second week of January 1977, I was assigned to Communications on the 12:00 midnight to 8:00 AM shift. My job was to answer 911 calls and also other non-emergency or routine calls and then transfer them to the police dispatcher. It was during the week so it was pretty slow. At about 3:00 AM, I received a call from an elderly lady who reported that her furnace had stopped working and her apartment was very cold. She stated to me that she lived alone with her cat and tried unsuccessfully to contact her fuel oil company for service. The weather outside was bitter cold. I asked the lady if she knew what the temperature was inside of her apartment. She put down the phone to check the thermometer on her furnace control. She stated that it was 52 degrees and dropping. Normally, a call like this is not police related but in this case I made it my business. I had an elderly woman who could potentially freeze to death. She could not get her oil Company on the phone. She tried several oil Companies but because she was not a customer, they would not come out. I made sure she was bundled up before asking her some questions. She assured me she had a blanket wrapped around her and her cat was snuggled up to her. I asked for her name, address, and telephone number, but most important, who was her oil company and their phone number. She gave me all necessary information. I called the "so called" emergency service phone number. I got an answering machine... so much for emergency service. I went into a file for owners of businesses and called the owner at home. A man answered on the 2nd ring. "Hello," he said. "Hello. This is Officer Meyerholz with the New Haven Police Department." "Yes, what's wrong?" "You have a Mrs. M*** who lives on Huntington Street and her furnace stopped and she needs emergency service immediately." He was annoyed that I called his home number. Too bad, I have a lady that's in real trouble. He said he was on the way to deliver oil of fix her furnace. One hour later Mrs. M***** called me to say the furnace man just left and her furnace was working and the apartment was getting warm. She thanked me and asked for my name. A week later, I received a copy of her letter to Chief DiLieto. This is what Policeman do. They get paid to help people, especially in emergency situations. •

BLOCKING DRIVEWAY RESULTS IN SHOOTING

IN the summer of 1968, one Saturday afternoon, I was dispatched to Boyd's Barber Shop on Dixwell Avenue, located just south of Munson Street. Like any barberhop, Saturday was the busiest day of the week. Children were out of school. People were off from work so Saturday was the day that barbers were the busiest and have a chance to make money. The nature of the complaint was a possible shooting. Two Police Officers were dispatched. I was the first Officer to arrive on scene. There was a fairly new Pontiac parked in the driveway. A man was slumped over the steering wheel. The man was not breathing and after closer examination, it appeared that he had a bullet hole in his left temple. Very little blood at the scene. I called for an ambulance and a Police Supervisor. My backup stayed with the man that was shot. I entered the barbershop with my right hand resting on my Colt 38. Not knowing who the shooter was, I was being very cautious. There were two barbers on duty. One of the barbers stated that he shot the man because he was blocking his driveway from customers wanting to park their cars in the backyard. He stated that he had warned the "cat" (man) to move his car. The "cat" replied, "I ain't moving s**t man," and turned his motor off. Then, he said, "I shot him." The man handed me, a loaded 25 caliber handgun. He stated that he felt justified in shooting the man because he was disrupting his business by blocking his driveway. The operator of the vehicle was taken to Yale New Haven Hospital where he was pronounced dead on arrival. His vehicle was towed to the police garage to be processed. At this point, I turned over the investigation to the Detective Division. The barber was subsequently arrested for a homicide. I do not have any further information as to the outcome of the investigation. •

ROOKIE ARRESTS DRUNK DRIVER

In December,1961, we were doing our second six months of probation on the 12:00 midnight to 8:00 AM shift. I had mentioned in another post that we kept busy making motor vehicle arrests while walking the beats downtown. At about 4:00 AM, one of my rookie classmates walked into Headquarters with his ticket book in his hand. I was standing at the front desk talking to my Lieutenant. He proudly announced to the Sergeant that he just arrested a drunk driver. "Wonderful Ladd. How did you do that on foot?" The rookie stated that he approached the driver who was waiting for a red traffic light on Grove and Orange streets and asked him for his license and registration. As the man produced these documents, the rookie detected an odor of alcohol on the man's breath. Remembering what he learned in police academy, he had the guy get out of his car and walk a straight line. The man kept stumbling so the rookie took out his ticket book and after looking up the State Statute on Operating a Motor Vehicle While under the Influence Of Alcohol Or Drugs, he wrote a ticket and handed it to the man. "Good police work Ladd. Very good police work. Where is the drunk driver?" "I let him go and told him to drive home slowly and do not drive again until he sobers up. He only lives off of Orange Street Serge." "What? You let him drive home, intoxicated?" "Yes Sergeant. He wasn't that drunk. Only a little drunk, sir." "Jesus, Mary and Joseph, Ladd. You new recruits are driving me to drink. What if he has an accident on the way home?" "It's Ok Serge. He said he has insurance." "Jesus Mary and Joseph. You are supposed to take him into custody." "How Sergeant? I don't have a car?" "You are supposed to call for a police car to take him into custody. You better pray he doesn't kill someone on the way home. You let a drunk driver, drive his own car home?" "I told him to be careful, sir." "Give me your ticket book Ladd. No more motor vehicle arrests for you tonight. Now get the hell out of here." I was laughing my ass off, but I didn't want the Sergeant to see me. All rookies make mistakes, some more than others. •

THE MOTHER FROM HELL

On Tuesday August 4th, 1964, at approximately 8:30 AM, I was dispatched to the home of a middle aged female baby sitter on Fillmore Street in Fair Haven. She was a woman with a clean and safe home who loves children, the perfect baby sitter. Julia informed me that she has been taking care of two children, age four and seven, for a long time while the mother worked in West Haven. This morning, her doorbell rang and she heard the two children screaming on her front porch. She ran down the stairs to discover the 4 year olds hands were both burned and blistered. The little boy cried that "Judith" burned me. She immediately called the Fire Department Emergency Unit and both children were taken to Yale (Grace) New Haven Hospital via ambulance. Julia stated that normally the mother from Valley Street drops off the children and rings the door bell and waits for her to come downstairs. Then they would chat for a few minutes, but this morning, the mother rang the bell and drove off, leaving the two screaming children on the front porch. When I asked her where I could locate the mother, she stated that the mother works in a machine shop in West Haven. She gave me the name of the Machine Shop and I notified my dispatcher to have the West Haven Police Department meet me at the city line on Kimberly Avenue. The West Haven Officer and I both drove to Universal Products on Water Street. After informing the shop foreman why we were there, he pointed to Judith Roman, age twenty-three, who was operating a machine. As we approached, she said, "What did Julia do to my children?" How did she know why we were even there? I placed handcuffs on her and led her out of the shop in front of all her coworkers and placed her in the back seat of my police car. I drove her to the Detective Division downtown, where they were awaiting her arrival. I then drove to Yale New Haven Emergency Room to check on the children. Has anyone ever seen a grown Nurse cry? Has anyone ever seen a grown Policeman cry? It happened that morning. I could not imagine the pain this little 4-year-old boy was going through. A complete and thorough investigation involving the Detective Division, the Yale New Haven Nursing staff, my knowledge and observations, statements from the baby sitter revealed the following: The 4-year-old was getting his little fingers caught in the torn lining in his coat as his mother tried to put his coat on so she turned on the toaster and forced his little hands into the red hot toaster and burned his little hands black, calling him a stupid little bastard. Both boys suffered from cigarette burns from the mother putting out her cigarettes on their little arms. She hated the children so much that they were not allowed to call her mom or mother, they had to call her Judith. This was the worst case of child abuse I have ever seen. Grown Nurses at the Hospital were crying as they treated these beautiful little boys. I also cried. It was difficult for me as a loving father of three children to believe that a mother could do this to her own children, her own flesh and blood. I followed the case until she was sentenced to prison. She spent years in prison and every time she was up for probation, I was there to make sure she never, never got out. Both boys were permanently removed from the home. The boys were adopted by a loving family and remained together. •

MENTAL ILLNESS NEEDS

As a Police Officer for twenty years, I dealt with many people with mental illness. There are so many degrees of mental illness from mild to severe.

One day I was dispatched to Headquarters on Court Street to meet with a lady. It was the summer of 1965. She lived on Orange Street near Edwards Street with her husband. She stated that her husband was acting very strange lately and she was worried and just wanted to talk to someone. Not necessarily a doctor but someone. My Sergeant told her he had just the right man and called for me. I was patrolling in Westville. I picked up the lady and drove her back to her house on Orange Street. We entered the second floor apartment through the front door. We climbed the stairs, not really knowing what I was dealing with. Her husband was sitting at the kitchen table drinking a cup of tea. Very casually, he offered me a cup of tea. I accepted the tea and sat down. He never asked why a uniformed policeman was in his apartment. I immediately noticed a small tube type radio on the table. The front was facing the wall and the tubes were removed and lying next to the radio. Then, we walked into the living room and I noticed the television was turned around with the picture tube facing the wall and it was unplugged. I am not a doctor, but this is not normal behavior. I finally asked him why the radio tubes were removed and why the television was facing the wall. He said, "Because, the whole world is watching me." He took me to the front window and pointed to the utility poles in front of his house. He showed me that the wires go from one pole to the other. From one street to another street. One city to another city. One state to another. All connected to watch people in their homes. He was convinced that the whole world was watching his wife and himself in the privacy of his own home. I looked at this wife. She had such sorry in her eyes. Such heartbreak. I am a Policeman, not a doctor, but it's my job to help people in need. I said, "Mister, if I bring you to the hospital, would you like to talk to a doctor who understands these things?" He said, "No ambulance?" "No sir. No ambulance." I called Headquarters to get permission to transport him to Yale New Haven Hospital. The Sergeant gave me permission but to use caution for my own safety. "Do you want me to send another policeman to ride with you Bob?" "No sir. I'm doing fine so far. This man trusts me." I placed him in the right rear back seat with his wife sitting behind me. As we drove he also mentioned that he no longer wears glasses because they can control your mind and people can read your thoughts. Upon arrival at Yale New Haven Hospital, I explained everything to the staff Psychiatrist. After a one-hour evaluation, the man was committed to Middletown State Hospital. He wanted a drink of water, but he would only take it from me because he thought the hospital would poison him and he trusted me. I took the lady back home and assured her that he would get the best of care that he needed. I never saw either one of them again. •

COUNTERFEIT $20.00 BILL

Sometime in the winter of 1967, I was dispatched to Railroad Salvage, located on Middletown Avenue near Ferry Street. The complaint was a report of a counterfeit bill. I parked my police car and walked in the front door. I knew Dorothy, one of the sales people, but she was off that day. The girl on one of the registers showed me a $20.00 bill and she stated that it looked counterfeit. Sure enough, it was on my list of counterfeit $20.00 bills. We closed her register so we could talk. I needed all her information, name, birth date, etc. We chatted for a minute telling her that I am a good customer and I love the store. I took the counterfeit $20.00 bill and put it in an evidence bag to send it to the US Treasury Department for processing. As I was leaving, the young lady said, "Officer. Did you forget something?" "No, what?" "You need to give me another $20.00 bill. My register will be short." "Miss, you want me to give you a $20.00 bill from where, my pocket?" "No. Doesn't the police department reimburse storeowners if they get stuck with a counterfeit bill?" "No. It's not our problem. It's your problem if you accept a counterfeit bill from a customer. That's why you get a list of known counterfeit bills." "Well, that sucks," she said. "I want my $20.00 bill back. Forget that I gave it to you. Give me back my $20.00 bill." "I can't do that Miss. It's counterfeit and I need to send it to the US Treasury Department. Don't you understand that? Mr. Vine will read my report and you are not in any trouble. I appreciate that you called the police." "Thank you. I will never call you again," she said. "I will pass it on to the next customer." "Then, Miss. You will be breaking the law." I gave up trying to explain that a counterfeit bill is worthless and if you get stuck with one, it's your problem. Employees of stores are not responsible for counterfeit bills. The company will absorb the loss. It's just common sense. •

Sometime after the May 21, 1969 murder of Black Panther Member Alex Rackley. The Black Panthers moved from Orchard Street to a one-family house on Sylvan Avenue. Law Enforcement Officials were aware that The Black Panther Party was heavily armed while residing in that house. The front porch was even sand bagged, possibly in case of a Police/Panther shoot out. Not sure exactly of the sand bags on the front porch. Gun permits were not needed at the time while inside a residence, so no one questioned the fact that it was a known fact that guns were inside that house. As I patrolled in that neighborhood, I was always aware of possible gun fire coming from that house and the possibility of being shot, but to avoid patrolling in the area would not be fair to the residents of the area that not only paid taxes to the city and state but who expected police protection. I did not avoid going past the Panther Headquarters nor were we ever told to avoid the area. I did receive some verbal abuse by being called a pig and "oink, oink" every time I passed that house. Not from Panther Members, but from local neighborhood youths. It was part of my job. I even named the house, t'he oink, oink house.' Like the old saying goes, sticks and stones will break my bones but names will never hurt me. The Black Panther Trials in New Haven brought so much civil unrest, it was a time for all Law Enforcement Officers to remain, calm, alert and not take sides. We were there for the protection of all people, including the Panthers. The trial at the Superior Court Building on Elm and Church Streets brought large crowds of spectators. Hilary Rodham was seen on the New Haven Green. She was a Yale Student at the time. Police Chief James Ahern at the time received national recognition for the way the Police Department handled the situation. It was a very difficult time for all Police Officers sworn to serve and protect all residents of New Haven. I was very proud to wear my blue uniform. That, to me, represented fairness and compassion for all people regardless of color, creed or nationality. Being called a pig constantly did not change my way of thinking to be fair to all residents of New Haven, Connecticut. I spent many nights sitting in a hot police van with other officers behind city hall. On standby in case anything serious broke out. We were just recovering from the 1967 New Haven riots when this new incident occurred. •

One morning in the fall of 1964, at about 1:30 AM, I was patrolling in the area of Whalley Avenue and the Woodbridge town line. A motorist flagged me down, flashing his headlights. I pulled over and he got out of his car and walked over to me. "Officer," he said. "Yes mister, what can I do for you?" "There is a lady walking on the side of the road on Amity Road near the Amity Shopping Center. She seems to be disoriented and crying." "Thank you, mister," I said. I made a U-turn and took a short cut near the Big Top Shop to Amity Road. I turned right and just up the road there was a white female in what looked like a blue and white waitress uniform. I pulled over and asked her if she was okay. She kept walking west toward Woodbridge. "Miss, are you alright?" She kept walking, ignoring me. "I'm a Policeman, please answer me." That got her attention and she stopped walking. "Are you okay?" "No. I just got fired from my job." I did not want to get involved in a person and private matter like that but I was concerned for her safety. "Where do you live Miss?" "In the Fowler Street Apartments." I offered to give her a short ride home. It was just one long block away. "Okay," she said and got into the front seat. For my own safety, when transporting females when I am alone, I radioed the dispatcher and told him I had a female in my car and I was taking her home to her apartment on Fowler Street. I also gave him my actual odometer mileage including the 1/10th. Example: mileage: 23930.7. As we drove that short distance, I discovered why she probably got fired from her job at The Lamplighter. She had strong liquor on her breath and she said she was sneaking drinks on occasion when she went into the kitchen to pick up food orders to be served and her boss caught her. Now we arrived at her apartment. I notified my dispatcher that we had arrived and gave him the ending odometer mileage. The dispatcher logged the mileage and actual time it took me to transport her. The dispatcher responded, "Roger car 21." Now, she started to cry and did not want to get out of the car. "Miss, I have a job to do. You are now safe at your front door and I need to leave, now." "Can't you talk to me for a few minutes?" "No, miss. Please get out. You are home safe now please get out." "No, you don't understand. I lost my F'in job," she said. She refused to get out of my police car so I had to call my Sergeant to meet me in front of the apartments. By now, with me idling in front of the apartments with my interior car lights on, for my own protection, and an intoxicated female in my front seat, I started to attract attention. Folks were looking out their apartment windows. Finally my Sergeant pulled up. I got out and walked over to him. I explained my predicament. "I'll get her ass out of your car," he said. He walked over and tried to reason with her. She ignored him. He said "Bob," in a loud voice, "call the wagon and lock her up for intoxication." She jumped out of my car and up the stairs and disappeared into the apartment. Then I got a lecture from the Sergeant. "You are too nice Bob and they take advantage of you." I agreed and we drove away. I just couldn't leave her there on the road, thinking to myself. •

LOITERING IN BIG TOP PARKING LOT

One Friday night in 1965, I was working the 12:00 to 8:00 AM shift. The Big Top Shoppe on Whalley Avenue was quite a popular place on the weekend, especially at night. Because I was permanently assigned to the Westville area, management at the Big Top asked me if I could pass through as often as time permitted as they were having a late night problem with young people congregating and loitering in the rear parking lot. This particular night, I was driving an unmarked police car. It was black and it had a whip antenna on the left rear fender but no overhead emergency lights. After leaving Station 2, I headed for Westville. I pulled into the Big Top driveway at approximately 12:15 AM. I backed in against the building next door and sat in my police car. With my hat off, just observing. To my right was a carload of teenagers pulled in and facing the brick building next door. They were enjoying the delicious food. Several other teens were out of their cars talking. Suddenly, I observed trash coming out of the windows from the car to my right, from both sides. Then, something hit my car. I notified the dispatcher that I would be out of my car at the Big Top with a carload of teenagers. My partner radioed that he was in route to back me up. I put on my hat and got out of the car. I walked around to the right side and observed mustard and catsup and some French fries that landed on my trunk. I was not too happy with this mess on my car. I told the carload of youths to get out of their car and clean up the mess, especially the mess on my car. They all got out and not only did they clean up their mess, but started to pick up the trash in the rear parking lot. One youth went inside and came out with a handful of napkins and cleaned the side and trunk of my car. The kids that were talking outside got in their cars and took off. One of the chefs was having a smoke break outside the back door. He said, "Damn. You taught those kids a good lesson. Wish they would listen to me like that." After that night, I made sure the kids didn't loiter or cause trouble when I was on duty. •

MAN ROBS AND KICKS PREGNANT NURSE IN STOMACH

On December 27, 1965 at 12:20 AM, I spotted an auto parked on Howe Street near Edgewood Avenue that was on the hot sheet and was reported stolen a few days earlier. Two young men occupied the stolen auto. They spotted our police car. As they attempted to flee on foot, Officer Christenson and I apprehended them both. They were both charged with taking a motor vehicle without the owner's permission. Something about one of these boys bothered me. After thinking about it for two days, I remembered a pregnant Nurse that was knocked to the ground for her pocketbook as she left work at the Yale New Haven Hospital last month. This assault and robbery had occurred about 4:30 PM when I was on the 4:00 PM to midnight shift. The Nurse described her attacker as a young male wearing a black sweatshirt with a certain symbol on the front. Thinking back, one of the young men had a sweatshirt with the same symbol. I arranged for a police lineup with the young man and had the Nurse come to the Detective Division to view the lineup. She picked him out of a police lineup of six young men and made a positive identification as the young man that violently knocked her to the ground for her pocketbook and kicked her in the stomach as she lay helplessly on the ground in the Yale New Haven Hospital parking lot on Frontage Road. Only a heartless animal would do that to a pregnant woman, to any woman. He was a spineless coward. He was detained until a warrant could be obtained from a Judge. Shaking the bars at the detention holding cell at the Detective Division, he called the Nurse a mother f'n bitch and threatened to get her. "I'll kill you bitch," he said to her. I befriended her and made sure she had a police escort after work every afternoon. If I couldn't meet her and escort her to her car, I made sure another Officer met her or had Hospital Security escort her to her car. Three months later, she gave birth to a healthy baby boy. She had to live with the thought that this animal caused serious injury to her unborn baby. She never saw him after his arrest. I never saw him after his arrest. Maybe he was put away for a long time. We didn't always get court dispositions. Incidents like this have only gotten worse in the society that we live in today. Everyone must be aware of our surroundings. Don't be paranoid but be alert. Don't be a victim. •

CHRISTMAS EVE FAMILY DISPUTE

On Christmas Eve, 1962, the night I realized just how much people, children in particular could hate a Policeman for doing his/her job. I was sent to an apartment complex off of Fountain Street about a loud domestic dispute between a husband and wife. As my back up partner arrived at the same time, we could hear a woman screaming from the apartment. When we walked into the unlocked front door of the apartment, it looked like a battle zone. Every Christmas gift under the Christmas tree was destroyed. The Christmas tree was knocked over. A horrible site that will always stay with me. The wife was beaten, bloodied and bruised. The two children were screaming and hugging their mother. The husband was about to attack me, but from my training I was able to put him down and get the handcuffs behind his back. I truly believe the husband would have killed his wife if my partner and I hadn't arrived when we did. Christmas Eve or not, we had no choice but to arrest the husband and get him out of that house or there would have been a homicide of a family member. Thank God there were no know weapons in the apartment. I could not get the husband to calm down. He remained in a rage even after we escorted him to a waiting paddy wagon, threatening to kill his wife when he got out of jail. He fought my partner and me all the way to the paddy wagon. I made sure the Sergeant at Headquarters put a high bond on him to keep him in jail as long as possible. We transported the wife to St. Raphael's Hospital while neighbors took the two children in. Our last thoughts were to call the Department of Children, Youth, and Families. My heart broke for the children. What I will never forget are the two children, a boy and a girl, punching our legs as we escorted their dad out of the apartment. They screamed, "Let my daddy go. Leave my daddy alone. I hate you, I hate you." I truly believe in my heart that we saved the lives of this family. What started this family dispute is unknown. Alcohol, drugs, bills, cheating? Neighbors said that they argued all the time, but never this bad. I was never sent to that apartment again. I saw pure hate in the children's eyes when we were there to protect them and in doing so, risking our own lives. More Policemen are killed responding to domestic disputes. Just part of what a Policeman does. To serve and protect. •

2 YEAR OLD CONSUMES RAT POISON

In the summer of 1963, Mary and I with our three children: Terry, 8, Alice, 6, and Bobby, 1, lived on 85 Willis Street, second floor. It was ½ block from Station 2 on Sherman Parkway. We had just moved from 229 County Street. Not realizing it when we moved in, the house had mice. The landlord, who lived on the first floor, converted his one car garage into a pigeon coup. As a hobby, he raised racing pigeons. Pigeon food attracted the mice. The landlord's daughter is on Facebook. To this day, the daughter and I remain friends. She recently told me that she hated those pigeons. With great caution, we used Decon rat poison and mouse traps to control the mice. A family on the third floor had three small children. One afternoon, thank God, I was off duty and home at the time, the third floor tenant came down the back stairs carrying her unconscious 2-year-old son. She had an empty box of Decon rat poison in her hand. The boy ate the whole box of rat poison, which she later told me was concealed under a console TV in the living room. I put the empty box of rat poison in my pocket to show the Emergency Room Personnel and then ran the ½ block to the police garage on the lower level of the police station at 710 Sherman Parkway. I took a spare marked police car without permission, not having time to explain to the mechanic why I needed that police car. The boy's mom was waiting for me on the sidewalk, holding her lifeless 2-year-old son in her arms. I drove as fast as I could safely drive to St. Raphael's Emergency Room. I radioed ahead for them to be standing by with a gurney for an unconscious 2-year-old boy. The chance of getting into a serious car accident driving my own personal car with no red lights or siren for protection was great. That's why I took the police car. The little 2-year-old remained hospitalized in an oxygen tent for more than a week. He did survive and was released maybe two weeks later from the incident. He made a full recovery. I was furious about the mouse infestation and I immediately reported the incident to the Board of Health. Not getting into any details, Mary and I bought a house in East Haven and we moved our family as quickly as possible. •

MEANING OF PISTOL EXPERT PIN

In the fall of 1962, a little over one year after being appointed to the New Haven Police Department, I was assigned my first police car – a 1961 Chevy Biscayne black marked police car. Designated as car #21, I was assigned to Westville. Everything west of Forest Road, from the West Haven city line, north to Whalley Avenue was my area of patrol. Car #21 was also designated as a major accident car, making me responsible for all serious motor vehicle accidents occurring west of downtown New Haven. However, I always found time to stop and chat with the children in my patrol area. Children are our future. I wanted children to see the blue uniform as their friend, their protector. Simply saying, I love kids. Many parents in those days would say, "See that Policeman? If you don't behave, he will take you away and we will never see you again." What a terrible thing to say to a child. One afternoon as I pulled into Cooper Place, my little friends were waiting for me. They knew that after 3:00 PM, Officer Bob would be coming. My shiny Pistol Expert pin on my uniform attracted the attention of a 6-year-old girl. "What's that for Officer Bob?" Trying to explain that to a youngster was difficult. A score of 70-80 was a Sharpshooter. 80-90 was a Marksman. 90-100 was a Pistol Expert. Explain that to a child? I just said I shot 98 out of 100 to receive that pin. Her little eyebrows raised and she looked at me and said, "People?" Boy, did I say that wrong. "No sweetie. We go to a shooting range at the police department and shoot at targets. The scores go from 70 to 100. I scored 98 so they gave me this shiny gold colored Pistol Expert pin." "Oh. Okay. So how many people did you shoot?" "None. A Policeman does not go around shooting people unless it is absolutely necessary to save an innocent persons life. Including the Policeman." "Oh. I understand now." Good. I had to clear that up fast. I didn't want my little friends telling their parents that Officer Bob shot 98 people. The story would get so distorted that it would have ended up, Officer Bob shot 98 people, today. •

In the summer of 1966, we had a big problem with pocket book snatches from female motorist's waiting for the red traffic light at Orchard and Henry Streets. In those days, most cars did not have automatic doors locks or even electric windows. Females waiting for that traffic light to change to green would have the passenger door unlocked and the window open. Small groups of young men would open the passenger door and grab the purse or pocketbook, usually sitting on the front seat next to the driver, and run with it. It happened daily and it was hard to warn motorists to lock all of their doors and close the windows. Most of the modern cars today have electric windows and automatic door locks; my vehicle doors automatically lock at 16 MPG. Some women would jump out of their cars and chase these kids, leaving their cars running in the middle of the street. You can't catch a kid, especially running with high heels on, that was never recommended. No women were immune to this crime. If you were a woman driving a car, it was assumed that you had your pocketbook sitting next to you on the front seat. It was by some miracle that their cars were not stolen, leaving their cars with the motors running. Finally we put a few plain-clothed policemen in the area to stop this blatant law breaking. After catching several kids and charging them with street robbery, the word spread to stay away from Orchard and Henry. There are cops at over the place. •

MAN WAS DRIVING WHILE UNDER SUSPENSION

One afternoon at approximately 6:00 PM, in the summer of 1966, I was traveling west on Sylvan Avenue. I observed an old Ford station wagon being driven by an elderly black man traveling slowly south on Winthrop Avenue. The Ford had a loud muffler and was physically in poor condition, one broken taillight. I pulled the vehicle over between Sylvan and Davenport Avenue. I cautiously approached the driver's side of the vehicle. The first thing I noticed was about five or six small children in the 3rd seat and an elderly gentleman was driving. A woman was also in the front passenger seat of the vehicle. As always, I politely asked him for his driver's license and vehicle registration, we did not ask for insurance papers in those days. The man stated that he did not have a driver's license. However, the registration was in order. I asked him to turn the engine off because it was noisy and exhaust fumes were coming from under the vehicle. He complied and turned the engine off. The kids in the back seat had their little noses pressed against the left side windows. Looking at me. "Where is your license, mister?" I" ain't gonna lie, my license is suspended Officer." Very seldom does an officer get an honest answer like this. Usually people lie and say its home or they lost their wallet. The registration was listed to a person on Orchard Street. The vehicle belonged to the man driving. I asked the lady if she had a driver's license. "No, Officer," was her answer. No other adults were in the car. Only the children. "Are these your children, mister?" "Yes Officer. They are all mine." I ran the man's record. No warrants, but he had a poor driving record, which caused him to have a suspended driver's license. The children really looked scared. At 6'1" and 245 lbs. with a gun on my belt, guess I looked scary to small children. I had to make a split decision to either arrest the man, tow the car. Find a ride for the family or give the man a break and move his car to the other side of the street because I stopped him on the cemetery side of Winthrop Avenue, which is no parking. Arresting him will result in a high bond because operating a motor vehicle while under suspension is a serious offense. He will go to court and probably pay a heavy fine, which affects his family who are the innocent ones. Maybe take food from their table, clothes off their back. I had full discretion to make a decision as long as it wasn't operating a motor vehicle while under the influence of alcohol or drugs, reckless driving or evading responsibility. None of the above. I made my decision. Everyone please get out of the car. I got in the car and started the engine and made a U-turn and parked the car legally on the east side of Winthrop Avenue. What a piece of junk that car was. "Mister, can your family walk to Orchard Street from here?" "Yes, Officer." "Okay." The man said goodbye to his family. "I'm going to jail," he said. "You are going to lock me up officer, right?" "No, I am giving you a break. One break only. If I see this car gone from this spot tonight, I am going to look for you and lock you up and throw the key away, understand?" "Yes, officer." "Now, take your family and go home. I better not see you driving this car again. Do you understand?" "Yes, I do Officer." I locked the car doors and gave the lady the keys. I said, "Do not give him the keys." The whole family walked east on Sylvan Avenue toward Orchard Street. The kids waved goodbye to me. I waved back. The next afternoon, the car was still parked where I left it. When I was a Policeman, we had full discretion to make intelligent decisions that could affect people's lives and the lives of their loved ones. It took courage but I took an oath to serve everybody. There was no black and white. I would make that same decision today. •

ELDERLY LADY AND NEIGHBORS

In the summer of 1969, I was sent to 15 Hotchkiss Street in regard to a neighbor harassment complaint. Upon arrival, a lovely old lady met me at the door. By old, I mean the age that I am now, late 70's or early 80's. She invited me in and offered me a cup of tea and at the same time, telling me the neighbors were out to get her. Why not, so I sat at the kitchen table. I knew that this would probably be a lengthy complaint. She had a laundry list of complaints about her neighbors on both sides of her house. As we sipped our tea, she complained that an unknown neighbor was cutting her garden hose. "I'll show you Officer when we finish our tea." Ten minutes later, we were in her back yard inspecting her garden hose. What I saw was a very old garden hose that had age cracks from being left outside summer and winter. She said that they were knife cuts. I tried to explain that to her but she insisted that the neighbors were harassing her. I wrote down everything she told me. I promised that I would look into her neighbor harassment complaint. She asked me for my name and wrote it down on a small pad. I thanked her for the tea and left. Several days later, the lady called headquarters and asked for me by name. I was dispatched back to 15 Hotchkiss Street. This time the lady seemed more upset. She led me around the house into her back yard and showed me her very, very old wooden fence. "See what they are doing to my fence?" "No ma'am. What?" "They are making holes all over my fence. They are ruining my fence. Can't you arrest them, Officer?" I did an inspection of the old knotty pine board wooden fence. What I observed was a normal occurrence when the knots from age and drying out fall out. There was absolutely no indication of anyone on purpose damaging her fence. Again, I tried to explain that the fence was very old and drying out from lack of sealant or paint. She would not listen to me. Again, I wrote down everything she was telling me and hoping that she would feel better. Seeing this older lady was like seeing my own mom. I was careful not to hurt or offend her. I left and reassured her that I would keep an eye on her house and property. One week later, I got the anticipated call to see the lady at 15 Hotchkiss Street. I had to ring the bell for a few minutes when she finally came to the door. She asked me to come in quickly and immediately closed the front door. I noticed towels on the floor. This time she had towels stuffed under the front and back doors. She asked me if I smelled anything. "No, what?" "They are trying to poison me with poison gas." I had to try to talk to her so I asked for a cup of tea. She was delighted. As she was heating water for the tea, in a roundabout way, I asked her if she had any children or grandchildren. She mentioned a son that lived in Litchfield, Connecticut. Somehow, I was able to get his name. Later that day, we were able to contact him and explain what was going on with his mom. Being careful not to say the wrong thing. Well aware that I was a Policeman, not a doctor, so I could not give any opinions as to what were my own thoughts. I let the son come to that conclusion. I was no longer dispatched to that house. Months later the house at 15 Hotchkiss Street became vacant. Hoping that this nice lady got the help that she needed. •

POLICE CAR HIT WITH GOLF BALL

In the spring of 1964, I was patrolling in my assigned area of Westville. I was driving my fairly new 1963 black Chevy Biscayne police car, designated car #21. It was equipped with the more modern "gum ball" type emergency light on top that revolved 360 degrees, making it a lot safer when responding to emergency calls. My old 1961 Chevy Biscayne had a stationary front and rear red light that just blinked on and off. This afternoon I decided to drive up to the Yale Golf Course, which was part of my assigned patrol area and check out the buildings. We were getting complaints of minor thefts of some of the equipment. As I was getting ready to cross one of the golf greens on a dirt road, I looked both ways. I saw nothing in the distance so I slowing crossed. Half way, I heard a terrible noise coming from the top of my police car. Pieces of red and white plastic came raining down off the windshield. I stopped. I opened the driver's door and looked at my gumball machine. It was shattered and in pieces. The red and white sealed beam bulbs were intact but the round plastic cover was shattered. What the hell happened? Three men ran over to my police car. One apologized for hitting my car with his golf ball. "What? How did that happen?" He explained that as he hit his ball, suddenly my police car appeared. They all thought the ball would go over my car. Nope? A perfect hit. I took the names of the men and assured them that it was my fault. Besides. There is no law about striking a police car with a golf ball on the books, anywhere in this country. I then proceeded to 710 Sherman Parkway, the police maintenance garage. I told the mechanic the truth as he looked at the top of my car with his mouth open, but Sergeant Nick O'Brien came out of his office and was not happy. "What is this BS I heard? You got hit with a golf ball, Bob?" "Yes, Nick. I have him the names of the men playing golf." Some more swear words came out of his mouth. "It's a brand new car, a new revolving emergency light. Where am I going to find and replace that light? Huh?" "I don't know Nick. I'm sorry." "Leave your car here," Nick said. "You can't drive it like that." Nick gave me the oldest spare police car he could find behind the fence. Here take that one. I was lucky the car even started. It took a good two weeks to locate and install a revolving emergency light on my 1963 Chevy. Nick got over it but occasionally I still heard about that emergency light. •

MEMORIES OF A RETIRED COP

RESIDENT REQUESTS RADAR ENFORCEMENT FOR SPEEDERS

By the summer of 1963, I was establishing myself as a Policeman that loved children and took my job very seriously in making sure that residents of my patrol area were safe while they slept snugly in their beds at night. Every twenty-eight days we rotated our shifts from 7:00 AM to 3:00 PM then to 11:00 PM to 7:00 AM and finally to 3:00 PM to 11:00 PM. Advancing our days off making it possible for all Officers to eventually get a Saturday and Sunday off. 7:00 to 3:00 shift, we had a lot of school traffic assignments excluding the summer school vacation. 3:00 to 11:00, we enforced motor vehicle violations and 11:00 to 7:00, paying attention to potential house and business burglaries. One day I was parked on Lake View Terrace and Ray Road. I was finishing up an accident report. I observed that a gentleman had parked behind me. I looked in my rear view mirror as he approached my police car on foot. He introduced himself as a long time Westville resident. I gave him my name as we shook hands. "Are you aware of the speeders on Ray Road?" he asked, "No sir, I'm not." The speed limit was posted at 25 MPH, as with most residential streets in that area. "Well, I have been complaining about speeders in our neighborhood for years and nothing seems to happen with my complaints." "I will certainly keep my eye out for speeders, mister." I said. "Can you arrange for the radar patrol to set up somewhere and catch some of these guys?" "I will request radar patrol in writing by contacting the Traffic Division, but I cannot guarantee or promise anything. The person in charge will make that decision mister, okay?" "Yes, Officer Bob," he said. "Thank you for your time" He seemed like a very sincere gentleman. I generated a report to the Traffic Division. One week later, the radar unit set up at that exact location at Ray Road, and Lakeview Terrace. The very first speeder clocked in excess of 45 MPH traveling east on Ray Road in a 25 MPH zone was this man. Yes, the same man complaining about speeders was himself, a speeder. As he was being issued the ticket for exceeding the posted speed limit, he told the arresting Officer to contact me. He stated to the Officer that he was the person that requested that radar be set up for speeders. "Ask Officer Bob and he will tell you. I'm the one responsible for you being here. That's right," he said. This man felt immune to receiving a speeding ticket but for the fact that he was the one that requested the radar unit in the first place. Let me go and forget the radar, he said. Of course that wasn't going to happen. He went to court and contested the ticket, telling the Judge it was his request and his idea to put radar on Ray Road. After a very brief jury trial, He was found guilty and paid a fine. •

ROOKIE CAN'T SHOOT STRAIGHT

Shortly after we were issued our Colt 38 special police revolvers in January 1961, we started training with the weapon. Captain Gilroy could not stress enough about gun safety. Being able to shoot straight and accurately was extremely important to not accidentally shoot an innocent bystander. After a few days in the classroom, we all went out to the outdoor pistol range on Sherman parkway. We would hand load six bullets and shoot at a silhouette "bad guy" paper target. The targets were attached to a line, similar to a clothesline. We would then reel in the target and check the results. Needless to say, some of us rookies were not even hitting the target. Some of us were hitting the wrong target. God knows where the bullets were going. After a few days of constant practice, we were doing much better. Captain Gilroy noticed one Officer was shooting to low. Every bullet struck the "bad guy" target between his legs (ouch). Captain Gilroy spoke directly to the officer in front of the whole class. He said, "Ladd, your main objective is the kill this man who is pointing a gun at you. Not to ruin his sex life." That brought a chuckle from most of us, but Captain Gilroy was serious. He talked about trigger pull and flinching as the Officer squeezed the trigger causing the gun barrel to drop. This resulted in the low shots. He instructed the Officer to load six more bullets and try again. We all stepped back and watched as the Officer put six shots right in the kill area. Six perfect shots to the chest area. Captain Gilroy commended the Officer for getting it right. As Captain Gilroy walked away, the Officer turned and whispered to me, "I was aiming for his head". By some miracle, we all graduated. •

SIDEWALK MECHANIC RIP OFF

In 1971, one afternoon in the fall, I was on radio car patrol duty in the downtown area. I came on duty at 4:00 PM. At approximately 5:30 PM, I noticed the traffic was unusually backed up at Church and Chapel Streets. I was stuck in traffic on Church Street traveling north. I finally arrived at the intersection. An orange colored Datsun (Nissan), model 510, was stalled in the middle of the intersection. With the assistance of several other motorists, we pushed the car to the curb in front of Liggett's Drug Store. The operator of the car was a black Yale Student from Nigeria. His name was Geti Ambwah. Geti opened the hood. Being mechanically inclined, I asked Geti to try and start the car. As the engine was turning over, I noticed a wire under the distributor was hanging loose. The main ignition wire came off the terminal on the distributor. I reconnected the wire. I said, "Okay, try it again." The car started. Geti thanked me and said he just had a new carburetor installed last week for $250.00. The carburetor was not new. Someone had spray painted the carburetor with silver paint. A very bad paint job causing silver overspray on the air cleaner. Geti informed me that a sidewalk mechanic on Portsea Street did the work. The next afternoon, I arranged to meet Geti on Portsea Street at the sidewalk garage at 4:15 PM. The so-called mechanic was surprised when Geti and I approached him. I wasted no time in telling him that the carburetor was not new or rebuilt but simply spray painted silver paint to deceive Geti. Mr. "S" agreed to give Geti his money back in full that Friday afternoon. I met with Geti that Friday evening and he was so happy that he got his full $250.00 back that he tried to hug me. "That's okay Geti. That's not necessary." Men hugging me are a no-no. Mr. "S" made Geti sign a piece of paper (torn brown paper bag) promising not to make trouble for him. To prevent anyone else from getting ripped off from Mr. "S" on Portsea Street, I did report the incident in writing to the Dealers and Repairers Section of the Motor Vehicle Department. Sidewalk mechanics are okay, as long as they do quality and honest work. This man was a thief. Geti and I remained friends for a long time, occasionally having a cup of coffee at the Dunkin Donuts on Church and Center Street.

•

MEMORIES OF A RETIRED COP

STOLEN AUTO RECOVERED

On January 31, 1978, at approximately 3:30 PM, I discovered a late model auto that was reported stolen from Orange, Connecticyt a few days earlier. The auto was parked on Henry Street, just east of Dixwell Avenue. The car was listed on the hot sheet as being stolen. The engine was still warm. The ignition was broken. A screwdriver was lying on the floor. Several teenagers were standing near the car but they took off as soon as I pulled up. I notified my dispatcher who notified the owner of the vehicle in West Haven, Connecticut. I was told that it would be awhile before the owner could respond from West Haven. I could not leave the car, being concerned that the thieves were just waiting for me to drive off. I stayed with the stolen auto protecting it from being stolen again, until the owner could arrive and arrange to have the auto towed from the scene. I was detained about 25 minutes past the end of my shift. This was a routine recovered stolen auto. Nothing unusual. •

THE DAY ST. PATRICKS CHURCH WAS DEMOLISHED

According to historic records, Saint Patrick's was built in 1877 and was considered the oldest Catholic Church in New Haven. The day Saint Patrick's was torn down, sometime in the late 60's; I was assigned to extra traffic duty. As I directed traffic for the many dump trucks and heavy equipment, as they knocked stone by stone to the ground to haul away, there were people standing on both sides of the street weeping as they witness their beloved church being demolished. I had to constantly tell the people to please stand back for their own safety. One elderly lady, dressed all in black wearing a black kerchief, wept as if she was at a funeral. Many were making the sign of the cross. As I recall, it took approximately four days to bring the church to ground level. It was a very sad thing to witness. How many people were baptized there? How many people were married there? How many people received their First Communion from there? How many people buried their loved ones from there? After the 2nd or 3rd day, the crowds dwindled. Suddenly, I noticed several demolition workers huddled in a group. As they were ripping up the old wide floorboards, thousands of coins were discovered lodged between the floorboards, some in absolute mint condition dating to the 1800's. The disposition of the coins was unknown. It was a civil and legal matter as to what happened to the coins. Getting back to my traffic assignment. Once the church was physically gone and the dump trucks were no longer parked in the street or on the sidewalk, the police were no longer needed for traffic duty. As sad as it was to witness this beautiful Church being demolished, I feel very proud to be a part of New Haven history. •

7 YEAR OLD BEATEN TO DEATH

The following story is very, very graphic and sad.

Sometime toward the end of 1969, one morning about 9:00 AM, I was dispatched to the second floor apartment of a home on Winthrop Avenue, just north of Edgewood Avenue. A 28-year-old mother and her 34-year-old boyfriend had transported her 7-year-old son to St. Raphael's Hospital Emergency Room. They told the nurses that they found the 7-year-old, unresponsive in bed. The boy was deceased. Later, I learned that the boy had been severely beaten. The Detective Bureau requested that I enter the apartment, forcing the door if necessary and look for any evidence of violence, blood, torn clothing, etc. Also, I was to remove all the dirty clothes from the hamper, especially the child's underwear and bring everything to the Detective Division. As I was doing a complete inspection of the apartment, I heard noise coming from a back room in the apartment. The door was locked. I knocked and a Yale student opened the door. He was a tenant of the couple. He asked me what was wrong. I told him that a small child from this apartment was taken to the Hospital and he was pronounced dead on arrival. "I knew it," he said. "Knew what?" "Last night, the boyfriend was beating the boy, again." "Why, was he beating him?" "Because the boy was crying and wanted a glass of water. The man screamed, "Go to sleep you little bastard," and struck him several times. I did not witness it but I heard it. As a matter of fact, I taped the beating," he said. "I put my portable tape recorder on the floor next to the boy's bedroom door and taped the beating." I listened to the tape. The beating was crystal clear and painful to listen to. "Why didn't you call the police?" "And lose my room?" he said. "It's hard to find reasonable rooms for students in this neighborhood. Take my tape player," the student said, "but I am not getting involved." I called the Captain of Detectives and told him what I had and that the witness was reluctant to come with me. "Bob," the Captain said, "place his ass under arrest as a material witness and bring him in with the tape player. Cuff the bastard if you need to." As we drove to the Detective Bureau, the man said, "There goes my room." I said, "You have much more to worry about that your room." I had all I could do not to punch him in the face. Both adults were charged with killing the little 7-year-old boy because he wanted a drink of water. I have deep seeded personal thoughts of what I think of this poor excuse for a mother who permitted her boyfriend to beat her child to death and the monster that beat this helpless little boy to death. The Detective Bureau had full change of this investigation. I was just a small part of the investigation and of collecting important evidence. I went home that afternoon and hugged my own children and shed a few tears. God bless this little boy. •

FATAL MOTORCYCLE ACCIDENT

In the fall of 1971, at approximately 1:30 AM, I was dispatched to a motorcycle vs. parked car accident on Sherman Parkway just north of Munson Street. Upon arrival, I observed a Harley Davidson motorcycle had struck the rear of a parked car in the 500 block of Sherman Parkway. The impact was so severe that the motorcycle had bent the rear bumper of the parked car into the trunk. Motor vehicles at that time had solid steel bumpers. The operator of the motorcycle that was traveling north toward Hamden was thrown through the rear window and exited through the front window. The operator was killed instantly. I found a cold can or beer at the scene that was still trickling beer on the ground. The Fire Department had dispatched the emergency unit to the scene. I obtained a listing of the parked car and the listing came back to a resident of the apartment complex at 537-545 Sherman Parkway. I went to the apartment to notify the owner of the parked car. After ringing the doorbell, the owner opened his door. I advised him of the motor vehicle accident involving a motorcycle and his parked car outside of his apartment complex. He got dressed and walked outside with me to examine the damage to his parked vehicle. I did advise him that the operator of the Harley was killed. His only question was, "Who's going to pay for the damage to my vehicle?" I could not answer that question not knowing if the motorcycle operator was covered by insurance. From the motorcycle registration, I gave him the name of the owner of the Harley. Judging from the extensive damage to the parked vehicle and the total destruction of the Harley Davidson, it was determined that the motorcycle was going at a high rate of speed before the impact. I had the Hamden Police notify the family of the 22-year-old operator of the motorcycle. The 22-year-old accident victim was transported to Saint Raphael's Hospital via ambulance. It is always very difficult to make such notifications, especially when the accident victims are so young. I had the parked car towed from the scene. I learned several days later that the parked car was a total loss. •

On Monday morning, February 6, 1978 I was working the squad A shift. 8:00 AM to 4:00 PM. I can't recall what the weather forecast was but heavy snow was definitely not forecasted. Just about noon it started to snow very lightly. I was driving a police car, #60, in the downtown area. By 4:00 PM, we had a full-blown blizzard. All police cars were called to the garage for tire chains. The dispatcher announced that all patrol units would stay on patrol until further notice. I thought about my wife Mary. She was driving a school bus in Hamden that day. Mary was driving for the New Haven Bus Company. At the last minute, all school buses were ordered to pick up the children at the schools. Most buses never made it to the schools. Mary got stuck in deep snow on Paradise Avenue in Hamden. A Hamden police officer came by and rescued Mary and after she told him her husband was a New Haven Police officer and he took her to Police Headquarters at 1 Union Avenue before another policeman took her to my daughter's house on Quinnipiac Avenue. We were all held over and not allowed to go home. The National Guard at the Goffe Street Armory brought in cots and set them up in the cafeteria so we could get some rest. However, travelers at the Union Train Station across the street were stranded, the Chief invited them over to stay in the Police Station and we gave up our cots to them. I spent the night guarding a Furniture Store on Grand Avenue that had the front window blown out. I sat in the most comfortable recliner I could find and guarded the furniture store from looters. Several times I had to draw my weapon and chase neighborhood people away from entering the open window. Before I went to Grand Avenue, the local television and radio stations broadcast for anyone with a snowmobile to please come to Headquarters. We needed transportation for Doctors and Nurses coming and going at the local Hospitals. I sent one guy with a snowmobile to pick up a doctor. He said, "Aw gee, can't I get a nurse?" "Next one will be a nurse," I said. He never came back. Finally by 9:00 AM the next day, we were relieved of duty. All our personal cars were snowed in by the snowplows. We were taken home in police cars. We were all exhausted from a long night away from our families. It took another two or three days before we were able to dig out our personal cars in front of 1 Union Avenue. Governor Ella T. Grasso did an absolute wonderful job in keeping the highways clear for emergency vehicles. She was one of our finest Governors. •

STUBBORN FEMALE PARKING VIOLATOR

One spring morning in 1968, I was dispatched to the Trailways Bus Station on Whitney Avenue, corner of Grove Street. I parked my police car and walked in to speak with the Bus Station Manager. The Manager took me outside and pointed to three automobiles that were parked between two signs on Whitney Avenue that read, *NO PARKING BETWEEN SIGNS – BUSES ONLY*. The buses that were picking up and dropping off passengers had to double-park, causing a traffic hazard. I looked around for the drivers without success. I called for three tow trucks and commenced to place parking violation tickets on the windshields while waiting for the tow trucks. I wrote and placed tickets on the first two cars. As I started to write the third ticket, I noticed a female sitting behind the steering wheel. I motioned for her to move. Nothing. She just stared at me. I wrote and placed a parking ticket on her windshield. She didn't even open her window and attempt to talk to me. First one and then two tow trucks arrived. I directed them to tow the first two cars. The third tow truck arrived. He backed up to her car, but still nothing. She just stared out the windshield. The tow drivers said, "Officer, I can't tow a car with someone in it." I said, "I know that. Just hook up to the front end and raise the car off the ground." He did and as the front wheels came off the ground the lady rolled down her window and said, "I'll move the damn car." She started the motor and sped off. The tow driver said, "What's her problem?" I said, "Guess she's a nut case." With the Bus Stop clear I left the area. Thirty minutes later, I got a radio call to meet an off duty Police Officer on Grove and Orange Streets. It was my friend Officer G.S.. I pulled up and he was standing on the corner laughing. He said, "Guess you met my wife?" "Where? At the Trailways Bus Station?" "Yep." "That was your wife?" I said, "What's her problem?" "She's stubborn, Bob." What can I say? Stubborn isn't the word. As a courtesy to my friend, I was able to lawfully excuse the parking ticket he handed to me. He said, I would only have to pay for it anyway because she doesn't work. I made it clear, but careful not to ruin a good friendship that his wife was rude and disrespectful and he agreed with me. Months later, Mary, I and other Policeman and their wives attended a Police Credit Union dance in Ansonia. My friend G. S. and his wife were there. I hardly recognized her because she never got out of her car and she did not recognize me out of uniform. After a few drinks G. S. talked me into dancing with his wife. He said, "While you are dancing, tell her who you are?" "Are you crazy G. S.?" Anyway, I did it. Guess I'm crazy. I asked her to dance and she said yes. Surprisingly she was very pleasant. I said, "I met you once Mrs. S." "Where?" "At the Trailways Bus Station." "That was you?" "Yes, it was me." She playfully beat on my chest and said, "You are so mean," but then apologized and told me she was completely embarrassed. "Why didn't you move your car when you saw I was tagging and towing all three cars?" "I don't know, really. I'm sorry." Mary told me that I took a chance dancing with her. "Yes, I know. I was holding on to my can of mace." •

MONKEY ATTACKS POLICE CAR

In the summer of 1967, I was on patrol in the Fair Haven area. It was about 2:30 PM. I was driving south on Quinnipiac Avenue. Just as I slowed down to turn right into Ferry Street, I noticed something dark jump on the top of my police car from the right passenger side. I thought it was a big brown dog. Whatever it was it came from a large apartment house that was on the North West corner. I pulled over to the curb and there was a monkey looking through my front windshield upside down. What? Am I on Candid Camera or something? I carefully got out of my police car and the monkey jumped right into my arms. I knew it had to be someone's pet. He was not a chimpanzee, smaller than a chimp but he had big teeth. Next thing I hear, this guy yelling to me from the porch, "Hey, leave my monkey alone. Give me my monkey." He approached me and the monkey jumped out of my arms and onto the sidewalk and then jumped into the guys arms. As he started to walk away toward the large apartment house, I stopped him. "Wait a minute, mister," I said. "This isn't over yet. This animal could have caused an accident. What if he bit me? What if he attacked a kid? Then, you are accusing me of trying to stealing your monkey." It's funny now, but at the time, it was not so funny. I took his name and address and did a report. He told me he was a Merchant Marine and lived right there on the corner. Also, he said the monkey had escaped a few other times but always returned on his own. After that day, every time I passed that intersection, I thought of that darn monkey and the Merchant Marine. I did a Google search of the apartment house on the corner. It's no longer there. It is now a fenced in paved lot. •

LONELY FEMALE PROWLER COMPLAINT

One evening in 1972, at around 11:30 PM, I was dispatched to a prowler complaint in the 200 block of Lawrence Street. The one family home was between Whitney Avenue and Livingston Street. This was an upscale neighborhood. On all prowler complaints, the Police Dispatcher would send two officers. I pulled up in front of the home with my partner Officer Bobby O'Brien pulling in behind me. A lady in a nightgown was standing on the front lawn. She asked me to tell the other Officer to leave and that she was embarrassed to have two police cars in front of her home. I waved him on. As he drove off, he yelled, "I'll be around the corner if you need me, Bob." I followed the lady through the front door and into the kitchen. It was a beautiful large two-story one-family house. The lady, I learned lived alone in this big house with two children that were away at private schools. She pointed to a window in the kitchen and indicated that a man was standing there looking through the window. I walked out into the back yard and discovered that there was a Bilco style metal basement door just below the window; a place where someone could stand and look into the window. After a complete search of the back yard, I re-entered the home through the back door. I advised the lady that the back yard appeared to be secure. She asked me if I wanted a cup of tea. Looking at my watch, 11:50 PM I said, "No thank you ma'am." Indicating I get off at 12:00 midnight. She asked me if I was married. "Yes ma'am. Wife and three children." "I have 2 children and I've been divorced for 4 years," she said. "That's nice ma'am." "My dad is a Yale Professor," she said. "Nice ma'am," I said, trying to be polite to her. She seemed very lonely. "Can I have your name please for my report?" Finally, I got her information and was walking out the front door. There was a formal foyer between an inner door and an outer door. She stopped me there and asked me if I would just hug her. Talk about an awkward moment. Believe it or not, I did but only briefly and left. She yelled, "You get off at midnight, come back for that cup of tea." "Okay ma'am." I got to Station 2 on Sherman Parkway and Bob O'Brien was waiting. He asked, "What the hell was that all about?" I told him everything. "Wow, Bob." He said, "Are you going back?" I said "NO." I went home. •

GUARD DOG GOES FOR WALK

When I patrolled Fair Haven in 1965-67, there was an Auto Body Shop on Mill Street, corner of Wolcott Street. It was called Putnam Auto Body. Frank and Nick were the owners, both very nice guys. A lady in the office was named Kay or Kate; maybe she was Nick's wife. Anyway, they had a big German Shepard dog. He was basically there to guard the business at night when the shop was closed. On night about 2:00 AM, I noticed the side door on Mill Street was wide open. Thinking I possibly had a burglary in progress, I radioed for back up. I removed my 38 Colt special from the holster and carefully entered the garage area with a flashlight in my left hand. I knew where the light switches were so I turned on all the lights. Everything appeared to be in order or secure in Policeman's terms. My backup arrived. I called Communications to get Nick or Frank's home telephone number. I called Nick and woke him up. "Nick," I said. "This is Bob M. from the Police Department. Sorry to bother you but your shop is wide open." "Bob, where's that F'en dog?" "He's not here, Nick." "Son of a Bitch. That GD dog learned how to open the inside garage door with his mouth and then he goes for a walk." "Nick. Isn't he here to protect your business?" "Yeah, he's supposed to watch the place, but he's been opening the door from the inside and taking a walk during the night. Making it easier for the burglar's to get in." "Some watch dog, huh Nick?" "Yeah. I'm getting rid of the SOB." Anyway, I secured the business and did a quick found open door report and left. The Dog? Haven't seen him since. This is Fair Haven, as I will always remember it. •

MEMORIES OF A RETIRED COP

POLICEMAN WITH CHILDREN IN POLICE CAR

In the fall of 1964, while patrolling in the Curtis Drive and Ray Road area of Westville, I got into a little trouble by giving my little friends a ride around the block in my police cruiser. This of course was done with the parent's knowledge and permission. I would ask each mother, personally, if I could take their child around the block once in my police car. Usually, I had three or four of my cherished little friends. One well-meaning mom called City Hall to make sure that her child was covered by insurance just in case Officer Bob got into an accident. This did not sit well with the Chief. The next afternoon, I found myself walking a beat on Newhall Street as punishment. What was not realized was that I love all children. It didn't take long before I had four kids walking the beat with me. I had two girls and two boys trying to hold my hands as we walked along checking for "crime". That early evening, I met some of the parents who lived off of Newhall Street and I got permission from them to take the kids to Campie's Pizza Restaurant, located on Winchester Avenue. Policemen do get lunch breaks. We all had pizza and cold sodas. The first question all kids ask is, "Did you ever shoot anybody?" "Why are you walking?" "Where's your car?" "Do you live in the Police Station?" "Do Policemen have kids?" After the pizza, we walked south on Winchester Avenue and then turned right into Starr Street. As we walked and talked, a gentleman sitting on his front porch apparently noticed a scene that was not normal, a white Policeman walking with four black children holding his hand. He warned the kids not to say anything to me because I was looking for information from them so I could put their mammas in jail. A terrible thing to say to a child but I didn't need to say a word. The kids told the man that I was their friend and to shut up and mind his own business. I don't condone children being rude to adults but I guess there are rare circumstances where this could apply. I believe this was one of them. I returned children to the safety of their homes. I thanked the parents for permitting the kids to enjoy a pizza with me. I really enjoyed their company. I love kids. This went on for a week until I got a notice from the Chief's Office that I would be transferring back to my old radio car #21 in Westville the next Monday. Seems like Westville moms wrote letters to some of the Police Commissioner's demanding that I be returned to Westville. I told my newfound friends that I was leaving but I would always remember them. Yes, the kids didn't want me to go and I didn't want to go. Monday afternoon I was back in Westville with a stern warning from the Chief's Office. Keep those kids out of the squad car. •

MEMORIES OF A RETIRED COP

POLICEMAN AND STANDING LADY BUS PASSENGER

One afternoon in May 1961, on the squad B shift AT 1600 hours, I was assigned to a walking beat on Whalley Avenue from Sherman Avenue to the Boulevard. The radio car that usually transported some walking beats left Headquarters on an emergency call. My Sergeant said, "Bob, walk over to Church and Chapel and catch the Whalley Avenue bus to your beat. In uniform you do not need to pay the fare." "Okay Serge, thank you." I walked over to Church and Chapel and caught the Whalley/Westville bus. I found a seat and sat next to a lady. The next stop we picked up several more passengers. By now it was standing room only. I was age 24 and seeing an older woman standing, I got up and offered my seat to her. She smiled and thanked me. As she was about to sit down, a teen aged boy, standing toward the rear of the bus, beat her to my seat and sat down. I said, "Hey young man. I got up and offered this lady my seat." "Oh, sorry. I thought you were getting off at the next stop." "No, I am not but you will be if you don't get your butt off that seat." He jumped up like a jack in the box and the lady sat down. At Broadway, many people got off the bus and there were plenty of empty seats. I found another seat and sat down until we reached Whalley and Sherman. That's where I got off. Not sure what happened to the young man. •

ROOKIE POLICEMEN IN BARBER CHAIRS

In July 1961, I was walking the Grand Avenue beat one afternoon from 4:00 PM to midnight. My beat went from James Street to Ferry Street. The weather was warm and I met a lot of friendly merchants on both sides of Grand Avenue. People were friendly in those days and Policemen were welcome almost anywhere: Shack's Hardware, Connecticut Auto Parts, Annie's, etc. There was a barbershop on Grand Avenue between Blatchley and Fillmore across the street from a school. One late afternoon, the barber was outside getting some fresh air. I stopped and talked to him and introduced myself. It was a small shop with two barber chairs. He had mentioned the fact that he often gave a key to his barbershop to the Policeman on the beat in case the Policeman wanted to get out of the cold or use the bathroom. I reluctantly took advantage of his offer and took the key. I can't remember his name, but I told him if I ducked in on a cold night, I would leave his shop the way I found it. This was before the Masonic Temple incident. In August 1961, half my class of rookies now rotated from the 4:00 PM to 12:00 to the 12:00 midnight to 8:00 AM shifts for the next six months of probation. One cold night in December 1961, I was walking that beat. I had a partner, another rookie. It was about 4:00 AM and I remembered the key to the Barber Shop. I said to my partner, "Would you like to get out of this cold and warm up?" "Where he said? Bartoromo's Bakery?" "No. I have a key to a Barber Shop, given to me by the owner." It was for the back door. So, we walked in the alleyway and entered through the back door. The heat felt so good. We did not turn on any lights and decided to just relax and sit in the two barber chairs. It was pitch dark. We removed our long overcoats. So comfortable we both fell asleep in the barber chairs. Next thing we woke up at about 6:45 AM. It was getting light and we had an audience of about six to eight people staring at us through the plate glass window. Now I know how monkeys feel when people stare at them. Remember, we are still rookies on probation and this was not good. We were so embarrassed and worried. We grabbed our overcoats and quickly put then on and went out the back door. No way we were showing our faces on Grand Avenue so we turned left into Blatchley Avenue and walked south for a block and turned right into Woolsey Street and walked to James Street. We turned right and walked to Grand and James. Seemed like everyone was staring and pointing at us. Finally at about 7:35 AM a police car picked us up to take us to headquarters. The next week, we were worried that we would be fired or suspended. For some reason, no one mentioned it. Finally, one night, I told my Sergeant Joe Perrelli about the incident. I had to tell someone. Sergeant Perrelli laughed and told me some stories when he was a rookie. Don't sweat it kid. A good cop never gets cold or wet. •

JAMES BROWN COMES TO THE NEW HAVEN ARENA

On February 20, 1970, James Brown came to the New Haven Arena to perform. I was on duty at that concert. All seats were sold out. Also performing that night was a well-known comedian named Pig meat Markham. I had seen Mr. Markham on one of the late night TV shows months earlier. We were on duty hours before the 9:00 PM performance. As we checked the building for any trespassers like we did the night of the incident with Jim Morrison of The Doors, I decided to knock on the dressing room door of Mr. James Brown. There were very few places a Policeman in uniform could not go. One of his attendants opened the door. I requested to say hello to Mr. Brown. The man asked me to come in and at the same time said, "Hey Jimmie, there's a Policeman looking for you. No really looking for Mr. Brown." Mr. Brown walked out of another room and greeted me. I said, "I just want to say hello to you Mr. Brown," and I shook his hand. I did not ask for an autograph, which would have been improper. I also shook hands with Mr. Pig Meat Markham. Seeing that they were getting ready to perform, I left and thanked them both. About 45 minutes later, Mr. Brown was escorted to the stage area. The crowd went wild, yelling and screaming. We tried to get folks to take their seats but instead they rushed the front of the stage. Officers on the stage kept the crowd from jumping onto the stage. Finally, in desperation trying to get the folks to sit down, Mr. Brown announced in a loud voice speaking into the microphone, said, "I want all the black folks to sit in their seats and the rest of y'all to keep standing." It worked and everyone sat down in their seats. No one was standing except for the Police Officers on duty. We had at least forty-five officers on duty inside of the Arena and another dozen outside for traffic control. What a concert it was. People really got their money's worth. There was a whole lot of smoke in the air. It was too dark to see anything but just inhaling the air inside of the Arena, I felt good. We all felt good. I'm surprised we didn't all start singing. In spite of the capacity crowd, we had no major incidents like the Doors concert. No arrests and no fights. It was a great crowd. Even after the concert, people left in an orderly manner. One of the best concerts I ever worked at. •

MEMORIES OF A RETIRED COP

POLICEMAN STOPS WANTED HOMICIDE SUSPECT

One afternoon, at about 2:00 PM in the spring of 1967, I was on radio car patrol in the Dixwell Avenue area. I believe it was a Sunday. Before I could see the speeding vehicle, I could hear the engine revving. A Pontiac sedan operated by a black male was proceeding north/west on Broadway toward Dixwell Avenue. I was operating a marked police vehicle. I was able to pull the vehicle over to the curb on Dixwell Avenue, just past Lake Place. I called the license plate in to the dispatcher and gave my location. This was standard procedure. I cautiously approached the vehicle and had a conversation with the driver who was alone. I asked for his license and registration, pointing out that he was exceeding the speed limit. The driver had his license in his wallet but then he bent over to open the glove compartment. This is when all Policemen become alert for any possible weapons in the glove compartment. I had my right hand on my gun, prepared for the possibility of him having a weapon in the glove compartment. The man handed me his New York vehicle registration. I asked him to sit tight and went to my car and called in his name, address, birthdate, etc. for warrants. The dispatcher immediately alerted me that the man fitting that name and description was wanted for a homicide in New York City. Back up in route, the dispatcher said. I did not want this to turn into a high-speed pursuit so I acted quickly and approached the driver with my Colt 38 police special revolver aimed at this face. I got him out of the car and face down in the street. I got him handcuffed behind his back. The man was cooperative at all times. He had no weapons on his person or in his car. In spite of his birthdate being one day off, it was learned that he was wanted for shooting a man to death in New York City the day before. A cooperating suspect, no matter how nice they appear could be a cold-blooded killer. I towed the vehicle for processing by the New York PD and sent the suspect to Headquarters in the paddy wagon. The next day, two New York City Detectives came and took him back to New York. They also towed his car back to New York for processing. All in the line of duty. A risk every Police Officer takes every time he leaves the safety of his home and puts on his uniform. •

NEW YORK DETECTIVES AND AUTOPSY

In the summer of 1962, I was just leaving headquarters at 165 Court Street at 4:00 PM, in route to a downtown walking beat when one of my Sergeants asked me to accompany two New York Police Department Detectives to Yale New Haven Hospital. A New York man had been killed in a motor vehicle accident the day before and they had to view his body because they believed the man had been wanted by the New York PD. I was still a rookie; I jumped in the back seat of the unmarked New York police car. We drove to Yale New Haven Hospital and parked at the emergency room entrance. We entered through the emergency room door and we walked that long and cold basement hallway leading to the morgue. I was in uniform and the New York Detectives displayed their shields on their business suits. I spoke to an attendant in the hallway and asked him where we could find the body of the man whose name was given to me. He pointed to a door leading to a room and said, ask them in there. A sign on the door read. *AUTHORIZED PERSONNEL ONLY.* "They should be able to help you." We walked in to this cold eerie room where a Pathologist and his assistant were performing an autopsy on another deceased man, which was nearly completed. I had to leave the room. I walked back into the hallway and leaned against the wall. I cannot and will not describe what I saw. In Police Academy we were supposed to witness an actual autopsy as part of our training, but we never did. As the shock wore off, the two New York Detectives came out and said, "Hey kid? What's wrong? Oh, the guy they are slicing up? That bothered you kid?" "Yes it did, Detectives." "You know what kid, we're going to treat you to a nice pizza and you will feel much better. Compliments of the N.Y.P.D. kid." That did it. I headed to the nearest bathroom and puked. I was so sick. Never felt that way before. They laughed and I puked. I will never forget that autopsy. Anyway, they took pictures and fingerprints of the deceased man who was in a cold storage locker and brought me back to Headquarters. They were still not sure if it was the man they were looking for. They made a few phone calls and before they left the Precinct, they asked me if I was okay. "Come to New York kid and we will show you some real gory stuff." All part of being a New Haven Police Officer. •

LINCOLN CATCHES FIRE AT GAS STATION

In the summer of 1968, I was patrolling on Ferry Street at about 1:00 PM. As I passed Ferry and Lombard Streets traveling south toward Grand Avenue, something caused me to look to my left. There was a gas station on the southeast corner. A Lincoln was parked at the gas pumps and a man had the hood open, assuming he was checking the fluids. Suddenly, flames shot out from under the hood. The man jumped back. Every police car was equipped with a fire extinguisher in the trunk. On pure instinct, I pulled over and ran back to the trunk with the car keys in my hand to open the trunk. I did not have time to call the dispatcher and request a fire engine. There were flames shooting out from under the hood. Hoping that the fire extinguisher was full, I grabbed it and ran across the street and was able to extinguish the engine fire by empting the contents of the fire extinguisher. It made quite a mess of the engine compartment and all over the fenders with white powder but the fire was out. It appeared that the fire started by the carburetor and melted the distributor cap and burned the spark plug wires. The thought of the gas station or gas pumps exploding was in my mind but instinct told me to put out that fire. Someone had called the Fire Department because a fire truck arrived on scene from Engine 10 on Lombard Street. The owner of the car reappeared with a brown bag in his hand. He bought me a six-pack of beer at a Package store next to the gas station. He thanked me for saving his car but I told him I could not accept the beer. Especially because I was on duty and beer in my police car would be a no-no. He insisted and put the bag on my front seat. Anyway, I called for a tow truck and towed his car to a local garage. The damage to this beautiful older Lincoln was confined to the distributor cap, rotor and spark plug wires plus a carburetor rebuild. I did a complete incident report of the car fire and was able to contact the owner a few days later. He told me that he planned a trip with his family the next week and he was grateful that I was passing by at that moment and thanked me for saving his car. This is what Policemen and Firemen do every day. Nothing heroic or unusual. We are trained and paid to do the job. I was at the right place at the right time. Yes, the next day, I enjoyed that six-pack of beer. •

SCHOOL BUS DRIVER ARRESTED WITH STOLEN CHECK

In the later 60's, my wife Mary drove a school bus for Chieppo Bus Company, located on Forbes Avenue. Mary talked me into taking a part time job on my days off driving a school bus and eventually driving a long distance coach. One day in the spring of 1969, I had just dropped off my kids at the Kimberly Avenue School. Another driver named Lee had dropped off his kids at another school in the Hill section of New Haven. Lee's school bus had stalled and would not start. He called the company and was told to leave the bus until a mechanic could look at it later in the day. Lee radioed for me to pick him up at Sacred Heart School. I drove over to Sacred Heart and picked up Lee. As we drove back to the bus terminal, Lee asked if I could do him a favor and stop at a bank to cash a check for his uncle. "Of course," I said to him. I pulled the bus into the parking lot of a bank on Congress and College Streets. As Lee walked to the entrance door of the bank, I found a two-day-old newspaper to read while he was gone. 10 minutes went by. No Lee. After about fifteen minutes, I observed a New Haven police car stop in front of the bank with two Officers entering the front door. Then, another police car arrived with another officer entering the front door of the bank. I'm thinking to myself, "It's a hold up and poor Lee's right in the middle of it." The Officers come out with Lee in handcuffs, being put in the back seat of a police car. I did what any off duty Police Officer would do, I got the hell out of there. As I was parking my school bus in the rear lot of Chieppo's, Nick Chieppo approached me. "Hey Bob, where's Lee?" I told Nick the story. Nick called the Police Department but was told it was a confidential investigation. That afternoon Lee got out on bond and came to the bus company. Lee told the following bazaar story which ultimately turned out to be true. Lee's older uncle asked Lee to cash a $300.00 check for him because the uncle had no ID, Lee agreed to do his uncle a favor. The check was stolen, but Lee did not know this. Finally Lee was exonerated and his uncle was arrested. Chieppo Bus stood by Lee and did not fire him until the case was resolved in court. I went to court with him and assisted in getting a warrant for his uncle. After it was all over, I realized just how easily innocent people can get involved in incidents like this. I visualized the headlines in the New Haven Register. "Local bus driver arrested for

MEMORIES OF A RETIRED COP

attempting to cash stolen check. Local off duty Police Officer charged with being the getaway bus driver." •

CIRCUS ANIMALS ESCAPE FREIGHT CAR

In May 1962, just after my transfer to Station Two on Sherman Parkway, I was assigned to the 12:00 midnight to 8:00 AM shift. I was finally going to get my own police car after walking the beat for more than one year. I was in training to learn the different areas of patrol in Station 2. I was riding with a seasoned Officer. At about 1:00 AM, we had an assignment to drive to the summit of East Rock Park and chase all the lovers from the various lovers' lanes. We started from the lower road and worked our way to the top. Signs were posted on the lower level, *NO PARKING FROM SUNDOWN TO SUN UP*. This gave us a legal right to have these cars moved. One car at a time, we used a portable spotlight that plugged into the cigarette lighter receptacle. There were no spotlights on police cars in those days. As we made our way to the top, one at a time, as the Officer drove the police car, I shone the portable spotlight on each car and told them they had to move. A few asked, "How come?" and we advised them it was a city ordinance prohibiting parking in East Rock Park after sunset. Well, as we approached the summit, we observed at least 8-12 cars parked. We decided to have a little harmless fun. One by one we would announce at each parked car that a Barnum & Bailey circus train had derailed in Cedar Hill freight yards off of State Street and two circus gorillas had escaped from one of the freight cars. They were last seen heading for the woods in East Rock Park. This made our job much easier because no one argued with us and most parkers (lovers) asked us to wait until they drove away. I never laughed so hard in my life. I can still smell the burnt rubber as they spun their tires driving off in the moonlight. One young man climbed over the front seat from the back seat, bare assed as a new born baby holding his pants in his hands. If I was a Police Officer today, would I do that again? Absolutely. We cleared the Park in twenty minutes. But, I don't think I could say gorilla with a straight face without laughing. I am laughing now. To be a good Police Officer it requires courage, strength, common sense but also have a good sense of humor. •

MEMORIES OF A RETIRED COP

HYSTERICAL FEMALE OPERATING UNREGISTERED MOTOR VEHICLE

On October 25, 1973, I was on patrol in the Kimberly Avenue area of New Haven, CT. At approximately 12:30 AM, I noticed the vehicle in front of me stopped for the red light at Kimberly Avenue and the Boulevard had expired registration tags from May 1973. Five months overdue. I pulled alongside of the vehicle and motioned for the female driver to pull over when the light turned green. When the light turned to green she pulled over. I parked behind her. I got out of my police car and approached her vehicle. The young woman driver was all upset. "I wasn't speeding, was I Officer?" she asked. "No Miss, but your vehicle registration expired in May of this year so you are driving an unregistered motor vehicle." The lady started to cry. I told her to please calm down. She was not going to jail. I was ready to call for a tow truck and tow this unregistered car off the street, then issue a summons to her for operating an unregistered motor vehicle and call for a taxi cab for the lady, but I decided to help her get home safely to West Haven. She promised to leave her unregistered car in her driveway until she could get to the Motor Vehicle Department and renew her registration. She stated her dad always takes care of all her motor vehicle needs but apparently he forgot to renew it for her. I followed her home to her driveway to make sure she was not stopped again by another Police Officer. She wrote a beautiful letter to Chief DiLieto. •

In the fall of 1966, a couple of weeks after the Fountain Street incident with my tiny 1959 Fiat model 500 Bianchina, I had another incident. To fully appreciate the size of this car, it had a 2-cylinder air cooled rear engine rated at 18 HP. It also had the suicide front doors that opened from the front. I was getting 54 miles per gallon. It only weighed 1050 lbs., with 10 inch wheel rims. I had left my football traffic assignment on Fountain Street and drove toward Station Two on Sherman Parkway in my uniform but with my police hat off. Not much head room in this tiny car, for my regular 3:00 PM tour of duty. I came down Fitch Street and turned right into Crescent Street. As I proceeded toward Fournier Street at the 25 MPH posted speed limit, I noticed in my rear view mirror, a big Pontiac crowding my rear bumper. I turned left into Fournier Street only blocks from Station 2. Just in front of the Animal Shelter, the Pontiac passed me in a reckless manner. Two men were in the front seat. They caught the red light at Sherman and Bassett Street. I pulled along the right side of their big Pontiac Bonneville. With the weakest horn anyone has ever heard, I hit my horn button. Beep, beep and looked up at the passenger. Looking around to see where the 'beep beep' was coming from, he finally looked down at me driving my tiny Fiat. By now, I put my Police hat on and said, "Tell the driver to pull over when the light turns green." The big Pontiac pulled to the curb just East of Sherman Parkway. I got out of my little Fiat at 6'1" 240 lbs. of mean looking cop and walked to the driver's side. "License and registration please." All the twi men could say was, Damn. Officer, where did ya all come from? I didn't see no police car?" "Look behind you," I said. The men asked if they could get out of their Pontiac. "Yes," I answered. Looking at the Fiat, the passenger asked, "Is that a police car?" I could not resist a laugh. He opened the door and I walked in. "Yes," I answered, "a new fleet of unmarked police cars." "Damn and double damn," the passenger said. Looking down at my tiny little green unmarked police car. The driver lived on Starr Street. I said, "Today is a verbal warning. Next time you get the ticket for improper passing." We shook hands and I excused myself telling the men I was in route to Station 2. Looking in my rear view mirror, they stood there scratching their heads in disbelief. •

PLAIN CLOTHES POLICEMAN AT DANCE

In the winter of 1965, I was assigned to work a dance at Yale University. They called it a mixer. This was an extra duty assignment. My Sergeant instructed me to dress in plain clothes and to blend in with the crowd and not look like a Policeman. I chose a pair of brown slacks and a white shirt, no tie and a grey pull over sweater to cover my 38 police revolver. The mixer was held on Elm Street near High Street. I arrived just before 9:00 PM. My assignment was to look out for any excessive drinking, underage drinking and drug use. Also gate crashers. (non-students). I stayed in the background and observed the dance floor sipping a cup of cola. A young woman, maybe age 19 sat next to me. She was sipping a cup of beer. "Hi," she said. "Hi, how are you? Fine thank you." Finally, she decided to find out more about me. "So, are you a student here at Yale?" "No, miss. Are you a student?" "Yes. Music School studying piano. I play the piano." "Really?" "Yes." "So, are you a parent of a student?" "No, miss." "A Professor?" "No, miss." Watching her as she sipped her beer, I finally whispered, "I am a Police Officer on duty working the mixer." "Oh no, am I busted with the beer?" "No miss, but after you finish your beer please don't have another one in front of me, okay?" I remember having my first bottle of Hull's beer at age sixteen at the stock car races at The West Haven Speedway at Savin Rock one Saturday night, so I sure wasn't going to go hard on her for doing what I once did myself. She walked away, but ten minutes later she came back with two Coca-Cola's; one for me and one for her. We chatted until the mixer was over at midnight. I wished her luck with her piano studies and she told me that she enjoyed talking to a real Policeman. My own daughter, Terry, was age 10 at the time. I made one more friend. •

One evening in the spring of 1965, I was dispatched to an apartment building on Fountain Street in regard to harassing and sexually explicit telephone calls. Upon arrival, I spoke to a young woman in her late 20's or early 30's. She reported that for the past week she had received several phone calls from an unidentified male caller. The calls got more progressively explicit and sexual in nature. In those days, there was no such thing as caller ID. In order to trace a call, the caller had to remain on the line for a long period of time while the phone company attempted to trace the call. Putting a tap on a telephone required the approval and signature of a Judge or in more serious cases, the FBI or similar agency. This complaint appeared to be some pervert calling and talking dirty to a female. I reassured the lady that I would give her apartment attention as my time permitted and not to worry. I forwarded a copy of my report to the Detective Bureau. Several days later I received a message to call the Detectives. I was told that the complaint did not reach a level whereas they would get involved. I called my Sergeant and we met at the ladies apartment. In the meantime she received two or three more obscene phone calls from this guy. We arranged for the lady to go along with the next call received and pretend to be interested in meeting him. The plan was for the complainant to meet the man at the Edgewood Avenue Park across from the duck pond. Several days later the lady got another call and she made a date with the man to meet her at the Edgewood Avenue Park. It was about 7:00 PM. She called Station 2 and spoke to my Sergeant. We had the lady meet me at Station 2 on Sherman Parkway. I parked my police car and got into the ladies car. The plan was for me to hide on the front floor in the front seat and apprehend him if he showed up. I had no idea what I was dealing with. The man could have been 6' 8" and 300 lbs. or 5' 2" and 120 lbs. Could have been armed or a complete lunatic. We drove to the Park at exactly 9:00 PM, the time she was to meet him. She backed her vehicle in against the hill leading to the play area on the Edgewood Avenue side, facing the pond. I had to crouch down on the floor. Very uncomfortable for me. I never liked these "stake outs". The lady had excessive perfume on and I had, well, I had to remain professional and a gentleman at all times. She was attractive. Not easy for me but necessary. We waited until 10:30 PM. The same car passed the ladies car three times but it never stopped. It slowed down and then sped off. No way of telling if that was the pervert. Finally, it was obvious he was not going to show up so the lady took me back to Station 2. We went inside and spoke to the Sergeant. I generated another lengthly report. I never received another call from the lady. •

In the winter of 1962, I was on duty in Fair Haven on the 4:00 PM to 12:00 Midnight shift. I had the dreaded traffic assignment on State and Ferry Streets at 4:00 PM. The assignment consisted of turning off the traffic light at that intersection and taking a position in the middle of the intersection and manually directing traffic for two solid hours. This was Route 5 and was heavily traveled by trucks before I-91 opened. There was a floodlight under the traffic light so cars and trucks could see the Policeman directing traffic, as it got dark. Between the trucks coming so close to the exhaust fumes, it was one of the worse and most dangerous assignments a Policeman could have. It was a full two hours doing manual hand traffic. This one day I was out there when a trailer truck traveling south toward New Haven came very close to me and the truck driver yelled out his open window, "That's a good way to get run over copper. Get out of the street you jerk." I had my police car parked on May Street just off of State Street. I stopped all traffic and left the intersection and turned the traffic light back on. I got into my police car and took off after this trailer truck. I was so mad. The nerve of this trucker. I caught up with him as he turned into East Street. I pulled him over and approached the truck on foot. I gave the dispatcher a description of the truck and the Connecticut license plate number. I did not ask for backup. I was going to handle this wise guy on my own. I jumped up on the running board and cautiously opened the driver's door. The driver was lying on the front seat laughing. I grabbed his leg to pull him out of the truck. It was my cousin Frankie (Junie) Murratti. The SOB thought it was funny. I wasn't laughing. "I should lock your ass up June Bug." That's what I called him, June Bug. He called me Bob Cat. Since we were kids he always pulled pranks on me. I was not amused and slammed his truck door and got in my police car and drove back to State and Ferry to finish my traffic assignment. We made up a week later when I went over to his house for coffee. I couldn't stay mad at him forever. Our mothers were sisters. I loved this wiseass cousin of mine. RIP Junie. •

12 YEAR OLD BURGLAR

One night in the fall of 1967, at about 1:30 in the morning, I was on patrol in the Fair Haven area. I was being observant for burglaries to gas stations. We had a rash of burglaries but nothing much was taken. Loose change from the cash register or desktop radios. It had to be kids because the expensive tools, jacks and tune up equipment were never touched. Brand new tires on tire racks were left alone. Tune up parts, etc. were never taken. As I checked the gas station garage on the South West corner of Ferry and Exchange Streets, I observed glass on the ground in front of the small door leading to the office. I called for backup and was able to carefully reach in and unlock the door. Flashlight in my left hand and 38 revolver in my right hand, I carefully entered the office area. I looked for and found the light switch. I turned on all lights including the garage area. I found a 12-year-old hiding under a car. I said, "Let's go. You got caught so don't do anything stupid." Of course, 12-year-old children never carry any form of ID. I placed him in my back seat but handcuffed him from behind for my own safety. He gave me his name, phone number and address, which was in the projects on North Front Street. I notified my dispatcher that I would be in route with a minor. The Youth Division was closed so I took him to the Detective Bureau. He was very cooperative but also seemed street smart. Then, I found out why he was like that. By now it was almost 3:00 AM. I called his mom. The phone rang approximately 14 times. I was ready to hang up when a females sleepy voice said, "Hello, who's this callin my phone this late?" I identified myself as a New Haven Police Officer. "So, what you want?" "Ma'am. I have your boy here downtown. He broke into a gas station on Ferry Street. I will release him to your custody until his court date comes up, okay?" "Don't bring that boy home here. I can't do anything with him. He runs the streets all night and won't listen to me at all. Do what you want. Keep him. I don't care and she hung up on me." The Sergeant said, "Take him to Juvenile Detention on Orange Street." We left headquarters on Court Street and I asked him if he had anything to eat today. "Nope," he said. "Do you like hamburgers and fries?" "Yeah." He lit up. "Okay, I am taking you to Juvenile Detention, but first I will swing by the White Tower and get you something to eat. Don't try to run on me, okay?" "I won't." We pulled up to White Tower and I took him in with me. We sat at the counter. The place was empty. I had a coffee and I ordered him a cheeseburger because that's what he wanted and fries and a coke. He was really hungry. He did not steal anything, but he did break in so that was a burglary, which I charged him as a Juvenile Delinquent. He was booked and as I was leaving he thanked me. It was probably the first time someone was kind to him in a long time. His mother didn't seem to care. This scenario is still very real today. Kids running the streets, unsupervised. •

POLICEMAN AND LOUD CAR RADIO

Sometime in the early 70's, I was given a special assignment to enforce the current law that more than three unregistered motor vehicles on one's property constitutes operating a junk yard without a permit. Because of my people skills, I was chosen for this complex job. I felt honored to be chosen until I attempted to enforce the law. I was given a list of gas stations and garages and also private properties where numerous abandoned or unregistered motor vehicles were observed. It was the worst assignment I was ever given. Not only was I threatened by business owners, but a few Police Officers who had relatives in the gas station, garage business were angry with me. I was given this important assignment and I vowed to follow through and do my best. One particular business was a small gas station/garage on E. Grand Avenue, just over the bridge on the right side (south side). The owner was a man named Charlie. On my list was five unregistered abandoned cars parked behind the gas station on the side of Quinnipiac Avenue. Using all my people skills, I walked into the garage and spoke to Charlie and advised him that he had to comply and remove all but 2 of the motor vehicles. Charlie took it personal and was very angry with me. In my entire life I always tried to turn negative things into positive things. Rather than say, "I'm right and you are wrong." I tried to compromise whereas everyone was happy. Charlie was not happy and vowed that his unregistered cars would remain on his property even if he had to go to jail. Charlie was a hard working business owner and I respected that. I was a hard working Police Officer doing my job. One day I pulled into the gas station and after talking and having a cup of coffee we were able to come to some agreement. With his dealer plates and the willingness to drive the cars occasionally so they were not considered abandoned, he was able to keep his cars on his property legally. I turned an enemy into a friend. One day Charlie talked about his 22-year-old daughter that just started driving. He gave her one of his used cars, a beautiful 8-year-old Cadillac. Problem was, she played her car radio to loud and it was annoying. They lived up the hill on East Grand Avenue. In the morning, she would come down the hill and turn left into Quinnipiac Avenue and proceed to Stiles Street and onto the Turnpike to work. I waited the next morning and pulled her over on Quinnipiac and E. Ferry. "What's wrong Officer?" she asked. "Miss, I have numerous complaints from residents that you blast your car radio in this area every morning." "Honestly Officer, I don't do that." I could not keep a straight face and I burst out laughing. She looked at me and realized it was a joke and started laughing also. "My father put you up to this, right?" "Yes he did." I handed back her license and told her to drive safely. If we could only turn every negative in our lives into positives, we would all live healthier and happier lives. •

DRUNK DRIVER

One Sunday afternoon in the summer of 1979, six months after retiring from the New Haven Police Department, Mary and I decided to take a nice relaxing country drive to the area of the Goodspeed Opera House along the Connecticut River. We pulled out on to Route 80 from our East Haven home and proceeded north. As I approached River Road, I observed a car in front of me driving erratically. He crossed over the double yellow lines a few times and then suddenly he veered over to the right and was driving on the shoulder kicking up dirt and stones. I am not a Policeman anymore and I have no authority to enforce any laws but this vehicle is going to cause a serious accident. Mary was worried. Bob, please be careful. I made up my mind that this vehicle had to be stopped. Thinking up ahead of where the red lights are and hoping that he has to stop for one. Just ahead was Totoket Road (Rte 22) and a little farther up the road was Forest Road. Bad luck, as we passed Totoket Road with a green light. His driving got more erratic. Mary pleaded, "Please be careful Bob. You are not a Policeman any more." Finally at Route 80 and Forest Road, the light turned red. He stopped. As I got out of my car, Mary said, "Bob, what if he has a gun?" I thought what if he runs into a family on a Sunday afternoon ride and kills them all? No options here. I had to stop him. I approached his vehicle with my retirement badge in my left hand. His driver's window was open. I smelled the booze. He was intoxicated. I stuck my badge in his face and put the car in park and removed the keys. I yelled to Mary to go to the North Branford PD right there on Forest Road and bring back a Policeman. No cell phones in those days. She did. In five minutes his car was surrounded with police cars. The policeman called him by name and remarked that he was just arrested last week for driving under the influence. They removed him and put him in handcuffs and towed his car away. We proceeded to the Connecticut River area and had a beautiful day. A possible tragedy was averted that day. •

FIRST TIME GIVING BLOOD

The very first time I ever gave blood was on January 9, 1962. This date was significant to me because it marked my one-year anniversary since I joined the New Haven Police Department. Secondly, a man, whom I never met, needed blood for a lifesaving open-heart operation. Open-heart surgery was something new and this stranger needed a lot of blood. I was only one of so many people that gave blood to this stranger so that he may live to enjoy his family for many years to come:

I was working an extra job on Elm Street and Church Street for the SNET. Two men were working below ground on telephone wires. I was directing traffic around the manhole cover. Another Officer passed me on foot and said he was on his way to 200 Orange Street to give blood to a man who needed open-heart surgery. I said, "Does it hurt?" "A little but it's a nice feeling to give blood." We broke for lunch so I walked over to 200 Orange Street on my lunchtime break and asked if I could give blood. A lady from The American Red Cross asked me if I have ever given blood before. "No ma'am. It's my first time." After giving my blood, I felt a little weak so they gave me some orange juice and a cookie and made me sit down. A few minutes later, I walked outside and felt better than I have ever felt. I have been giving blood ever since that day. It is such a small thing to do, but after giving blood, something happens to your body. I can't explain it but when I leave the donation center, I feel much younger and so much better about myself. It is the very best gift you can give to another human being. •

LOVE LETTER

In November 1963, while patrolling in the Westville area, I received a love letter from a sweet little Jewish girl. The name Meyerholz, I guess, could be construed as a Jewish name. Well, anyway, this little girl had mentioned or hinted that someday I could take her swimming in the pool at the Jewish Community Center, located on Chapel Street. As it was, I was a member of the YMCA, being a Catholic. I told her that I did not have a membership at the Jewish Center. Then she said, "You are Jewish aren't you Bob?" "No honey, I am not Jewish." With than she slowly walked away and disappeared into her house. The next day, all the other kids were standing by the curb, waiting for my daily visit to say hello. She was not with the other kids. The next day, the same thing, she was not there. I was actually sad because she was one of my favorite little friends. On the third day, she was standing there holding hands with her mother, a lovely lady. The mom asked the other kids to leave for a few minutes because my little friend had something for me. She handed me this large pink envelope addressed: To Bob. It contained the sweetest love letter that started:

"Dear Bob. I love you very, very much. The rest is very personal and will remain that way."

On the letter was a drawing of a heart in red crayon. Inside the heart was written, "Love means you, Bob" and signed, "Love." On the back there were round circles with the word LOVE inside with a sting attached.

When I asked what they were, she simply said, love balloons. This is the most cherished item in my scrapbook. It is so fragile after being there for almost fifty-three years. We are still friends and she has grown into the most beautiful woman. Mary and I met with her four years ago for dinner. I had my scrapbook with me and showed her the letter that I had kept for so long. Water stained and fragile. True friendship should last a lifetime. It requires love, trust and respect. •

SUPPLEMENTS

The following pages are various images that I have included, gathered throughout my time as a New Haven Police Officer. These images are supplements from some of the stories that I have told. •

Dear Chief McManus,

I am writing to tell you about one of your officers Robert Meyerholz.

If this young man saved my husband life, he is without a doubt the finest and most efficient gentlemen that I have ever come in contact with

I am so indebted to the young man. I am really lost for words in describing this young man. I have mentioned his name to other

people and he is loved by
all the children and most
of all missed by all adults.

He is a credit to our
New Haven Police force.

Please Mr Mr Mamos please
thank him for me as I
am unable to convey it
myself.

Thanking you.
Mrs William Guesthouse
79 Brooklawn Circle
New Haven, Conn.

February 25, 1964.

Mrs. William Greenhouse
89 Brooklawn Circle
New Haven, Connecticut

Dear Mrs. Greenhouse:

Your letter of February 20th, 1964, commending Patrolman Robert
A. Meyerholz for assistance rendered to you and Mr. Greenhouse
at a time of serious trouble was most pleasing to me.

This letter will be called to the attention of the Honorable
Board of Police Commissioners at their next meeting. A copy of
the letter will be placed in Patrolman Meyerholz' file for future
reference, and another copy will be sent to the officer to call
his attention to the fact that you appreciate his efforts so great-
ly.

Thanking you for calling this matter to my attention, I am,

Sincerely yours,

FRANCIS V. MCMANUS
Chief of Police.

Copy to: Ptmn. Robert A. Meyerholz
Pct. 2

Dear Chief Biagio DiLieto,

It is nice to know that you have on your police force, officers whom with all their other duties can make time to be a friend when a person is in need.

In this case officer Robert Myerholtz showed compassion, and sincere friendship when at three in the morning I was without heat and could not receive any answer from my oil companies answering service. Officer Myerholtz helped me, by finding who the owner of the fuel company was, and aroused him at his home and told him of our need.

I am very grateful, that you have this officer on your force, because he was so considerate as to take over my burden and to make it easier for me.

Sincerely yours,
Mrs. D. Mallijek

DEPARTMENT OF POLICE SERVICE

NEW HAVEN CONN   06519   FRANK LOGUE MAYOR   BIAGIO DILIETO   CHIEF OF POLICE

10 May 1977

Officer Robert Meyerholz
Uniform Service

Dear Officer Meyerholz,

I am proud to inform you the Board of Police Commissioners has
voted to award you a CERTIFICATE OF COMMENDATION for your
actions and effective cooperation with Officer Terrance Heffernan on
15 April 1977. On responding to a dispatch of a robbery in progress,
you radioed a description, which enabled Officer Heffernan to give
chase to the suspect until he crashed his car and escaped on foot.
But, given his more complete description, you soon apprehended the
suspect, found to be in possession of burglary tools. He confessed
to the robbery in question and eight other burglaries in the same
area. Through your professionalism, and especially your excellent
use of the communication facilities, you ended the continued threat
of a systematic night burglar.

The New Haven Department of Police Service has attained a national
reputation for efficiency, progressiveness, and professionalism. This
reputation, and the Department's standing in the community, are en-
hanced by the outstanding performance of members like you, and on
behalf of the Board and the Chief, I want to take this opportunity to
compliment you for a job well done.

Your Certificate of Commendation will be presented to you formally
and publicly when the Department holds its next Award Ceremony.

                    Sincerely,

                    Clarence Butcher, President
                    Board of Police Commissioners

MEMORIES OF A RETIRED COP

4/25/77
4/25/77

81 Marvel Road
New Haven, Conn. 06515

Chief Biagio DiLieto
New Haven Police Department
One Union Avenue
New Haven, Connecticut 06509

Dear Chief:

Seeing that you get more than your share of bitchy, cranky,
go-to-hell mail, I thought you might appreciate hearing from a
particularly pleased resident of New Haven whose home was
recently burglarized, to inform you personally that the excellent
work of your department resulted in the prompt apprehension of
the culprit and the recovery of our property.

Last week our home in Westville was broken into while we were
sleeping, and a number of items, including an heirloom pocket
watch, were stolen. During the early morning hours Officer
Meyerholz responded for an initial investigation, and was
followed by Detective Buffaloe and a representative of the lab
whose name I do not recall.

Each of your staff was considerate, polite, gracious and
thoroughly professional in his conduct.

We were informed a few days ago that the alert actions of officers
Davis and Meyerholz resulted in the apprehension of the burglar,
and subsequent questioning and search by other members of the
department produced extensive evidence of numerous burglaries.
Among the evidence were our belongings -- some of which we
didn't even realize were missing.

My sincere thanks to members of the department who were involved
in the case, and to all those who worked behind the scenes in
support roles. We are very pleased and satisfied with the fine
work of our city's police force, and wish to express to you and
to them our personal gratitude for their efforts.

My kindest regards and best wishes.

                                    Sincerely,

                                    Byrne Stoddard
                                    F. Byrne Stoddard, Jr.

Made in the USA
Charleston, SC
26 July 2015